'*Gendered Hierarchies of Dependency* compares the experience of female accountants in Germany to those in the UK. Kokot-Blamey finds greater equality in the UK, but at the cost of weakened professional relationships and less stable tenure. The comparison exposes an important question neither country has answered: how can fairness at work be achieved without denying our interdependence? This insightful book is a valuable addition to the comparative study of accounting and to the literature on gender at work.'

Matthew Gill, Author of *Accountants' Truth*

'Kokot-Blamey provides a fascinating and in-depth account of women's careers in professional accountancy in Germany and the UK. Her powerful analysis identifies that sexism, job insecurity, and gendered hierarchies of dependency persist under neo-liberal capitalism. She challenges preconceptions about women's (and men's) careers to argue for a more compassionate and caring approach to professional work and family life that offers a nuanced alternative.'

Kathryn Haynes, Professor of Accounting, Newcastle Business School, Northumbria University, UK

'The book brilliantly illuminates the functioning of the accounting profession in regard to gender. Drawing on a rich body of empirical material, Patrizia Kokot-Blamey offers a compelling comparative analysis of how women partners make sense of careers, sexism, motherhood, and job security in Germany and the UK. A thought-provoking book!'

Elisabeth Kelan, Professor of Leadership, Essex Business School, University of Essex, UK

'Motherhood and work and family demands remain key barriers to women rising in business organizations such as accounting firms. While the "working mother challenge" has been examined by scholars for decades, it remains to be resolved. Moreover, few books link women and mothers' personal experiences to macro forces such as how liberal and coordinated economies and occupational labor markets create ongoing rigidities reinforcing gendered job and societal hierarchies. An exception is Dr. Patrizia Kokot-Blamey's book, *Gendered Hierarchies of Dependency: Women Making Partnership in Accountancy Firms*. Using a cross-national sample, Dr. Kokot-Blamey skillfully examines the motherhood career paradox: while professionals such as accountants must work full-time and often long hours in order to make partner, the demands of motherhood culturally and practically in countries such as Germany necessitates part-time work, which relegates many mothers off the partner track. Yet she argues that liberal economies are not necessarily any better. Other social forces such as the lack of supportive structures for working mothers limits women's agency in many ways that reduce their labor market value and security. Kokot-Blamey questions whether creating standardized career structures that offer the illusion of individual "choice and autonomy" are truly satisfying solutions for women who seek to personally control their bodies and reproductive experiences crossing work and non-work boundaries. Scholars and managers seeking a thoughtful current analysis of the complexity of truly supporting mothers' careers across societies should read this fascinating book.'

Ellen Ernst Kossek, Basil S. Turner Distinguished Professor of Management, Krannert School of Management, Purdue University, USA

'*Gendered Hierarchies of Dependency: Women Making Partnership in Accountancy Firms* provides an original and accessible account of the persistence of gender inequality at the top levels of organizations despite the attention paid to equalities and diversity policies. Drawing on organizational studies together with feminist political economy and the ethics of care, this book provides a comparative, interdisciplinary analysis of the processes leading to these outcomes. It provides a stark reminder of the pressure employers place on workers even at high levels in organizations to comply with their conditions or else face redundancy and that, while there has been a profound change in women's lifestyles, limitations remain, not so much from the fact that they care, but that many men do not.'

Diane Perrons, Professor Emerita Feminist Political Economy, London School of Economics and Political Science, UK

Accountancy is an elite profession, wielding its influence in every step we take in business and political life, from takeovers to bankruptcies and from Brexit to war: we need accountants to help us see the bigger picture and to enable us to trust one another in public life. But for much of the profession's history, women were excluded from it and, while we have seen great advances in women's access to the profession, women remain significantly underrepresented at the top of the hierarchy and amid partnership ranks across the industry and globally. Importantly, there are noteworthy differences in the severity of this underrepresentation across national borders which remain underexplored.

Gendered Hierarchies of Dependency considers this underrepresentation of women at partnership level cross-nationally and through a feminist lens, analysing interviews with female partners in Germany and the United Kingdom. In doing so, Kokot-Blamey innovatively merges insights from accountancy and organization studies, political economy, and the feminist ethics of care literature to contribute to contemporary debates about women at work, neoliberalism, and the capitalist fiction of the autonomous self. Beyond career advancement to partnership, Kokot-Blamey examines several timely issues such as the persistence of discrimination and sexism at work, motherhood, and weathering recessions and economic crises in accountancy. Revealing important insights into the day-to-day working and private lives of modern elites, this book shows how hierarchies are negotiated differently across borders, but that the outcomes are always gendered.

Gendered Hierarchies of Dependency

Gendered Hierarchies of Dependency

Women Making Partnership in Accountancy Firms

Patrizia Kokot-Blamey

Great Clarendon Street, Oxford, OX2 6DP,
United Kingdom

Oxford University Press is a department of the University of Oxford.
It furthers the University's objective of excellence in research, scholarship,
and education by publishing worldwide. Oxford is a registered trade mark of
Oxford University Press in the UK and in certain other countries

© Patrizia Sofia Kokot-Blamey, 2023

The moral rights of the author have been asserted

All rights reserved. No part of this publication may be reproduced, stored in
a retrieval system, or transmitted, in any form or by any means, without the
prior permission in writing of Oxford University Press, or as expressly permitted
by law, by licence or under terms agreed with the appropriate reprographics
rights organization. Enquiries concerning reproduction outside the scope of the
above should be sent to the Rights Department, Oxford University Press, at the
address above

You must not circulate this work in any other form
and you must impose this same condition on any acquirer

Published in the United States of America by Oxford University Press
198 Madison Avenue, New York, NY 10016, United States of America

British Library Cataloguing in Publication Data
Data available

Library of Congress Control Number: 2023931904

ISBN 978–0–19–968845–6

DOI: 10.1093/oso/9780199688456.001.0001

Printed and bound in the UK by
Clays Ltd, Elcograf S.p.A.

Links to third party websites are provided by Oxford in good faith and
for information only. Oxford disclaims any responsibility for the materials
contained in any third party website referenced in this work.

Acknowledgements

I am thankful to the respondents for being so generous with their time and for sharing their experiences with me. Their stories, their tenacity, and their willingness to persist have given me much food for thought about what it means to be a working woman today. I am grateful to the publisher that I have the opportunity with this book to share these impressions with a wider audience.

Professionally, I have been fortunate to receive support from many ambitious women and a few men. I thank Aparna Barua Adams, Alexandra Beauregard, Evelyn Fenton, Marina Fielder, Marina Franchi, Chris Grey, Grace James, Elisabeth Kelan, Gill Kirton, Natasha Marhia, Rainbow Murray, and Chris Statham for support and advice, a helping hand over the years, and/or for reading some of this work. I am especially thankful to Diane Perrons for her guidance and patience with me and for dedicating her scholarship to improving women's lives. I am grateful to Christina Scharff, who is both a friend and an inspiration to me as a scholar, and whose comments and feedback are invaluable. I thank Tessa Wright for friendship and collegiality—and for reading one chapter too. I thank Susan Lawrence for giving me space to think, for her generous insight, encouragement, and consistently good counsel over many years. I am grateful to my colleague and now coauthor Sarah Riley and her family for twelve years of friendship and support in weathering the ups and downs of working in academia. A special thank you to Sreenita Mukherjee for research assistance for this book, and for the many stimulating discussions with past and present PhD students. I can't wait to see what the future holds for you.

And to my family: this is my first book, and my thanks go to my parents Ursula and Peter for supporting me over the years and for their determination, inspiration, and hard work. I cherish the memories shared across many summers with my paternal grandmother Zofia, who recently left us. And I am grateful to my late maternal grandmother Rosa. I have so many wonderful memories as a young child, of building dens together, eating kiwis, walking everywhere, and mischievous trips to the local allotment. Like my own mother, she too had a keen sense of survival and an inspiring sense of resourcefulness. I thank my in-laws for their support and for loving our boys, who are always delighted to see them. I thank my children for their patience with me and the love and joy that they bring to our lives.

Finally, I thank my husband John, who changed my life for the better in less time than it took to complete this book. Our children are the greatest gift to me, and motherhood my most formidable teacher.

Acknowledgement of Sources

A shorter version of Chapter 3 was published by Emerald in 2014 as 'Structures and relationships: women partners' careers in Germany and the UK' in the journal *Accounting, Auditing & Accountability Journal*, 27(1): 48–72. Reprinted with permission. A shorter and earlier version of Chapter 4 was published by Elsevier in 2015 as 'Let's talk about sex(ism): cross-national perspectives on women partners' narratives on equality and sexism at work in Germany and the UK' in the journal *Critical Perspectives on Accounting*, 27: 73–85. Reprinted with permission. An earlier version of Chapter 5 was published by Elsevier in 2021 as 'Mothering in accounting: feminism, motherhood, and making partnership in accountancy in Germany and the UK' in the journal *Accounting, Organizations and Society*, 93. Reprinted with permission.

Contents

List of Tables   xv
Key terms, Firms, and Acronyms   xvi

1. **Introduction: Feminism, Capitalism, and Dependency**   1
   Dependency, Capitalism, and the State   4
   Feminism, Women's Careers and Capitalism   11
   Scope and Limitations   15
   Outline of the Book   17

2. **Accounting Matters: Mapping Women's Underrepresentation in Accountancy**   19
   Mystery and Professional Closure—the Making and Ascent of Accountancy   19
   Herstory: The Entrance and Rise of Women in the Accounting Profession   22
   Professional Organization and Women's Representation   23
   Women's Advancement at Big-4 Firms   27
   Women's Representation and Advancement in Accounting Research   29
   Work-life Balance, Flexibility, and Motherhood   34
   Conclusion   37

3. **Making Partnership in Accounting: Career Histories, Structures, and Relationships at Work**   39
   Women's Career Progression in Germany   41
      The role of friendships at work in German small and medium-sized firms   41
      Relations with managers and career advancement in Big-4 firms in Germany   44
   Women's Career Progression in the United Kingdom   46
      Making partnership in the Big-4 firms in the UK and the role of standardized career structures   47
      Making partnership in small and medium-sized firms in the UK and the role of ads and recruiters   50
   Managing Others and Developing Talent as Partners   52
      Managing others in Germany   52
      Managing others in the UK   57
   Conclusion   59

4. Sexism at Work — 63

'We are all equal, but women need to make a choice' — 66
Equal Opportunities in the Accounts in the United Kingdom — 71
'Taking it with a bit of humour': Dismissing or Problematizing Sexism at Work — 74
Time and Age — 78
Being Different at Work — 81
Conclusion — 85

5. Mothering in Accounting — 88

Matricentric Feminism and Experiences of Difference — 89
The Maternal Body as Taboo at Work — 92
Mothering and Motherhood in Accounting — 93
  Germany: the maternal body as social pollutant — 95
  Germany: childcare as mother's care — 98
  The UK: contracts and household economics — 103
  The UK: reversing gender roles as good household economics — 106
Conclusion — 109
  Between a rock and a hard place: motherhood as institution and the unencumbered norm — 110
  Centring mothers in accountancy — 112

6. Job In/security and Work Centrality — 115

Recessions and Reunification — 118
  The economy and entering the profession — 119
  The economy, redundancies, and pay freezes — 124
Work Centrality and Work-life Balance — 134
  Work, other life domains, and work-life balance — 138
  Work stress, health, and fertility — 143
Conclusion — 148

7. Gendered Hierarchies of Dependency, Feminism, and the Commodification of the Self — 150

The Cost of Embeddedness and the Cost of the Commodification of the Individual — 152
Feminist Visions of Equality — 155
Domesticity, Marriage, and the Family under Neoliberalism — 159
Resisting the Upside-down World in Feminist Visions of a Future under Capitalism — 160

Appendix — *163*
  Methodological Note — *164*

References — 167
Index — 189

List of Tables

1.1	Respondent characteristics	16
2.1	Comparison of proportion of women in accounting profession in UK and Germany	25
2.2	Percentage of women in the profession	26
3.1	National and organizational dimension in respondents' accounts of career advancement	40
5.1	Marital Status and childcare arrangements among the respondents	94
6.1	Respondents who referred to recession/economic downturn as a factor in their career advancement	119
6.2	Respondents who referred to the German reunification and the internet boom as a factor in their career advancement	119
6.3	Respondents who referred to redundancy rounds	125
6.4	Work centrality and how respondents described the focus of their 'work-life' balance	138
A.1	Respondents' characteristics, Germany	163
A.2	Respondents' characteristics, United Kingdom	164

Key terms, Firms, and Acronyms

Abbreviations

CME	Coordinated Market Economy (Varieties of Capitalism framework by Hall and Soskice (2001))
FRC	Financial Reporting Council (UK organization)
IASB	International Accounting Standards Board
LME	Liberal Market Economy (Varieties of Capitalism framework by Hall and Soskice (2001))
M&A	Mergers and acquisitions
SME	Small and Medium-sized Enterprise
Stb	Steuerberater (German certified tax consultant)
VoC	Varieties of Capitalism

Big-4 Firms

Ernst & Young (EY)
Deloitte
KPMG
PricewaterhouseCoopers (PWC)

British Professional Institutes

ACCA	Association of Chartered Certified Accountants
CIMA	Chartered Institute of Management Accountants
CIPFA	Chartered Institute of Public Finance and Accountancy
ICAEW	Institute of Chartered Accountants in England and Wales
ICAS	Institute of Chartered Accountants in Scotland

German Institutes and Associations

WPK	Wirtschaftsprüferkammer (professional institute of chartered accountants in Germany. Membership is mandatory)
IdW	Institut der Wirtschaftsprüfer (association of chartered accountants in Germany. Membership is voluntary)

1
Introduction

Feminism, Capitalism, and Dependency

Chartered accountancy is considered an elite profession. And, as elsewhere, while women have made advances in accessing the profession, they remain widely underrepresented at the top. This underrepresentation varies across borders and has a socio-economic and political context and, in this book, drawing on interviews with sixty women who made it to partnership in Professional Service Firms in Germany and the UK, I explore how this might matter. It is a specific interdisciplinary contribution to existing research on women's advancement, drawing on the organization studies literature on women's careers, gender, social capital, networks, and homophily, but doing so within a frame informed by political economy on the one hand, and the feminist ethics of care and related literature problematizing the effects of advanced capitalism on women and workers more broadly, on the other. This framing will be introduced in this first chapter.

There are many more women in the UK accountancy profession than there are in Germany. In fact, there are many more chartered or chartered certified accountants—fifteen times more. The question that motivates this book is not which way of working results in more women at partnership level, but what the costs are of getting there in each context; to acknowledge that hierarchies are negotiated in different ways across borders and that this has variegated implications for women. Chapter 2 contributes to the accounting literature by introducing the profession comparatively and bringing together existing research on its history, women's entrance, and women's advancement within it. Comparatively little is known about the profession in Germany and how things work in practice, and this book therefore also contributes to learning about it. The focus on female chartered accountants who made it to partnership as well as the study's cross-national framing is novel and advances our knowledge of the careers and lives of modern elites in the professional services industry.

Chapter 3 draws attention to how the women interviewed in the UK were comparatively much clearer about the standardized career structures they were expected to navigate to advance to the top. At the same time, they were much more likely to talk about themselves, their private and public lives, and their careers, in commodified terms. In Germany, in contrast, respondents talked about the significance over the years of experienced friends and family relations in the profession, the support received by informal mentors, or benign father figures, or—where such support was lacking—the various steps they took to manoeuvre themselves into positions where supporting relationships were more likely. This focus on market-type structures in the UK in contrast to relationship-based careers in Germany affirms wider institutional differences. After all, the UK is the exemplar of a Liberal Market Economy (LME), while in Germany the focus remains on institutional coordination within a wider ordoliberal framework, and negotiations and coalitions are part and parcel of political life. But what does this mean from a feminist perspective?

The implications for women are teased out in Chapters 4 to 6 in relation to discrimination (Chapter 4), motherhood (Chapter 5), and work centrality and job insecurity (Chapter 6), and brought together in the conclusion and discussion in Chapter 7. The analysis shows how the sort of relationships the German female partners drew on at work, and the dependencies that came with these, of loyalty and discretion, may inhibit one's ability to name sexism and discrimination when we encounter them. In contrast, the formalized structures in the UK afforded more space to challenge such behaviours from a rights-based and arm's length approach. Similarly, the blurring of lines between private and public life in Germany in the entanglement of such relationships of dependency meant that motherhood, and the expectations with which it burdens women specifically (i.e. how women ought to behave, whether it is acceptable to forgo motherhood, and how one ought to mother) was everyone's business at work in Germany.

One of the key juxtapositions in the talk of the German respondents was that mothers should work part-time but that partnership is a full-time commitment, effectively disqualifying mothers from the top of the firm hierarchy. This is tricky in a population where 80 percent of women become mothers at some point in their life with over 70 percent of these women going on to be working mothers (Statistisches Bundesamt, 2019). In contrast, while in the UK women did not have to justify how they wanted to mother, problematically, at the same time, the unencumbered norm did not budge for motherhood and it was left for individual women to work out in private how to organize care for their children within the household in order to continue working like normative fathers might, often effectively relinquishing mothering to their husbands.

The market-like mechanisms that governed the UK respondents' careers did not judge them and their ways of mothering, but at the same time these structures also did not always provide for them. In the UK, the female partners interviewed, despite being organizational elites, often talked with little agency about working patterns while being acutely aware of economic downturns and recessions and the impact of these on *their* market value. Chapter 6 confirms just how much work dominates the lives of women working at this level, and the struggles and tensions the women tackled while trying to shape their lives at home and at work.

In both countries, the respondents talked about unpleasant experiences at work. But the women in Germany also shared how they trusted those they worked with, how they joined firms that their friends worked at. The German respondents frequently likened making partnership to a long-term commitment, for some even akin to marriage. This resonates with a focus on coordination and cooperation that is more specific to Coordinated Market Economies (CMEs) such as Germany. In the UK, a focus on standardization, competition, and performance, would, at times, turn against the women. Unlike their German counterparts, they witnessed and administered redundancies and even experienced being made redundant themselves in response to economic shifts. Here, the lack of relationships of trust at work perhaps meant that, as women, they were more vulnerable. Chapter 6 and Chapter 7 problematize the ways in which this standardization of human resource management, under the guise of organizational justice and fairness, also depersonalizes, and discourages relationships, thus isolating workers, while at the time being susceptible to bias and manipulation, but without anyone risking being held accountable to it. In contrast, the German partners, while being more exposed to intrusive views, behaviours, and judgements of others, particularly men, and struggling with blurred boundaries of work and home, could rely more often on relationships of trust to weather crises together. In Germany, the monopolist status of the profession was also working as it was meant to: as a closure mechanism controlling the supply of accountants, therefore making it more difficult to join the profession, but also ensuring that the women interviewed could depend on their qualifications and their relationships with others to see them through, and confidently seek new opportunities when they felt they needed or wanted to.

The book thus asks what, then, do we gain when we let go of the messy but enduring and often dependable relationship-based hierarchies the women relayed to me in Germany, and what in turn do we give up?

Dependency, Capitalism, and the State

The research is set in Germany and the United Kingdom and one of its premises is that the national context of the women's experiences matters. A number of frameworks developed in the 1990s and early 2000s, which seek to capture cross-national differences in how we do things at the level of the state and the political economy, informed my thinking. These include Hall and Soskice's (2001) Varieties of Capitalism, but also Esping-Andersen's Three Welfare Regimes (1990). In this book I particularly take forward the former, despite the criticism it has received since its conception, some of it from feminist writers. Developed in the sphere of political economy, the Varieties of Capitalism approach, in its original form, introduces a continuum of capitalism and two extreme models on either side—Coordinated Market Economics (CMEs) and Liberal Market Economies (LMEs)—and a spectrum of mixed-market economies in between (Hancké, Rhodes, and Thatcher, 2007; Molina and Rhodes, 2007). Coordinated Market Economies and Liberal Market Economies are distinguished on the basis of five spheres: industrial relations, vocational training and education, corporate governance, inter-firm relations, and the relationship between firms and their employees (Hall and Soskice, 2001). The firm is placed at the heart of the theory; however, a relational view is taken. The main distinction between LMEs and CMEs is the way institutions interact and how this interaction is coordinated, and it is this point that I draw upon in particular in this book: while actors in LMEs rely predominantly on the market as a coordinating drive, collaboration and relationships are key in CMEs. Firms and companies adapt their strategies accordingly, and the economy will, according to Hall and Soskice (2001), develop different institutional comparative advantages, with radical innovation more likely in LMEs and incremental innovation more likely in CMEs. Britain and Germany are often placed at the two extreme ends of the spectrum (Estevez-Abe, Iversen, and Soskice, 2001; Hall and Soskice, 2001), making it a good fit with this research project.

German firms, accordingly, rely on strong networks and the maintenance of relationships with other institutions such as unions or professional organizations as well as rivals to coordinate in terms of training, research, and financing (Busch, 2005; Hall and Soskice, 2001) and in overcoming crises

(Weishaupt, 2021). Here, trust and relationships, built on the idea of mutual dependencies, are encouraged. In contrast, LMEs such as Britain rely largely on market forces as a coordination mechanism. The welfare system then complements and/or replicates these differences in focus to some extent. For example, the labour force in CMEs is able to depend on a relatively generous security net, and this encourages investment in industry-specific skills. In contrast, the labour force in LMEs will usually only be able to draw on a very slim level of welfare support and thus focuses more on investing in general skills, which enables smoother transitions in and out of the labour market (Estevez-Abe, Iversen, and Soskice, 2001).

The VoC, like other typologies at this level, has a number of shortcomings and critiques commonly note that it is overly simplistic, that it lacks dynamism, and that it is Western-centric (Gould, Barry, and Wilkinson, 2015), and gender- and class-blind (Estevez-Abe, 2002; Mandel and Shalev, 2009; Rubery, 2009). Estevez-Abe (2002, 2005) has been at the forefront of critiquing the gender blindness of the VoC and focuses specifically on the second dimension: vocational training and education. Estevez-Abe argues that women are more limited in the labour market in CMEs due to three disadvantages when compared to men: higher risk of layoff due to family dependencies, lower rate of return on specific skill investments due to a lower amount of time spent in the labour force on average, and less chances for skill formation as women's childbearing phase may coincide with the time to form those skills. In addition, she notes that firms, in the absence of perfect information, will be more prone to practicing statistical discrimination in CMEs as they too anticipate a lower return on their investment. These disadvantages then result in a gender-bias in human capital in CMEs such as Germany, while LMEs, where general skills are more valued, are, according to Estevez-Abe, relatively more gender-neutral. In line with this, as will be discussed in more depth in Chapter 2 which focuses on the profession, the chartered accountancy qualification in Germany is in practice not readily transferable to other industries, while the equivalent qualification in the UK is transferable and often seen as a stepping stone. Yet, Mandel and Shalev (2009) have also noted that this gender bias in skill formation does not hold true for all women and that the intersections of class with gender need to be considered.

Indeed, Rubery (2009) also questioned Estevez-Abe's argument, stressing that a wider, more comprehensive perspective must be taken. Specifically, she critiques the functional distinction between firm-specific and general skills, pointing out that Soskice and Estevez-Abe describe the occupational labour market for women in Germany, often considered the archetypical CME, as 'functionally equivalent to jobs requiring either no training or general educational skills at a low level' (2009: 196) and further highlighting that this neglects the role of occupational labour markets in ensuring that skills remain valued once women return to the labour market following a period of childrearing—very relevant in the context of accountancy. In addition, it underplays the role of informal firm-specific training in LMEs. Referring to research by Crompton and Sanderson (1990), Estevez-Abe substantiated her critique by focusing on highly educated women in LMEs, who, in order to protect their career prospects while moving in and out of the labour force, may choose to enter careers which require a licence to practice or accreditation, such as the accountancy profession.

Nonetheless, even in occupations where, through accreditation, skills are supposedly rendered more time-insensitive, there are what Rubery (2009: 197) calls 'major scarring effects' for women leaving and re-entering the labour market in terms of future earnings. In addition, the Varieties of Capitalism and Estevez-Abe's work on skill formation presume that economic actors in the labour market, both employers and employees, make informed choices about the skills they invest in or the employees they 'choose' to hire, retain, or promote. Rubery (2009) noted that this potentially exaggerates the role of employers in maintaining gender segregation in the labour market, which disregards the wider system of 'loosely interrelated practices, processes, actions and meanings that result in and maintain class, gender, and racial inequalities within particular organizations' (Acker, 2006: 443). As examples, Rubery (2009: 199) specifically names recruitment decisions made on the basis of internal employee referrals, 'promoting a long hours culture (such that willingness to work paid or unpaid overtime is effectively a job requirement) or creating and maintaining a male work culture that is not conducive to gender-mixed working'. Furthermore, Estevez-Abe's (2002, 2005) argument also focuses in more detail on the underlying premise that women are more likely than men to interrupt their work to take care of family responsibilities, which reflects the prevailing gender segregation in the domestic labour market (Doucet, 2006). Geist (2005), for example, finds that domestic work is not shared equally in any of the three welfare state regimes, but that an equal distribution is less common in conservative welfare regimes than in liberal or social democratic regimes. This difference is largely attributed to structural constraints in conservative labour markets which are often aligned with CMEs.

Ann Orloff (2009; 2011) has also contributed significantly to the gendering of typologies of this kind, and her work connects the comparative literature on welfare states and capitalism, with the literature on feminism and post-maternalism that I turn to in the next section and draw on across the book. Orloff, in 1993, argued that the comparative literature on state social provision has neglected to consider gender and the full effects of provisions on women. These remain valid critiques. Nonetheless, these typologies also allow us to consider how things we take for granted might be done differently in two nations which are relatively close geographically. Hall and Soskice (2001: 18) introduce the notion of institutional complementarities, noting that 'nations with a particular type of coordination in one sphere of the economy should tend to develop complementary practices in other spheres as well'. For example, CMEs would usually adopt policies that offer relatively high levels of social protections (Mandel and Shalev, 2009; McCall and Orloff, 2005) as they need specialist and highly qualified staff to benefit from its institutional comparative advantage that is incremental innovation. These social protections signify also what Esping-Andersen (2000) defines as de-commodification, which is at the heart of his three welfare regimes typology. Esping-Andersen defines de-commodification as a 'a citizen's relative independence from pure market forces; it captures one important dimension of freedom and constraint in the everyday life of advanced capitalism' (2000: 353). It stands for the degree to which citizens have to rely on the labour market to survive. The higher their ability to survive without entering the labour market, the higher the de-commodification effect and thus social protection. In contrast, liberal welfare regimes provide only the bare minimum of social protection, thereby encouraging citizens to enter and remain in the labour market. Here, the labour force would be unwilling to invest in highly specialist vocational skills in the absence of high social protections, as finding new employment with very specific skills would prove more difficult than with general skills. In contrast, Hall and Soskice's conceptualisation of a CME can often be found to be paired with a social policy approoach along the lines of Esping-Andersen's 'corporatist' welfare state regime, where social protection and so-called 'de-commodification effects' are higher (Mandel and Shalev, 2009). Here too then, dependency and the extent to which individuals are expected to function unsupported are at the heart of the model. The VoC does not function as a critique of capitalism per se, but it acknowledges variations and the implications for citizens, for firms, for competitive advantage of different economies, thus bridging various spheres.

Despite its critics, analyses of policy interventions to economic crises suggest that the VoC continues to offer a meaningful framework to think about cross-national differences at this level and that governments will resort to institutional legacies when reacting to crises (see Chung and Thewissen, 2011, for an analysis of reactive policy strategies to the financial crisis of 2008;

and Bariola and Collins, 2021, or Beland, Cantillon, Hick, et al., 2021, for such analyses in relation to the coronavirus pandemic).

There is an ongoing debate about the charge that CMEs and LMEs are converging—i.e. that CMEs too are becoming more and more liberalized and market-focused. However, Germany's liberalism is of a different kind. For example, Weishaupt (2021), in an analysis of Germany's response to the financial crisis of 2008/2009 and the coronavirus pandemic of 2020, notes: 'In Germany, two sets of culturally embraced economic ideas traditionally dominate—one about fiscal discipline and price stability, and one about the Social Market Economy, which includes a generous welfare state. These two at times competing visions are bound in an opaque and occasionally incoherent narrative of German "ordoliberalism"' (2021: 5). Ordoliberalism *is* understood as a type of neoliberalism but one that 'calls for a *strong* state, mainly to contain market power' (Beck and Kotz, 2017: 14).

Young (2017) argues that ordoliberalism developed as 'the German concept of neoliberalism (and) originated in the 1930s, in opposition to the Anglo-Saxon *laissez-faire* liberalism of self-regulating markets and the totalitarian alternatives in the form of fascism and communism' (2017: 32). Ordo here refers to *Ordnung* or *order* (Young, 2017: 34). Ordoliberalism sometimes carries negative connotations, more recently due to Germany's commitment to fiscal discipline and its dominance in pushing for austerity measures in other EU member states following the financial crisis of 2008, often with painful consequences for citizens in those countries. And some argue that neo- and ordoliberalism are essentially one movement (Wilkinson, 2019). But, at the core of ordoliberalism is a pledge to the social market economy, and for the government to work with social partners to deliver this. In the German context, this is a commitment made by the centre right Christian Democrats, in power until recently (2021). Reviewing Germany's response to the financial crisis, Weishaupt (2021: 7) writes: 'Chancellor Merkel repeatedly stressed that the "Social Market Economy was more than pure capitalism, but a societal conviction" (Frankfurter Rundschau, 5 November 2008)' and 'CSU chief Horst Seehofer stated that Germany had "the best economic order of all: the Social Market Economy" and that, as long as he was in power, "neoliberalism was stone dead" (cited in Neumann and von Hammerstein 2008)'. Weishaupt reminds us of this commitment to coordination, and to maintaining often complex and conflicting relationships between partners such as unions and private sector employers, from a centre-right party that has dominated leadership in Germany's political life over the past seventy years. Weishaupt traces the often messy and frustrating interplay between these, the media, and the government on the path to delivering solutions to crises and decision-making. Relationships here are long-term; they are not easy and they require commitment, but they are maintained nonetheless. At the same time, not everyone can have an input, because relationships have a history and thus, by definition, exclude those who are not party to them, who do not share that history, or who are unable to show up—the latter often including vulnerable or marginalized groups. But those in the relationships are also constrained: expectations of conformity, of taking views from one another and accepting criticism, as well as expectations of reciprocity, all matter (Sennett, 2012). And trust and reciprocity vary across national and cultural boundaries as Dietz, Gillespie, and Chao (2010) show. This is one of the core ideas taken forward and explored throughout the book at the organizational level. Relationships, at work and in the private sphere, are mediated by frequency of interaction, reliability, and trust—but also by similarity (McPherson, Smith-Lovin, and Cook, 2001). This is what we call homophily, which has gender, race, and class implications, amongst others. Women working within male-dominated professions are especially at a disadvantage when negotiating their way through relationship-based organizational spaces, because relationships at work favour homosociality (Holgersson, 2013; Lipman-Blumen, 1976) and are enacted in organizational bureaucracies where masculinity and power are interlinked, producing and maintaining gendered power relations vertically as well as horizontally (Acker, 2006; Collinson and Hearn, 1994; Kanter, 1977). This is where relationships between managers and the managed have the capacities to turn into gatekeeping relationships of dependency that are gendered in their unfolding and effects.

The 1990s saw a move away from the idea of 'female deficit' in management studies and the associated focus on the 'training of women' in, for example, assertiveness or leadership, and towards looking at organizational practices and the extent to which gender and gendered outcomes are produced and reproduced at work by how we organize it and ourselves within it. Here, the focus in affecting practice then moved towards concentrating instead on restraining discretionary behaviours and bias by, predominately, male managers in recruitment and hiring (Goldin and Rouse, 2000), salary and bonus setting (Abraham, 2016; Healy and Ahamed, 2019; Joshi, Son and Roh, 2015; Kulich, Trojanowski, Ryan, Haslam, et al., 2011), performance management (Heilman, 2012; Rivera and Tilcsik, 2019), and so forth, by focusing on the adoption and development of more transparent performance management systems, and investing in training, for example on unconscious bias or diversity—not without critiques (Anand and Winters, 2008; Osman, 2021; Noon, 2018; Williamson and Foley, 2018). But despite large investments in diversity and inclusion drives by employers (Kumra and Vinnicombe, 2008), and despite extensive sets of legislation on equal opportunity in the workplace, forty-five years after Kanter's (1977) *Men and Women of the Corporation*, men still dominate the top of organizational hierarchies, and the way we organize work still favours men's careers and reproduces and maintains class and racial inequalities endemic in wider society. True, there are more women in work (Acker, 2006; Amis, Mair, and Munir, 2020; Holck, 2018). But the focus on cutting of ties, on cutting discretionary behaviour, of rewarding performance and not experience or seniority—a focus on professionalization, marketization, 'merit', and competition—went hand in hand with a neoliberal acceleration of capitalism, with globalization and the rise of the financial services industry. This is what Sennett (2012: 192) terms 'a new figuration of global investment and shareholder value' where the focus is firmly on short-terminism. This manifests itself in different patterns. At the organizational level, within the Anglo-Saxon context he focuses on, Sennett critiques the rise of a 'fetish of assertiveness'—a rise in our tendency to associate effectiveness with assertiveness, especially in 'leadership' (Ames and Flynn, 2007; Santora, 2007). But this inhibits the potential for cooperation. Sennett (2012) calls for the return to a 'subjunctive mood', a move away from 'I think' and back towards 'I would have thought' which opens a space for others to join in and think together. He notes that 'the subjunctive mood is most at home in the dialogical domain' where the point of a discussion is not its resolution 'by finding common ground. Though no shared agreements may be reached, through the process of exchange people may become more aware of their own views and expand their understanding of one another' (2012: 19). But this is precisely an output that performance management systems cannot cope with. Sennett as well as Scharff (2016) note the ways in which we now compete with ourselves, heightening our anxieties about our own worth, that is so tangled up in our working lives, and consequently accelerating our withdrawal (Sennett, 2012). Sennett observes:

> Modern labour is increasingly short-term in character ... Within organizations, social relations are also short-term, managerial practice recommending that teams of workers be kept together no more than nine to twelve months so that employees do not become 'ingrown', that is, personally attached to each other. Superficial social relations are one product of short-term time; when people do not stay long in an institution, both their knowledge of and commitment to the organization weakens. Superficial relations and short institutional bonds together reinforce the silo effect: people keep to themselves, do not get involved in problems, which are none of their immediate business, particularly with those in the

institution who do something different. In addition to material and institutional reasons, cultural forces today work against the practice of demanding cooperation. Modern society is producing a new character type. This is the sort of person bent on reducing the anxieties which differences can inspire, whether these be political, racial, religious, ethnic or erotic in character.

(Sennett, 2012: 193)

This cultural space of a new modernity is marked by a neoliberal logic that cannot cope with dependency (Stephens, 2012) and insists that the individual be responsible for health, wealth, and general well-being, never mind one's circumstances. It drives individuals to act as entrepreneurial subjects who 'relate to themselves as if they were a business, are active, embrace risks, capably manage difficulties and hide injuries' (Scharff, 2016: 108). There is a fear of workers becoming 'ingrown' or connected. Because connections that are meaningful supersede our neutrality and draw us into complex webs of reciprocity. Much of what Sennett describes—the short-term-ness of our ties to organizations and others at work—is captured by the idea of the 'the boundaryless career' (Arthur and Rousseau, 1996) in the Anglo-Saxon organizational and management literature. But it is a culturally specific phenomenon. In Germany the level of job transitions within the quarter century from 1984 and 2010 actually decreased (Kattenbach, Schneidhofer, Luecke, et al. 2014), for example. But there are notable convergences, as outlined above.

In this book, I introduce and analyse the respondents' accounts in relation to their career histories, their experiences of discrimination and sexism, motherhood, work-life balance, work centrality, and job in/security, and explore how the extent to which this absence of relationships at work might matter in shaping our experiences of gender relations at work throughout our career history—what is the cost of this shift away from each other and towards the unrelational performance-orientated self from a gender perspective?

Feminism, Women's Careers, and Capitalism

Feminist scholars have a strong tradition of exposing and critiquing the effects of capitalism on women (see e.g. Fraser, 2017, 2013, 2009; Perrons, 2021; Rottenberg, 2014). For Fraser, feminism's 'signature insights' and 'insurrectionary spirit' relate to 'its structural critique of capitalism's androcentrism, its systemic analysis of male domination, and its gender-sensitive revisions of democracy and justice' (2013: 2). Like McRobbie (2004), for example, she notes a turning point around 1990 which saw a 'broader cultural shift from the politics of equality to the politics of identity' (Fraser, 2013: 2), and 'towards a moment of definitive self-critique in feminist theory' (McRobbie, 2004: 256). Fraser (2013: 2–3) highlights a '"dangerous liaison" between feminism and marketization' henceforth, and these critiques are taken forwards here and in forthcoming sections. For example, in Chapter 4 in particular, I draw on analyses emanating out of cultural and media studies by UK-based writers such as Rosalind Gill, Angela McRobbie, Catherine Rottenberg, or Christina Scharff, who problematize women's relationship to feminism within a neoliberal cultural frame that expects us to treat ourselves as entrepreneurial selves, and run our lives 'as if we were a business' (Scharff, 2016: 108). These contributions are enriched by the insights of Foucault and the concept of governmentality (see e.g. Rottenberg, 2017, 2014; Scharff, 2018, 2016, 2011; and Foucault, 2010 [1979]) uncovering the ways in which neoliberalism seeks to convert human subjects into human capital (Bauman, 2000; Brown, 2015; Rottenberg, 2017) and, in the case of middle-class women, predicates future fulfilment 'on careful sequencing of career and maternity and small (self-) investments in the present' (Rottenberg, 2017: 332) with reproduction and care work 'outsourced to other women deemed disposable since they are neither considered strivers nor properly responsibilitized. The emergent neoliberal order is slowly expunging gender and even sexual differences among a certain strata of subjects while it simultaneously produces new forms of racialized and class-stratified gender exploitation' (Rottenberg, 2017: 333).

Rottenberg (2017: 345) paints a bleak picture of the future for women and work, emphasizing the role of technology in severing the ties between women's bodies and motherhood. These are important critiques of our times and of feminism, and I draw on these contributions at various points in the book. They are insightful in that they help us unpick and advance our theoretical engagement with ideas of how power manifests itself in society and how we might respond to it (Oksala, 2013).

Yet, more broadly, I feel inspired by ethics of care feminists who also offer a normative perspective of how things ought to be. These recognize the ways in which human beings are embodied and embedded in social relations and institutions, which has implications for women in all spheres of life. Women's reproductive capacity, for example the ability to bear and nurse children, and the fact that we do most of what has become known as 'care work' or 'caring labour', matters at work and at home. But how we relate to one another at work is a function of our wider socio-political and economic environment, as well as our varying feminist legacies. The project was motivated by a desire to learn about the respondents' experiences on the way to partnership as women and exploring how these experiences might differ across borders. The focus then is not on where more women can rise up the hierarchy to partnership faster, but on acknowledging different ways of doing things and thinking about the outcomes of these differences for women at work and at home. It is a specific feminist contribution to an evolving and growing body of literature on inequality in the labour market and in organizations.

But what does it mean to do feminist research? As Letherby (2003) notes, feminist 'researchers start with the political commitment to produce useful knowledge that will make a difference to women's lives through social and individual change' (2003: 5). But feminism is also a political project and as such can mean different things to different people. As a movement it developed differently in different places. Offen (1988), for example, notes that feminists in the UK and US took a rights-based approach focusing on gender equality in access to positions of power and all spheres of social life, while, in contradistinction, the 'European' movement focused on 'sexual difference rather than similarity within a framework of male/female complementarity; and, instead of seeking unqualified admission to male-dominated society, they mounted a wide-ranging critique of the society and its institutions' (Offen, 1988: 124). Women's reproductive capacity and the question of motherhood straddle these varying legacies in often uncomfortable ways. The problem is not that women work, for as Gilman (1903) reminded us, women have always worked, and all industries were once domestic. But it is through the industrial revolution and under capitalism that we work in frequently large, adult-only spaces that are removed from our homes, denying the centrality of care and the dependence of little children (Bueskens, 2016) in particular. Any form of economic organization where production is organized outside the domestic sphere is tied to feminism's dilemma with the sameness/difference dogma—the extent to which we believe that men and women are different and what that might mean for the roles we occupy at work and in caring for others. We have seen at least two extremes since the second World War in Europe and the UK, both oppressive to women: on the one hand, a focus on difference and a division of labour under a capitalist breadwinner model where the mother is isolated and to remain in the domestic sphere, giving herself to mothering and entirely economically dependent on a man, and on the other hand, a focus on sameness and the full integration of women into the labour force which necessitates in turn the complete institutionalization of the child, either during working hours, or, as practiced in some cases in the German Democratic Republic, in so-called

'Wochenkrippen'[1] or Wochenheime for six days and nights a week (Stary, 2018). The child and its care are invisible from an employment perspective in both contexts, but while the former ascribes it with an all-consuming need for its biological mother, the latter denies any needs for the mother, the father, the wider family, or attachment to these at all. This dilemma is at the heart of ethics of care approaches to feminism where dependencies—not necessarily of children—take centre stage. This literature argues that it is not women's 'independence' that should be our aim, but rather the organization of society around an understanding that we are all dependent at different points in our lives, at birth, in ill-health and old age; that independence, autonomy, and the rational self are capitalist fictions, and that women, by virtue of performing most of the care work around the world, are more likely to be subjected to a 'derivative dependency' (Fineman, 2000; Kittay, 1999) which must be supported rather than exploited or passed on to others.

Kittay (1999) puts forward a powerful argument when she asserts that a

> conception of society viewed as an association of equals masks inevitable dependencies, those of infancy and childhood, old age, illness and disability. While we are dependent, we are not well positioned to enter a competition for the goods of social cooperation on equal terms. And those who care for dependents, who must put their own interests aside to care for one who is entirely vulnerable to their actions, enter the competition for social goods with a handicap. Viewed from the perspective of the dependency critique, we can say: Of course, women have not achieved equality on men's side of the sexual divide—for how could women abandon those they leave behind on their side of the divide?
>
> **(1999: xi)**

Kittay notes our 'nested dependencies', the fact that we are 'interdependent', thus stressing the need for social cooperation and reciprocity as central to a functioning welfare state; to support both those cared for and those doing the caring. It recognizes the individual as entangled with a place, and its socio-economic and political context, as well as with people, and that these affect one's capabilities (Kittay (2011) uses this term following the work of Nussbaum and Sen (e.g. 1993) in all spheres of life, including the workplace. Fineman (2008; 2017), also drawing on insights from feminist scholarship and disability studies, takes a broader approach in her conceptualization of 'vulnerability theory', in which she criticizes the formulation of the current legal subject, based on liberal individualism and imagined to be independent

---

[1] E.g. like state sponsored boarding school for babies and toddlers, sometimes starting at the age of six weeks, from Monday morning to Friday evening.

and autonomous. Instead, she proposes that the legal system holds the state responsible towards a 'vulnerable subject'. Here, instead of making provisions for specific groups on the basis of, for example, sex, disability, age, race, and so forth, the term vulnerability is instead applied to all, acknowledging that vulnerability is universal to our 'embodied humanity' which, for example, 'carries with it the ever-constant possibility of dependency' (2008: 9), beyond the years of early childhood and old age. Both Kittay's and Fineman's approaches are insightful reminders of how the 'ideal worker' debates within organization studies are embedded in wider legal and sociopolitical structures that are variegated in their willingness to commit to taking responsibility for the care of dependents and dependency workers—a point I explored above.

The focus on dependencies, in and outside of work, in a book on women's careers in accountancy is relevant because, as Chapters 2 to 6 will show, women's reproductive capacity always matters. When it is spoken about it can be intrusive. This comes to the fore, for example when Barbara, a participant in this research, is told that she has not been assigned a project of significance because she is in her early thirties and may get pregnant. Similarly, it is there when it is not spoken about, and indeed when reproductive matters such as pregnancy and birth, and the challenges these can pose to working women, are disavowed, which can make the workplace terribly unfair. An example is the case of Apoorva in Chapter 5, where she is told that all partners can come and go as they please—a supposedly gender-neutral arrangement with gendered outcomes—that leaves her working with a newborn baby by her feet.

Scope and Limitations

The book examines the narratives of sixty female partners in accounting and professional service firms in Germany and the United Kingdom. There is further information about the research methodology employed in the Appendix. The respondents were all partners in accounting firms, with most being full equity partners and some noting a salaried partner status. The group was relatively homogenous, as—unfortunately—might still be expected in a project studying elites (see Table 1.1.). Chapter 4 shares the women's accounts of being different at work, speaking of age, accent, race, and ethnicity. The vast majority of the women interviewed were white, middle-class, and married, heterosexual women. Half of them had children. A representation of the respondents' characteristics is offered in Table 1.1 and respondent profiles are included in Appendix Table 1 and Appendix Table 2 at the end

Table 1.1 Respondent characteristics

Respondents/Country	Germany				UK			
Respondents/Firm Size	Small	Medium	Large	Total	Small	Medium	Large	Total
Number of Respondents	9	9	12	30	4	18	8	30
Age								
30–39	2	0	1	**3**	3	3	4	**10**
40–49	4	3	10	**17**	1	12	2	**15**
50–59	3	6	1	**10**	0	3	2	**5**
Socio-Economic Background								
Working Class	0	3	0	**3**	1	4	2	**7**
Medium Class	8	5	11	**24**	2	12	6	**20**
Upper Class	1	1	1	**3**	1	1		**2**
Ethnic Origin								
White-British/German	9	9	10	**28**	3	16	7	**26**
White-Eastern European			1	**1**				**0**
European Union			1	**1**			1	**1**
Asian or Caribbean British					1	1	1	**3**
Marital Status								
Single	0	1	3	**4**	0	2	2	**4**
Divorced	1	1	1	**3**	0	0	0	**0**
Married	7	5	4	**16**	4	15	6	**25**
Partnered	1	2	4	**7**	0	0	0	**1**
Children								
0	4	4	9	**17**	2	8	2	**12**
1	2	3	3	**8**	0	1	2	**3**
2	3	2	0	**5**	2	9	4	**15**

of the book. The Appendix also includes a methodological note, which provides more information about how data was collected, interviews conducted and analysed and how categories such as gender, class and ethnicity were constructed.

The analysis offered in this book is interdisciplinary, and this is one of its key strengths, drawing on readings particularly from political economy and the feminist ethics of care literature. It is qualitative research, and therefore one of its key limitations is that we cannot generalize. But we can theorize from it and, in doing so, I am particularly interested in thinking about the potential and applicability of the frame employed in organization studies;

also with a view to producing a normative perspective of what we might want to see happen in our workplaces and in our communities. The latter is something that Chapter 7 is concerned with and, in particular, the question of what we ought to care about when it comes to women and equality at work.

Interdisciplinarity always also introduces a set of challenges, and I think that one of these involves a sense of trepidation around how to join up conversations and debates in different fields that can employ different languages, where terms may mean different things, and where scholars have different habits of how to go about things (see e.g. Rhoten and Pfirman, 2007; or Szostak, 2007). For example, the terms in/inter/dependence are employed in the ethics of care literature, in the sociological literature on the effects of the new or accelerated capitalism, and in the literature on neoliberal feminism, and I too employ these terms in relation to the respondents' experiences at and around work. It is not always used in precisely the same way, even where these literatures overlap. There is a case to be made here that this way of employing terms across boundaries brings limitations with it, as well as opportunities to ask, and seek to answer, questions that may encourage new, productive avenues of inquiry. And I think that there is already a tradition of such explorations in scholarship that authors such as Richard Sennett, Eva Feder Kittay, or Ann Orloff have always pursued themselves. But I hope that, in the spirit of this being my first monograph, the reader will forgive instances of interdisciplinary awkwardness.

Outline of the Book

This book comprises seven chapters. This concludes Chapter 1 which introduces the key findings and frames employed.

Chapter 2 introduces the accounting profession and offers an overview of what we know about women's entrance and advancement to partnership in accountancy in Germany and the UK. It provides a snapshot of some of the latest research and current statistics. It will be of interest to anyone who wants to learn more about the history of the profession and women's advancement within it and those who wonder about the differences of the professions across borders—a topic that remains underexplored.

Chapter 3 focuses on an analysis of the career histories of the respondents. It highlights the role of dependency between respondents and their line managers or supervisors on the way to the top and examines how these dependencies are patterned cross-nationally. It asks what dependency in the workplace does to women and their careers-both being dependent on others and being able to depend on others. It also introduces a comparative curve in relation to women's career advancement.

Chapter 4 concentrates on the respondents' narratives on sexism, discrimination, and equal opportunities in the workplace, relating the ways in which respondents pointed to sexism in professional service firms, or indeed denied its existence, to their relationships with their line managers. It employs the literature on post- and neoliberal feminism in its analysis, and also considers how the respondents made sense of being othered or being different at work from an intersectional perspective.

Chapter 5 moves from an exploration of the respondents' lives at work to the subject of motherhood, at work and at home, exposing the ways in which partnership always also requires one to be an unencumbered worker, and how this was done in different ways in practice across borders. It also considers the different roles fathers play in the lives of these women.

Chapter 6 discusses work centrality and job in/security and considers the extent to which the female partners interviewed felt secure in their positions when faced with fluctuations of the economy. In this way then, the book moves from an exploration of the respondents' lives at work towards an acknowledgement of how our working lives intersect with our private lives in gendered ways and to an examination of how both are subject to a wider economic, political, and embodied reality.

Chapter 7 contains the discussion and conclusion, with the focus returning to making sense of dependency at work and women's advancement under capitalism. It problematizes the matter of women's time and presence and the commodification of the self from a cross-national perspective. And it considers how we might go about tackling the challenges ahead from a feminist perspective, resisting an upside-down future under capitalism.

2
Accounting Matters

Mapping Women's Underrepresentation in Accountancy

This chapter focuses on the accountancy industry and its emergence as a profession. The first section focuses on why we all should care about accountants and women's standing in the profession. It reminds us of the importance of accounts, accountants, and accounting in organizing our everyday lives, our relation to the state, how it enables trade, and the health and wealth of businesses and their shareholders in the globalized market economy of the twenty-first century. It considers why accountancy is a protected occupation in the first place—what is it that makes it worthy of professional closure and a Royal Charter in the UK for example? Section 2 focuses on the entrance of women into the profession and women's advancement since. This is quite a UK-centred literature that has had a leading role in advancing our understanding of professionalization more widely, and of professionalization also as a political project. There is only a relatively small literature here that explores this in Germany, which I introduce as well. The final three sections provide an overview of women's advancement in practice and how it is represented and explored in the academic literature.

Mystery and Professional Closure—the Making and Ascent of Accountancy

Ruth Hines (1988), a critical accounting scholar-turned-poet, once likened accountants to sorcerers. What Hines was referring to was accountants' role in deciding what constitutes an asset, what constitutes its worth, and doing so with a degree of discretion that renders the process inscrutable to many of us. It was this description of accounting that first raised my interest in a profession that is stereotypically considered to be boring, rigid, and overly regulated, but that wields its influence in every step we take in business and political life, from takeovers to bankruptcies, and from Brexit to war—we need accountants to help us see the bigger picture, to enable us to trust one

Gendered Hierarchies of Dependency. Patrizia Kokot-Blamey, Oxford University Press.
© Patrizia Sofia Kokot-Blamey (2023). DOI: 10.1093/oso/9780199688456.003.0002

another under capitalism that the things we claim to have are real, even when they cannot be seen in trade and in business. Accounting and accountants thus matter in the organization and regulation of our public lives. They bring order and simplify things (Gill, 2009). It is an example of a successful professionalization project, which, however, is always also a project of exclusion. Chartered accountants, as they are known in Britain, are also called 'public accountants' internationally, and the term *public* here is related to the status of the profession in many countries as what is essentially a government-sponsored monopoly (Lee, 1995). This monopoly status, which means that only professionals examined by certain government-recognized institutes may call themselves chartered accountants, or Wirtschaftsprüfer, is granted by the state on the basis that a profession performs a service to the public (Lee, 1995; Witz, 1992). It is the latter that distinguishes the professions, such as law and medicine, from occupations. Bedard (1989) notes that '(t)he essence of all professions—including public accounting—lies in the expertise of its members. Recognising that some complex tasks require special competence, society may licence performance of those tasks exclusively to designated professionals' (1989: 113). Indeed, as more detailed bankruptcy legislation was introduced in the UK in the second half of the nineteenth century, the services of accountants became more and more valuable; however, it also attracted incompetent individuals, leading a British judge in a bankruptcy case in the early 1870s to conclude that 'lawyers are gentlemen' and 'accountants are ignorami' (Markus, 1996: 15). The establishment of chartered accountancy institutes to regulate and oversee training and qualifications was therefore deemed by some a necessary step to ensure the public's trust in the profession (Markus, 1996). Others, however, argue that the primary motivation for seeking occupational closure—that is to create educational and professional barriers to entry—was to gain market control and thereby ultimately the power over supply and demand of professionals. The introduction of new bankruptcy laws, for example, would have meant that lawyers could perform some of the tasks accountants usually performed (Lee, 1995). The first professional institute of this kind in the world was founded in Edinburgh in 1853 (Shackleton, 1998), while the profession united in Germany in the early 1930s (Markus, 1996). Nowadays, chartered accountants engage in a range of activities, including M&A transactions, management consulting, tax advisory, and so forth—a matter of controversy. However, public accountants also carry out statutory audits in publicly listed companies and limited companies of a certain size, and thereby, presumably, perform a service to the public by ensuring that the accounts of companies represent a 'true and fair' view of 'reality' (Walton, 1993; also see Gill, 2009)—what

Ruth Hines was referring to in her poetic contribution to critical accounting scholarship. Yet, while accountants are therefore performing a public service in terms of assisting fraud prevention and helping the public trust in markets, they are at times not liable if fraud is left undetected, prompting some to criticize the monopolist status of the profession as unwarranted (Canada, Kuhn, and Sutton, 2008; Doralt, Hellgardt, Hopt et al., 2008; and Lee, 1995). In Germany, the profession's status is receiving similar scrutiny due to the role of Wirschaftsprüfer in a number of scandals, for example, relatively recently, the insolvency of Wirecard, which set off another critical debate about the influence of Big-4 firms in politics and business (Scholtes, 2021).

The monopolist status is also one of the reasons why public accountancy is considered by some to be an elite profession (Macdonald, 1984, also see Willmott, 1986). One way this elite status can be exemplified is by noting the involvement of chartered accountants and public accounting firms in scandals (see Low, Davey, and Hooper, 2008; Tinker, 1985) and major events in economic history: the collapse of energy trader Enron in 2001, for example, or the bankruptcy of Lehman Brothers in 2008. And also the role of accountants in providing public challenge to going concern assumptions during recent bank collapses (e.g in the case of Credit Suisse (ICAEW, 2023)). It highlights the ways in which accounting firms are—partially due to their assumed role as 'guardians of the public interest' (Sikka, Willmott, and Lowe, 1989)—in a position of power and one that grants them access to information that is not generally in the public domain.

Tinker further points to the impact of accounting regulation in maintaining the status quo of class, gender, and race relations through its concealed role in wealth distribution:

> Members of a society are interconnected through their economic and social interdependencies: employees to investors to consumers to taxpayers to mothers to welfare recipients to students to insomniacs. Accounting information is not merely a manifestation of this myriad of interdependencies; it is a social scheme for adjudicating these relationships. We are all costs and revenues to each other; everyone is potentially a benefactor and a victim in the accounting nexus of social decisions.
>
> **(Tinker, 1985: foreword)**

Accounting and its standards are socially constructed, and the conclusions that arise from following accounting procedures have specific economic implications. Dahl (2005) argues that the study of elites enables a better understanding of the power structures involved between different actors in society. And, indeed, Tinker (1985: 81) describes 'accounting practice is a means for resolving social conflict, a device for appraising the terms of exchange between social constituencies, and an institutional mechanism for arbitrating, evaluating, and adjudicating social choices'. In addition, the power of the profession is demonstrated by its involvement in setting the global standard-setting procedures it then ensures are kept to through audits too, which is, to be fair, the prerogative of a self-governing profession and thus several members of the International Accounting Standards Board (IASB) are chartered accountants (IFRS, 2022). Standard setting affects businesses around the world and has the capacity to further complicate regulation, thereby stimulating demand for accountancy services (Lee, 1995). And according to the ICAEW (2021), close to 20 per cent of FTSE 100 Chief Executive Officers are accountants, with two thirds of Chief Financial Officers being former Big-4 firm employees (Accountancy Daily, 2020). The involvement of accountants in various past and present history-shaping events demonstrates the influence of accountants in decision-making in the business world. But, examining *her*story (Lehman, 1992; Kirkham, 1992) in accounting shows that women were kept from sharing in this influence for much of the profession's past.

Herstory: The Entrance and Rise of Women in the Accounting Profession

Unlike other professions such as law or medicine, the scope of the accountant's tasks was historically ill-defined, and by the mid-nineteenth century 'no clear means of differentiating the accountant from other classes of worker such as clerk had yet been established' (Kirkham and Loft, 1993: 519, also see Loft, 1992). In similar ways to the doctor-nurse dichotomy in medicine, the work of women accountants was cast off as inferior and 'mere bookkeeping' in the accounting profession. As more individuals claimed to be accountants, some of the elite among them started the professionalization project in a more organized manner by seeking a Royal Charter. High education standards were set, which excluded many women and working-class men. Interestingly, Kirkham and Loft (1993) note how middle-class women who were interested in the profession were discouraged through discursive practices that alluded to women's 'emotional' nature, which was deemed unfit for bankruptcy and insolvency-related work—a key focus of accountants at the time. Evans and Rumens (2020) too show how the professionalization of accountancy is significantly gendered in its origins. In Scotland, meanwhile, the Royal Charter was obtained and phrased in such a way that when women were attempting to enter the profession at the beginning of the twentieth century, the question was whether or not the Royal Charter permitted the admission of female apprentices at all or whether women would have to form their own society and seek a new Royal Charter (Shackleton, 1999). Professionalization projects of this kind lay the ground for the creation of elites by restricting the supply of professionals in the market in ways that are controlled by the elites themselves. This then acts as an additional barrier to women as well as working-class men, among others (Jacobs, 2003). In their work, Kirkham and Loft (1993) show how, through repetitive discursive practices, the professional accountant was 'constituted, in part, as something that is "not a clerk or a bookkeeper" and, in part, as something that is "not a woman"' (Kirkham and Loft, 1993: 507).

In England and Wales, women gained the right to vote in 1918, and the Sex Disqualification (Removal) Act became law in late 1919. It was only then that the Society of Incorporated Accountants and Auditors formally admitted women, when by law they were no longer able to exclude them. That year, Mary Harris Smith gained honorary fellowship status with the Society, having first applied for admission in 1888. She became the first female chartered accountant in the world (ICAEW, 2015). In Scotland, Isobel Clyne Guthrie applied for indenture to the IAAG (Institute for Accountants and Actuaries in Glasgow) in the autumn of 1915, with the financial backing and support of her father David Guthrie (Shackleton, 1998), a well-known Glaswegian accountant. It took four more years and the passing of the Sex Disqualification (Removal) Act to allow her to pursue her professional goals. The law clearly made a difference to these women's lives (also see Kirkham, 1992).

The history of women's entrance into the profession in Germany is not well documented, but Markus (1996, 2021), referring to the membership lists included in professional publications of the 1950s, notes that only a handful of women could be identified as professional accountants at the time.

Professional Organization and Women's Representation

The proportion of women within the profession is a point of departure in a comparative discussion of Germany and the United Kingdom. In the UK, access to the profession has improved vastly. Nevertheless, at the very top of the profession, women remain disproportionally underrepresented. In this book I want to explore the stickiness of this underrepresentation and why, despite decades of research, and a public and credible commitment to gender equality by industry leaders, the profession remains marred by sex discrimination lawsuits and a lack of women at its helm. There are differences in how the professions are organized, which warrants acknowledging. In Germany, there is only one main professional institute, called the Wirtschaftsprüferkammer (WPK), which is a corporation under public law supervised by the Federal Ministry of Economics and Technology. All those who may carry out public audits are members of the WPK. There is also the Institut der Wirtschaftsprüfer (IdW), which acts as an association, and the majority of Wirtschaftsprüfer in Germany are also members of the IdW, although membership is voluntary. In the UK, on the other hand, there are a number of accountancy institutes that professionally organize 'public' accountants, i.e. accountants who may conduct audits. These include the Institute of Chartered Accountants in England and Wales (ICAEW), the Institute of Chartered Accountants in Scotland (ICAS), as well as the Association of Chartered Certified Accountants (ACCA). In addition, there is the Financial Reporting Council (FRC), which acts as an independent regulator in the UK. The latter also provides data over its UK membership. In contrast to Germany, the UK associations are not under direct supervision of the state and are therefore mostly 'self-governed'. The audit industry is much larger in the UK than in Germany. There were 14,614 public accountants or Wirtschaftsprüfer registered in Germany in January 2022 (WPK, 2022), working in 3,013 registered audit firms. There are also 2,135 Vereidigte Buchführer (ibid.) who are able to do audits in smaller companies, but this title was phased out in 2005 and integrated into the Wirtschaftsprüfer qualification.

In contrast, ICAEW alone had 133,332 registered members in the UK and the Republic of Ireland in 2020,[1] with ICAS and ACCA adding another 20,237 and 103,293, bringing the total to 256,862 (FRC, 2021)—around fifteen times more than in Germany, but less than twice the number of firms (which is also in decline falling to 4,745 audit firms registered at the end of 2021, down from 5,007 at the end of 2020 FRC, 2021; 2022). Interestingly, the profession is perceived differently in both nations. The weekly *Der Spiegel*, for example, describes stereotypes of the Wirtschaftsprüfer as *'free, feared, and overpaid'* (Stehr, 2013). In contrast, in the UK, Jeacle (2008) refers to stereotypes of *'boring bookkeepers'* in her study on impression management in the profession in the UK; and Walker, in a piece for *The Guardian* (Walker, 2014), equally refers to auditor stereotypes as *'Grey men and women, boring bean counters'*. Vieten (1995) notes that the Wirtschaftsprüfer qualification was much more exclusive than the UK equivalent due to the comparatively very small size of its

---

[1] In 2021, the ICAEW revoked its Recognized Accountancy Body (RAB) status in Ireland. https://www.icaew.com/regulation/working-in-the-regulated-area-of-audit/brexit-removal-of-audit-rights-in-ireland.

membership and high failure rates in the professional qualification exams of over 50 per cent. Indeed, *Der Spiegel* (2013) describes the WP exam as one of the hardest exams in Germany. This is in line with the Varieties of Capitalism literature where liberal market economies such as the UK are more likely to encourage the development of general skills which are transferrable in a job market offering comparatively little security, and countries such as Germany are more likely to encourage the development of highly specialized skill sets, which are less transferrable.

In Germany, only 18 per cent of Wirtschaftsprüfer (WPK, 2022) (see table 2.1), or public accountants and auditors, are women, up from 16 per cent in 2015 and 12 per cent in 2005 (WPK, 2015; 2005). When looking at the age composition, women make up 35 per cent (a relatively small number, at 113) of WPs under 30, 28 per cent of WPs between 35–39, and 18 per cent of WPs between 55–59 years of age, dropping to 13 per cent for those aged 60–64. This points towards us seeing a higher proportion of women qualifying now than in the past. This is lower than in other professions in Germany; for example, women make up around 35 per cent of lawyers but there are over 166,000 lawyers in Germany (BRAK, 2019). In the UK (see table 2.2), women's representation across the relevant institutes varies remarkably: while 48 per cent of ACCA members are female, the ICAEW and ICAS only have a female membership rate of 29 and 35 per cent respectively. Across all seven accountancy institutes, which also include the CIPFA, AIA, CAI, and CIMA, women make up approximately 37 per cent of its membership, up from 29 per cent in 2005 (FRC, 2021; 2014; 2005).

This more pronounced underrepresentation of women in Germany will partially reflect historical differences in education systems and training routes. Historically, German students were the oldest University graduates in Europe (with an average age of 28 at graduation in 2003), but this has converged significantly with the introduction of the Bachelor and Master

Table 2.1 Comparison of proportion of women in accounting profession in UK and Germany

	UK & Republic of Ireland (ICAEW, ICAS, and ACCA)	Germany
Registered public accountants	256,862	14,614
Registered firms	5,007	3,013
Proportion of women	37%	18%

Sources: FRC (2021); WPK (2022)

Table 2.2 Percentage of women in the profession

Institute	% of women as full members in 2020
German Wirtschaftsprüferkammer	18
Average across three UK Professional Institutes (ACCA, ICAEW, and ICAS)	37
UK–ACCA	47
UK–ICAEW	29
UK–ICAS	35

Sources: FRC (2021); WPK (2021)

system across the EU as part of the Bologna process, and in Germany, too, the average age of students graduating with a first degree is now 23 compared to around 22 in the UK (Statista, 2022a; Little and Tang, 2008 OECD, 2014. In addition, qualified public accountants in Germany are more likely to work in audit than their UK counterparts and are thereby tied to the seasonality of the industry in relative terms. In contrast to their UK counterparts, German auditors who do not regularly engage in audits risk losing their registration. ICAEW or ACCA qualified individuals therefore have a wider choice of careers to pursue upon completion of their training and it is often seen as a stepping-stone.

The extent to which the professional institutes involve themselves with a quest for gender equality is limited. In a report celebrating the sixty-year anniversary of the profession in Germany for example, the WPK merely acknowledges that female membership rose from 4 per cent at the end of the 1980s to 8 per cent by the end of the 1990s. It produces annual statistics of its membership, which includes sex and age. The professional institutes in the UK take more of an interest, with blogs and reports. The Financial Reporting Council, like the WPK also, produces annual statistics to its membership which include age, sex, and race, and in its report for 2021 (FRC, 2021) notes that it has requested a further breakdown of its membership demographics from firms on characteristics such as disability, sexual orientation, religion, and gender reassignment, as well as indicators of class. It produces more information on, for example, hierarchical composition, noting that in 2020, among the 26 public interest entity (PIE) audit firms surveyed, women made up over 50 per cent of manager positions, over 32 per cent of directors, and just over 18 per cent of partners. When dissected by size, interestingly, women made up only about 9 per cent of partners in firms with less than 200 employees but over 20 per cent of partners in mid-tier (200–2,000 employees) and large firms (2,000+ employees).

Women's Advancement at Big-4 Firms

There is no doubt that the Big-4 firms, which employ over 1.12 million people worldwide (Statista, 2022c, d, e, f), have shown a consistent interest in gender equality, diversity, and inclusion more broadly (or more recently with a focus on Diversity, Equity, and Inclusion, which brings a somewhat different set of commitments with the meaning of what might be considered achieving equity in particular being subject to debate). They invest heavily in interventions and reports and are some of the most widely studied organizational contexts, because of this commitment and their willingness to give access to researchers, often commissioning research themselves both on the representation and inclusion of women and more broadly on the subject of a diverse workforce. The Big-4 firms are regularly counted among top employers for women and thus deserve closer attention. At entrance level, Big-4 firms are relatively committed to ensuring that 50 per cent of their new recruits are women, although in 2021 PwC (PwC, 2021) noted that only 43 per cent of its graduate intake in the UK were female. Across firms, women's representation declines with each step up the career ladder, and progress at partnership level has stalled. For example, KPMG shows that while women make up 46 per cent of senior managers, only 35 per cent of directors and 26 per cent of partners are female, and this is broadly representative of the other three firms. Deloitte reports that 24 per cent of its partnership are female, and PwC shows that 23 per cent of its equity partners are women, and that percentage is 24 for EY in the UK (EY, 2021). Making comparisons over time and even across firms and across countries can be tricky. Firms periodically adjust and change how they report these statistics over the years. For example, some are clear that they are referring to equity partners only, others do not make this distinction explicit, some firms include directors and principals in their statistics, and so forth. What is clear is that progress has stalled over time. In 2007, the Big-4 firms reported between 15 and 21 per cent of female partners. Specifically, what can be determined from more outdated sources is that women held 6.5 per cent of all partner and director positions at Deloitte in 1993, and that this number rose to 14 per cent in 2000 (Deloitte, 2000) and 21 per cent in 2007 (Deloitte, 2008)—a 1 per cent improvement per annum on average until that point in time.[2] In a 2015 UK report (Deloitte, 2015), Deloitte noted that its ambition was that 25 per cent of its partners should be female by 2020, which means that it has missed this target, albeit narrowly. Clearly, for all firms the proportion of women at partnership level has hurdled across 20 per cent and towards 25 per cent or a quarter of positions at that level. Fortunately, there is now a reversal in a frustrating recent trend of reporting the rate of women among those promoted to partnership, rather than also publicly noting the proportion of women at that level, which has had an obscuring effect. Women in the profession in both Germany and the UK also suffer a significant pay gap, and while women are as or more likely to receive a bonus than men, men receive significantly higher bonuses.

Lawsuits and employment tribunals remain an issue in the industry. Many readers will be familiar with the US case of Price Waterhouse v. Hopkins—a prominent case of sex discrimination with relevance well beyond the accounting profession. In 1983, Ann Hopkins filed a sex discrimination claim with the US Equal Employment Opportunity Commission against the accountancy partnership, which is now known as PricewaterhouseCoopers, after her candidacy for partnership had been placed on 'hold' (Hopkins, 2005; US Supreme Court, 1989). Hopkins had been with the company for five years and was proposed for partnership after she played a vital part in securing the group's biggest contract at the time, an implementation project worth around 30–50 million US dollars. Partners who had voted against her promotion had commented that she was 'Macho', 'Overly aggressive' and was in need of 'a course in charm school', and following the next nomination cycle, Hopkins was informed that she would never be partner and subsequently sued for admission to partnership, back pay, and the costs of the lawsuit. While the claim was filed in 1983, Hopkins won the case in 1991, following several appeals, which reached the United States Supreme Court. This case demonstrates very clearly the ways in which promotion to partnership is partly negotiated through sex and gender, or sex stereotypes. The question is not whether Hopkins was 'macho'—but whether being 'macho' would have also been an attribute held against a man in the partnership hierarchies. Hopkins failed to conduct herself in what her peers perceived to be a 'gender appropriate' manner and was held accountable (West and Zimmerman, 2002: 12; Kokot, 2015) and thankfully, after eight years, the courts agreed with Hopkins that this was unacceptable.

But sex discrimination lawsuits, particularly in the US and the UK, are an ongoing occurrence in the industry. Besides individual complainants against

---

[2] Not all companies provide the same data and it is not always available for years prior to 2007.

various accounting firms (Webber, 2021; Childs, 2018; Wigdor Law, 2018, Ghouri, 2021), in 2021, after ten years, KPMG agreed to pay 10 million US dollars to settle a class action lawsuit including claims by around 450 women claiming pay and gender discrimination (Tax Notes, 2021). In June 2011, class representative Donna Kassman filed a lawsuit against KPMG claiming 'systemic discrimination in pay and promotion, discrimination based on pregnancy, and chronic failure to properly investigate and resolve complaints of discrimination and harassment' (Sanford Heisler, 2015). In the UK, in 2018, Accounting Today reported a survey by Source Media which said that 34 per cent of female accountants have experienced sexual harassment over the course of their careers (Accounting Today, 2018), which is above the rate of 30 per cent among women in the general population reported by the 2020 Sexual Harassment Survey commissioned by the Government Equalities Office (2021). The *Financial Times* (Marriage, 2019) ran a story in 2019 based on interviews with twenty former employees in Big-4 accounting firms that complained about sexual harassment or discrimination and who found themselves unsupported and frozen out. The FT also unveiled the use of restrictive non-disclosure agreements in the industry as part of settlement deals upon resignation or dismissal.

Women's Representation and Advancement in Accounting Research

There is now a significant literature on gender and women's advancement in accountancy. There was a strong focus from the 1990s on the historical development of the profession which contributed to our understanding of women's entrance to accountancy (as discussed above), and the role of professional closure in keeping women (people of colour, and working-class white men) out. This is quite a specific development to accounting and contributed significantly to the field of management and organization studies and understanding the role of professions. In line with wider developments in how we approach the study of inequalities, labour economists showed an interest in studying accountants. For example, Schaefer and Zimmer (1995) focused on accountants to explore the gender pay gap, arguing that within such a homogenous group, differences in human capital endowments, thought to be one of the primary explanatory factors of the gender pay gap in the 1980s, would be minimal. Their analysis of US census data from 1989 to 1991 unveiled a 49 per cent pay gap among US accountants, and the authors point to differences in age, firm size, marital status, academic qualifications, and work experience as significant factors in explaining this gap. While Schaefer and Zimmer only attributed minor explanatory power to the 'fertility decisions of women', this variable was, of course, correlated with work experience. A strong focus on differences between women and men's decision-making, attitudes, and intentions, and the study thereof in relation to differences in occupational outcomes, is evident throughout the 1990s and around the turn of the century (see for example Nichols, Robinson, Reithel, and Franklin, 1997). Chia (2003), focusing on junior auditors in Hong Kong, for example, points to differences in 'career drivers' between men and women. More specifically, he found that male junior auditors placed higher importance on material rewards, while female respondents were more driven by the 'search for meaning and affiliation than male respondents' (2003: 104) and suggested that 'public accounting firms can utilize the information … to create environments that provide opportunities for the junior staff to satisfy their respective career drivers, if the firms want to retain them' (2003: 107). While not without merit, this stream of research resulted in resistance and lively debate, not only because its conclusions and suggestions would, if put to practice, likely increase rather than decrease the gender pay gap, but largely because of its uncritical engagement with gender as a variable (Alvesson and Billing, 1997; Haynes, 2008a). Haynes (2008a) presents a powerful critique of this body of research, noting that it is not variations in attitudes, intentions, and perceptions between men and women that result in different outcomes, but the underlying assumptions, gendered structures, and cultures that produce difference and maintain inequality in opportunity as well as outcomes. What assumptions, for example, underlie the way we organize work, and how may this result in disadvantages in terms of access to opportunity and inequality in outcomes?

Gebreiter (2021), interviewing university accounting graduates, shows how the graduate recruitment practices of especially Big-4 firms shape the expectations of students upon themselves. Examining socialization processes of accounting trainees (Anderson-Gough, Grey, and Robson, 2005; Durocher, Bujaki, and Brouard, 2016; also see de Vries, Blomme, and de Loo, 2021, for a broader discussion on socialization when becoming an accountant) and the construction of professional identities (Kornberger, Justesen, and Mouritse, 2011; Haynes, 2008a) makes visible how space and time are casually drawn upon as markers of performance and commitment in ways that are inherently gendered (Acker, 1993, 2006; Castilla, 2008; Martin, 2006). This too can be traced historically (Evans and Rumens, 2020). Measuring performance by relying on the image of the 'ideal worker' (Baker and Brewis, 2020; Dwyer and Roberts, 2004; Foster and Wass, 2011; Welsh, 1992), who is frequently constructed around the 'image of a white man who is totally dedicated to the work and who has no responsibilities for children or family demands other than earning a living' (Acker, 2006: 448) underlies many of the unequal outcomes for women: firstly, because female executives are more likely to be part of dual-earner couples than men in similar positions, and secondly, because women in heterosexual relationships are, on average, more likely to take over a larger share of domestic responsibilities (Bunting, 2020; Gallie and Russell, 2009) as part of said dual-earner couple. This stream of research has resulted in important insights into day-to-day social and discursive practices (Anderson-Gough, Grey, and Robson, 2000; Carmona and Ezzamel, 2016; Dambrin and Lambert, 2012; Kyriakidou, Kyriacou, Ozbilgin, et al., 2016) that make it difficult to compete for and combine high-ranking positions in accounting firms and professional service firms more broadly with other responsibilities and pervade even the most well-meaning of equal opportunities programs (Kornberger, Carter, and Ross-Smith, 2010).

The accounting academy has repeatedly criticized firms for practicing and retaining a 'macho' culture that encompasses and is maintained through gendered career advancement processes (Kirkham and Loft, 1993; Windsor and Auyeung, 2006). Kumra and Vinnicombe (2008), focusing on the partnership process in one Big-4 firm in the UK, concentrated in more detail on these processes, or more specifically consultants' perception of these processes. They found that women were more concerned about the self-managed nature of career advancement, as well as the 'necessity to "fit" a mould in order to succeed within the firm' (2008: 69). The former related to factors such as the 'presence of an informal system of project assignment allocation alongside a formal resource management system' (2008: 69).[3] This is an interesting finding in the context of this research, as the degree to which these informal systems operated differed both from a cross-national and organizational perspective. The interviewees in Kumra and Vinnicombe's (2008) research noted that the mould they felt they needed to fit included a person with '"gravitas", good technical expertise and skills, those who were overtly ambitious, good team players and who worked well with clients' (2008). They were, however, also under the impression that they needed to be likeable, and that partners were more likely to promote people who were similar to them. Carter and Spence have shed further light on what the process to partnership looks like more broadly, taking a Bourdieusian approach. Bourdieu was particularly interested in making sense of class and family

---

[3] Project allocation is important as it can impact on the individual's ability to develop a high-profile client list and 'grow' with the client over time.

and its relation to attitudes and dispositions, the ways in which these have generational properties that are internalized and embodied, shaping future behaviours and actions (Bourdieu, 1990). In their work, Carter and Spence (2014) emphasized the importance of social capital in making partnership, being able to build networks and convert these into economic capital. In fact, they found that social skills were seen as a key distinction between partners and non-partners and that this was also practiced more widely where any new acquaintance had the potential to become a future client (also see Spence, Carter, Belal, et al., 2016). Jeny and Santacreu-Vasut (2017) note the importance of language and how language within the workplace reproduces gendered assumptions about who can be an accountant and who can have a career in accountancy. In Germany, a recent contribution by Downar, Ernstberger, and Koch (2021) shows the distribution of those who move up, those who stay put, and those who move on. Comparing career status in 2013 and 2018, the study shows that among 343 senior managers tracked in 2013, 35.9 per cent remained at that level five years on, 16.6 per cent made director, 18.4 per cent made partner, and 22 per cent left their firm. They also note that importance of titles in Germany, with 23 per cent of those moving up to partner status from director having a PhD and foreign CPA licensures, as well as being a Steuerberater/certified tax advisor also being advantageous. Most importantly, they state very clearly that 'female and foreign senior managers are less likely to make partner even when controlling for other determinants' (2021: 11), also pointing to family commitments.

Accounting scholars have been exceptionally creative in the study and capture of exclusion in the industry (and beyond). For example, Bujaki, Durocher, Brouard, et al. (2021), analysing the representations of diversity in photographs used for recruitment of new accountants in Canada, found that women and ethnic minorities were in 52 per cent and 22 per cent of the photographs respectively, in line with their representation among the general population, but mostly in subordinate roles and constructed as outsiders. This is a contribution to a significant literature on the ways in which annual reports reproduce norms and stereotypes (Beattie, 2014; Benschop and Meihuizen, 2002; also see Bujaki, Durocher, Brouard, et al., 2021).

There is a host of research coming through exploring women's careers in the profession in specific geographic settings as well, many of which have contributed to bringing new angles to the study of gender and women's representation more broadly. In Malaysia too, women can access the profession but remain significantly underrepresented at senior levels, and in their interview-based research, Adapa and Sheridan (2021) point to gendered work practices and blatant sex discrimination by clients as a key barrier. For example, reporting that female accountants were less likely to look after high-income clients, that some clients would refuse to work with women, and a concern at firm level that women may request flexible working or maternity leave. Also with a focus on Malaysia, Sian (2021) discusses women's experiences of leaving the profession (off ramping) to focus on family commitments and later, through government incentive schemes, returning to the profession (on ramping). Sian notes the important role of the home environment and husbands' support in facilitating women's careers. There is a wider literature here that brings in international perspectives on understanding accountants' careers with regards to gender (e.g. see Kamla, 2012; Ogharanduku, Jackson, and Paterson, 2021; Vidwans and Du Plessis, 2020) and race (see e.g. Annisette, 2003; Kim, 2004; Sian, 2007; Wiese, 2006), but also intersectionally (Castro and Holvino, 2016; Sadler and Wessels, 2019). There is also a significant and insightful literature acknowledging and critiquing the profession's role in colonialism and empire-building (Annisette and Neu, 2004; Chua and Poullaos, 1998, 2002; McNicholas, Humphries, and Gallhofer, 2004; Neu, 1999).

Many of the above cited works also draw attention to the importance of context—be it related to culture, region, or geography; organizational context; or home context. Women are more likely to work in smaller firms than men, which not only impacts on earnings but also on the range of clients and other day-to-day activities (Bertrand and Hallock, 2001; Ely, 1995). Within the accounting literature, many authors distinguish between small, mid-tier/medium-sized, and large Big-4 firms (McManus and Subramaniam, 2009; Patten, 1995). Patten (1995) for example appears to make the distinction on the basis of the firms' scope—local, regional, or, in the case of the Big-4 firms, global. Others have in the past focused on the number of professionals (McKinley, Pany, and Reckers, 1985) or the number of partners present at the firm (DeAngelo, 1981). Firm size is often studied with respect to audit quality (DeAngelo, 1981) and audit pricing (Choi, Kim, Liu, et al., 2008). A widely cited study in this respect was done by Loeb (1971), who found that professionals in the bigger firms in the US upheld higher ethical values than their counterparts in smaller firms. And this has persisted as a dominant view (Doyle, Frecknall-Hughes and Summers, 2014). It relates back to the way trainees are socialized into 'professionalism' on the job and Weeden's discussion of how, in Big-4 firms, all aspects of 'behaving, acting, talking, looking' (Weeden, 2002: 48) are institutionalized. Goetz, Morrow, and McElroy (1991) note that this 'may reflect the idea that a larger firm can encourage the development of professional attitudes through three avenues: organizational structure, practice mix, and legal exposure. Larger firms tend to have more structure, and more bureaucracy' (1991: 160). Not only is there a firm-size element to the ways in which organizational structures work, but there also appears to be a cross-national one (also see Spence, Dambrin, Carter, et al., 2015). However, this is unlikely to occur in similar ways in smaller firms, which may imply that firm size is a determining factor in the way day-to-day practices are shaped by the organizational context. Adapa, Rindfleish, and Sheridan (2016) also focus on small and medium-size firms in regional accounting firms in Australia, highlighting the significance of geography as well as firm size, and through interviews with men and women at different levels note the ways in which gendered stereotypes are internalized. They found that having a career and making partnership in accountancy was not seen to be compatible with part-time work, for example. Both men and women interviewees noted that this is a key issue for women in accounting, rather than a universal one. Focusing on SME accounting firms in Malaysia, Adapa and Sheridan (2021) also argue that small firms may accommodate flexibility more but are also more susceptible to client demands and related misogyny (both Adapa, Rindfleish and Sheridan, 2016 and Adapa and Sheridan, 2021).

Work-life Balance, Flexibility, and Motherhood

There is also a significant literature on work-life balance and 'flexibility' (see e.g. Crompton and Lyonette, 2011). Recurring themes evolve around the difficulties of working part-time and being recognized, the long hours culture in the profession, and a conflation of working long hours with performance and commitment as explored above. In a quantitative study on the subject of work-family conflict and burnout based in the US, Buchheit, Dalton, Harp et al. (2016) showed that, while accountants felt that alternative working arrangements to support work-life balance were available, especially those working in Big-4 firms did not feel that these were viable in allowing employees to remain effective in their jobs. Taking a performative approach (Butler, 1990, 2004), for example, Kornberger, Carter, and Ross-Smith (2010) illustrate how the term 'flexibility', rather than enabling women to organize their work flexibly, was routinely employed in a way that put the onus of flexibility, and accountability, on female employees rather than employers.

The broader issue of the implementation of 'gender blind' policies and practices which have very real gendered effects and outcomes comes through repeatedly in research on questions of work-life balance (Smithson and Stokoe, 2005). Smithson and Stokoe (2005) note how, while firms were seeking to make provisions gender neutral, respondents in their talk implied that work-life balance remains a women's issue. It is unclear whether the fault lies with the people or with the policies and returns us to the question of whether such policies, at firm level but especially at state level, ought to be designed to support what we can see, or to nudge what we would like to see. For example, in a study on Korean accountants, Kim, You, and Lee (2022) found that work-life balance provision was consistently more important for women than men, across generations. This was not associated with career success.

I talked about differences in feminism in Chapter 1 and this approach to an ungendering of social policy and practices at firm-level is a specifically liberal way of going about things, but is also becoming more pronounced in other contexts as part of a wider trend towards liberalization, also mentioned in Chapter 1. This has been effectively problematized by Orloff (2006) and Stephens (2012). As a result, there is a reluctance to talk about why there is a dissonance between men's and women's perceived need for work-life balance provisions, and why our respondents seemingly refuse to internalize the gender neutralization in which the work-life balance narrative has been clothed and offered to them. It is part of a wider scholarly reluctance to talk about sex difference and subjects such as fertility, pregnancy, birth, maternity and mothering, motherhood, and the fact that women carry out most of the care work around the world. Women's and men's experiences diverge sharply when women become mothers. While 'childless men and women earn comparable amounts, it is only if and when they start to create families that fathers' earnings begin to accelerate, while the salaries of mothers start to stagnate' (Jensen, 2014: 345). The vast majority of the gender pay gap is not a gender gap, but a maternal one (O'Reilly, 2016; Sullivan, 2022; also see Bryson, Joshi, Wielgoszewska, and Wilkinson, 2021). It captures in one single figure the financial exploitation women are subjected to in public and private life; because it has been consistently tracked, budged little, and is probably one of the most leisurely denied hard facts with real economic consequences for half the population in both countries.

Within the literature on gender and accountancy, and the broader literature focusing on professional service firms introduced in Chapter 1, there is acknowledgement that the arrival of children impacts on women's careers (Alvesson and Billing, 2009; Whiting and Wright, 2001). Lightbody (2009), investigating the retention of women in accountancy, finds that further tensions arise as children reach school age, and later turn into teenagers, and that the number of children per household hugely impacts on women's experiences as mothers and accountants. In all these works we learn something about the working lives of those with children, but this is often a side effect of treating the status of becoming or being a mother as a variable in a similar way that gender (or rather sex) in accounting too is often handled as such (Haynes, 2008c, Haynes, 2017). For example, some quantitative studies consider the 'effect' of children on accountants' careers (Anderson, Johnson, and Reckers, 1994; Windsor and Auyeung, 2006) or examine whether or not childcare requirements may be motivating alternative work arrangements (Johnson, Lowe, and Reckers, 2008), and children and childcare are often discussed by and with, usually female, accountants (see e.g. Anderson-Gough, Grey, and Robson, 2005; Kornberger, Carter, and Ross-Smith, 2010) as one of a number of career-related concerns. Interestingly, in a number of studies there is an, at times implied, acknowledgement that becoming a mother is, in the vast majority of cases, a bodily experience that may require some thought of women that is not required of men, for example through pregnancy and the related restriction to move jobs when trying for a baby (a UK issue), feelings of 'letting down others' when not being in the office as a result of the physical act of having and caring for a child (Baker and Brewis, 2020), being unable to attend work due to children's ill health (Whiting, Gammie, and Herbohn, 2015), or through communicating an understanding that women may forgo having children or not take full advantage of employment rights in order to be able to work like men and to avoid the risk of being seen as 'a "female" other' (Baker and Brewis, 2020: 2; also see Barker and Monks, 1998; and Hantrais, 1995; Buchheit, Dalton, Harp et al., 2016). But the literature that specifically focuses on mothers in accountancy and professional service firms and makes space to investigate the transformative potential of becoming a mother is small (Dambrin and Lambert, 2008; Haynes, 2008b and Haynes, 2008c; Lupu, 2012).

Dambrin and Lambert (2008) focus on France in their analysis of mothers in accounting and drawing on twenty-four interviews with male as well as female auditors at different levels, find that becoming a mother is deemed to have costly effects on firms and clients. This echoes findings by Anderson-Gough, Grey, and Robson mentioned above (2005: 486). In their work, one of their respondents, an audit trainee in the UK, for example, noted that you 'don't mention kids around Partners' and that it is 'a case of helping them to forget that you are actually a woman'. They also found that mothers employ a number of tactics to enable themselves to better combine maternity with their work in accounting, including seeking careers in specialisms which are more predictable and less seasonal in their time commitment, such as tax (also see Khalifa, 2013). Haynes (2008b) also examines women's transition to motherhood from an identity perspective, and, drawing particularly on the oral histories of five ICAS and ICAEW qualified women, found that the mothers were under pressure to construct for themselves the identity of a '"high flying working mother", undertaking "macho maternity" (Smithson and Stokoe, 2005: 161), where women maintain their work responsibilities right up to the moment of labour, and/or during a short maternity leave' (Haynes, 2008b: 631). Some rejected this, and in trying to construct an appropriate mother identity for themselves also looked towards an identification with their own histories of being mothered—something that Lowinsky (1992) has termed the return to the Motherline. Not all firms were welcoming of this resistance to the 'high flying working mother' narrative, and some participants in Haynes' study reported being mommy-tracked and expressed their frustrations, while others found that firms took a flexible approach. Haynes (2008b) also pays attention to the ways in which the mothers were themselves, on the one hand, concerned with feeling guilty towards their firms and, on the other hand, feeling sad and anxious about leaving their infants. Further, Haynes (2008a) examined women's transition to motherhood from a maternal and embodied perspective, drawing on oral history narratives from fifteen women working in accountancy in the UK. In the accounts she shares, her participants describe coping with bodily changes on the one hand, for example noting the physical aspects of pregnancy such as tiredness or being unable to dress in ways deemed appropriate, and even being unable to continue working due to pregnancy-related complications, and their desire to work as if nothing had changed on the other hand. These are dilemmas of sameness and difference which come through across this small number of studies and warrant further scrutiny, something that will be discussed in more depth in Chapter 5. Haynes (2008a) considers these sameness and difference narratives in her work, and interestingly equates those of difference with inequality. Yet, as O'Reilly (2016a) and Bueskens (2016) argue, experiences of difference may not necessarily be perceived as oppressive, and indeed while connoting sameness with equality fits into a context marked by liberal feminism such as the UK, it was not a key strategy of the feminist movement in other European contexts (Offen, 1988), as outlined in the Introduction.

Conclusion

The accounting academe has been exceptionally creative in thinking about the different ways in which inequalities at work manifest themselves, and this chapter also hoped to provide an overview of these literatures and their contributions to broader debates, beyond accountancy. This chapter brought together key statistics and literatures on women's entrance to and advancement in the profession in Germany and the UK. The statistics, side-by-side for both countries, give an interesting insight into just how different they are. We know a lot more about gender equality in the UK profession; there are more women, and many more accountants, facing more flexible career paths. The next few chapters will return to these insights gained to consider the extent to which context may affect women's experiences at work in the public and private spheres.

3
Making Partnership in Accounting

Career Histories, Structures, and Relationships at Work

This first analytical chapter pays attention to respondents' experiences of career advancement and how these differed cross-nationally and across organizations. The process of making partnership has been examined before (see e.g. Carter and Spence, 2014), as discussed in Chapter 2. Here the focus is on female partners' careers and across borders. What emerged from the data were complex narratives in which the respondents described how they negotiated their way simultaneously through webs of relationships on the one hand, and organizational structures on the other. Importantly, the extent to which the respondents could depend on either, differed across both dimensions. In addition, the outcomes of these hierarchies of dependency were gendered in both contexts but in different ways. The management of relationships at work and the standardization of progression ladders are key parts in many HR drives designed to foster merit-based practices. Social capital and economic outcomes are linked (Woolcock, 2010), and access to networks that facilitate careers (or housing, health, and wealth) are gendered, classed, and racialized (Smith-Lovin and McPherson, 1993). Castilla summarizes the changes observed in the US over time, noting that 'under the old employment system, lifetime jobs with predictable career advancement and stable pay were virtually guaranteed. Pay raises were given on the basis of seniority or granted automatically to all employees at the same percentage levels … However, this traditional model of employment has gradually been replaced by market-driven employment strategies, including merit-based reward systems and other performance management practices' (2008: 1481). It is in line with the observations shared by Sennett (2012) and discussed in Chapter 1 that we are also seeing a move towards short-terminism here. And from a Varieties of Capitalism perspective, it aligns with a liberal market economic context where the focus is on demand and supply, competition, and market value, rather than relationships of trust.

In the accounts analysed below, one can see that the partners interviewed in Germany still relied on relationships as a primary means to progress and that they shared some ambivalence about the introduction of formal procedures. I was surprised by how much the women in Germany felt able to depend on friendships and family relations in their careers and how these types of relations were mostly absent in the working lives of the women in the United Kingdom. There was also a firm size dimension, with women in smaller firms in Germany talking about close personal friendships and mentors and those in larger firms more likely to talk about professional relationships with managers. The partners in the UK instead highlighted the ways in which they engaged with the structures in place and the formal as well as informal processes that are reproduced in any organization on a daily basis. Those two themes of relationships and structures intertwine in many ways in modern organizations and are to some extent inseparable, but the analysis points to a shift in the way the terms interact with one another in the respondents' narratives across organizations and national borders.

Table 3.1 provides some details on the comparative aspects with regards to the key themes and differences. While respondents in Germany noted the involvement of friends and family in career advancement, in the UK one of the key themes was headhunters and recruitment agents.

Interestingly, this difference is also represented in the respondents' narratives where they talk about internal structures or the absence thereof. For example, only four of the thirty German respondents said they have

Table 3.1 National and organizational dimension in respondents' accounts of career advancement

	Germany		UK	

Respondents who mentioned the involvement of friends and family

	Number	Total Interviews	Number	Total Interviews
Small firms	8	9	1	4
Medium-sized firms	6	9	2	18
Big-4 firms	4	12	1	8
Total	18	30	4	30

Respondents who mentioned the involvement of recruiters/headhunters

	Number	Total interviews	Number	Total Interviews
Small firms	0	9	3	4
Medium-sized firms	0	9	9	18
Big-4 firms	2	12	4	8
Total	2	30	16	30

had regular performance reviews during their career, although incremental, firm-wide salary hikes were referred to by all German respondents.

In contrast, twenty-two of the thirty women in the UK described highly formalized structures and internal hierarchies with regular performance reviews and salary discussions, and made less frequent and less central references to informal structures and processes in their narratives.

Women's Career Progression in Germany

The role of friendships at work in German small and medium-sized firms

Lincoln and Miller, back in 1979, distinguished between instrumental ties, which develop through working together, and primary ties, which are social in nature, with both occurring simultaneously in organizations. The latter was mostly referred to in smaller firms in Germany, with more women in Big-4 firms relying on instrumental ties in their work. Primary ties are more likely to be homophilous—that is, more likely to involve very similar people—with sex a key characteristic (ibid; McPherson, Smith-Lovin, and Cook, 2001). Friendships played a decisive role in the career advancement of women partners in medium-sized and smaller firms in Germany, where much advice and knowledge was shared across firms. Elenor, a partner in a medium-size firm, for example, relied on a male family friend throughout her career in accountancy, noting that her '*biggest fear was to sit around at Siemens for a whole year checking accounts receivables that start with the letter A*'. He told her '*this is how this works*' and '*this is how that works*' and '*this could be interesting ... *' (Elenor, medium-sized firm, Germany, 51/0). He suggested where she should apply and she joined one of the firms he had favoured, which interestingly, as discussed in Chapter 4, had only invited her to the interview as a result of drunken 'banter' at a party where her future colleagues had challenged her boss to consider a woman for the job. In our interview, Elenor recalled how her friendship gave her access to a crucial base of expertise outside of her own firm throughout her years as a trainee. She relayed asking him whenever she was unsure about how to proceed with a client project or a complicated tax question. This sort of external network functions as an important source of information, and enabled Elenor to uphold an expertly qualified identity within her own firm (Arthur and Rousseau, 1996; Eby, Butts, and Lockwood, 2003; Sullivan and Arthur, 2006). After qualifying at the medium-sized firm, Elenor's friend asked whether she was interested in joining the firm where he had since made partner. Elenor stressed the benefits and risks involved: on the one hand, joining a small and less established firm but gaining independence as a partner, and, on the other hand, staying with her employer and having more financial security as an employee in a larger organization but risking never making partnership. Elenor applied and was interviewed by another partner at the firm, a process she had agreed with her family's friend to preserve 'objectivity'. Her mentioning this shows her awareness that there is a line drawn somewhere between networking and nepotism, and that she is perhaps not sure where her friendship falls here. Her family friend is older and perhaps also acts as a professional father figure, taking her under his wing—but the cost is the illusion of her independence.

Other partners recited similar situations. Anita too was persuaded to enter the profession by a close family friend. She recalls:

'Well, the founder of the firm was a friend of the family and so I witnessed what a tax adviser does, you know that wasn't really what my family was into … and … I went to University … and throughout the time I worked here (at our friend's firm) already, or did internships. So that was here as well' (laughs).

(Anita, medium-sized firm, Germany, 45/1[1])

She emphasized throughout the interview that she very much enjoyed working there. While qualifying, Anita actively applied to larger firms and successfully joined another firm as a director. She stayed with that firm for two and a half years, travelling the world. Then her family friend asked her to return to his firm as a partner.

'Was this offer a surprise to you?'
'Well, we remained in contact throughout'.
'So they just happened to need someone?'
'I think it was good timing in terms of the structure and it was good timing for me as well and so we got together'.
'How did the negotiations work out?'
'Well, we negotiated the conditions over dinner … It's kind of like a commitment for life (laughs)'.
'Is it really? Do you feel like that?'
'Yes, in this small organization. I mean what does commitment for life mean? Of course, you can get out of everything. But in a way it is like a marriage'.

(Anita, medium-sized firm, Germany, 45/1)

---

[1] This depicts age and presence or number of children.

Her views on partnership as a commitment for life akin to marriage puts her relationship with her family's friend into perspective: trusting and knowing one another are crucial when making such a commitment. Anita was very young in comparison to the existing partners when she rejoined the firm and needed time to build a strong client base. It demonstrates that the firm's trust in her, knowing her well, was more important at that stage than her immediate ability to contribute financially to shared profits.[2] Knowing and trusting each other well, in public and in private, were recurring themes in the accounts of women working in smaller and medium-sized firms. The partners recognized, and were respectful of, their interdependence at firm-level.

Vanessa, for example, now a partner in a small firm, shared how uncomfortable she was with the idea of sharing power equally with people she did not know very well, an idea which was mooted when she discussed partnership with another firm a few years earlier:

> 'He (the managing partner at the firm) wanted to sell shares and imagined a firm with five partners where everyone holds 20 per cent, but I didn't like that either. I said, I don't want to sit at a table when I am 50 and fight over the colour of the stationery and no one has the power to make a decision. I don't want that. It doesn't work. I've seen too many firms break down like that …and you know those three men (who then made partner there)? None of them are partners there now'.
>
> **(Vanessa, small firm, Germany, 44/0)**

After entering the negotiations, Vanessa pulled out of the discussion and a few years later joined another partnership that she had worked for in the past. Trust, built on long-established relationships, was one of the factors lacking in the proposed scenario, and she felt reinforced in her hesitation as the partnership dissolved years later. Elisabeth also shared concerns about trust at this level and the concerns she had when her firm was seeking to grow by merging with another firm. She says:

> 'Well, when you have to get together then you also share liability risks and all those things … And it also wasn't easy for me, because from the perspective of my department and also my personal career development, there was no reason to merge … and it was entirely driven by the audit department … Decisions like

---

[2] The partnership agreement will determine what percentage of profits is shared and what share each individual has. In some firms, a points-based system is adopted in which the amount of points the individual has depends on various factors such as seniority and responsibility. The amount of points a person is assigned may be reviewed each year and determined by either a committee or the managing partner. Some firms also share equally in profits.

that aren't easy and you think: is it right? or is it wrong? and shouldn't we rather take the small firm path and we actually have a very good relationship among the partnership and … you don't know how that develops in a bigger round. So, the uncertainty isn't exactly small and that's why it wasn't an easy decision for me to make'.

(Elisabeth, medium-sized firm, Germany, 55/0)

Elisabeth, Vanessa, and Anita emphasize the interdependence of themselves with the other partners, acknowledging the sharing of risks and liabilities and that the relationship among partners matters for the functioning of the firm. This was a common thread in the narratives of women partners in small and medium-sized firms in Germany.

Relations with managers and career advancement in Big-4 firms in Germany

While partnership in medium-sized and small firms in Germany was frequently experienced through long-term friendships or acquaintances and based on trust, 'alliances' or informal mentoring arrangements—instrumental ties—which were developed at and confined to work were more often described by the respondents in larger firms. One example is Brigitte, a partner at a Big-4 firm. In order to find a job after graduating, Brigitte wrote letters to some of the regional partners she had heard about. One of them invited her to an interview and employed her, albeit in a separate division, and she saw him as an informal mentor throughout her career. She explains:

'Well, he was really kind of my mentor over the years … and it was relatively clear that if I perform and fit in that I would develop further. And this person, who I think of as a mentor, did what he promised me and there were several face-to-face meetings where we talked about how I imagined my professional development and what I would like to achieve'.

(Brigitte, Big-4 firm, Germany, 41/0)

This continuous support through an informal mentoring arrangement with an established firm partner was important and helped shape and direct her aspirations. In contrast to Elenor, Anita, and Vanessa in the smaller firm context, however, this was not a friendship, but a relationship that operated entirely in the public sphere and emerged there—she established this without drawing on her family or existing social networks. One in three of the respondents working in Big-4 firms in Germany mentioned similar types of informal mentorship arrangements and instrumental ties. Where such relationships were lacking, respondents took the initiative to appeal to individuals to consider them. This is in stark contrast to the accounts in the UK, which were much more framed by organizational processes and procedures.

Nadja, a partner at one of the Big-4 firms, recalled how, during the merging of various firms, entire departments suddenly became obsolete. While she followed the unit she had been working in immediately before the merger, she was not quite enjoying her role. She says:

'So then I went to the other part of the firm'.
'How did you do that?'
'Just like that (laughs) … Of course there are managers,[3] with whom you will have worked and they had to change units too and then you just ask "Do you want me?" "Would you take me with you?"'

(Nadja, Big-4 firm, Germany, 46/0)

Nadja drew on past relationships with managers and a shared working history to advance and move. Throughout the conversation she emphasized that things were much 'simpler' back then, and she credited many of her achievements to her ability to, firstly, work hard and, secondly, make people 'want to take her with them', which are arguably interrelated.

Beate similarly shared how she manoeuvred a move into a different team to navigate around a manager who was unsupportive. She says:

'I saw that this was a subject area where I could become more independent and … I really wanted to leave (the team I was working in) because I noticed that I wasn't going to advance, with the partner at the top. I realized they wouldn't let me get big'.

(Beate, Big-4 firm, Germany, 44/1)

She worked actively on being involved in the establishment of a new unit. She recalls:

'The special unit was led by someone who was in another regional office. I worked with the team over there loosely for a year and I noticed that the atmosphere was completely different … There was already a network for this specialism. Now, it's a whole service line … but back then those were the beginnings and I noticed that they were all getting together and so I linked myself in … consciously. I even went

---

[3] She used the term 'Vorgesetzte', which translates to 'supervisor', or 'line manager'.

46   Making Partnership in Accounting

and looked up the contact. Nobody here knew about him, but I said "right, this is a network, it's run by so and so and I want to be part of it, I want to contribute".

(Beate, Big-4 firm, Germany, 44/1)

Rather than talking about a firm-wide process of promotion, a recurring theme in the interviews in Germany was the absence thereof in their accounts. Instead, the focus was on finding supporting line managers to work with and 'linking oneself in'. But as a result, some partners felt they really faced an information gap about how the process *ought* to work. Manuela talks about this in the absence of clear guidelines or a mentor who could demystify the process to making partnership for her. She recalls:

'I thought to myself: well, why am I not moving forward? … and so at one point I just thought now I have to get active about this and so I made a presentation and just sent it to my manager who is in another city. So, I just presented it, without having a reason really because I thought "well, she just has to know what it is that I do here" and so she said ok and she said that she understood and would pass on my presentation. And then one day the head of tax was here and I asked him for a meeting and gave him my presentation as well. But he didn't give me much hope that it would work and I was quite disappointed … and two weeks later, suddenly, they told me I had passed the first step on the way to partnership and then suddenly I was a partner'.

(Manuela, Big-4 firm, Germany, 47/0)

Manuela proactively sought opportunities to demonstrate her contributions to the firm. What happened beyond this point remains unclear. Her account again emphasizes how important working relationships were in the case of the German respondents and how dependent they were on a manager to take an interest.

Women's Career Progression in the United Kingdom

In contrast to the respondents in Germany, in our conversations the women partners in the UK placed the emphasis not on people, but on an internal system of structures for appraisal and promotion. Relationships at work were often formalized and limited by time and location. Mentoring was described as part of a manager's job rather than something that is extended to people one cares about. When asked to comment on their own career advancement, the respondents in the UK talked about the importance of understanding the system and structures around them, which, in contrast to the web of relationships encountered in Germany, was more often described as a performance-related set of hierarchies. In the following, I will first discuss the case of the Big-4 firms in the UK, before moving on to a discussion of the narratives encountered at small and medium-sized firms.

Making partnership in the Big-4 firms in the UK and the role of standardized career structures

The female partners I interviewed in Big-4 firms in the UK emphasized the internal organizational structures that they had learned to understand and work with. In the early years of career advancement, some respondents encountered a standardized, almost automatic process. This does not mean that relationships at work did not play a role, but rather that they were bound and limited by the structures in place, which allowed the relationships to be, at times, fleeting, yet sustainable and often unemotional. Christiane, for instance, notes:

> '… one of the things about the accounting profession is that you count the years and you know roughly what grade you should be … but I wasn't sort of systematically thinking, you know, "Oh I better work towards that" or asking people "When am I gonna be a manager?" I just kind of assumed that I would (be)'.
>
> **(Christiane, Big-4 firm, UK, 43/2)**

In the UK, the appraisal systems—up until manager or senior manager level—were often described as fixed and structured. It was a system in which the respondents were taken from one step to the next with the help of different partners and managers. For example, Dunja, a partner at a Big-4 firm, recalls the process of gathering support for a promotion:

> 'You have to have a whole network of support around you … You have to get at least five partners to sign your form, to say they consent to supporting you going through to director. And similarly, you need the same in terms of going through as a partner'.
>
> **(Dunja, Big-4 firm, UK, 39/2)**

This is an interesting contrast to Manuela's account in Germany, who did not know what the process was, even when she was already quite senior, and the account of Beate, who noticed that being in the right unit could change her prospects dramatically. In Dunja's case the process is clear. It also involves reaching out to others and forming instrumental ties, but in a more contained context where this would be expected, making it less risky to reach out to managers and partners for support. There are formal and informal elements in the way career advancement is negotiated here. Asked how she managed to successfully convince the required number of partners, Dunja notes:

> 'Well, I mean, people do think about people's careers here and so it should be discussed as part of your appraisal sessions and obviously with your mentor. So, your sort of career development should be discussed in terms of your objectives: what you want to do, how you want to achieve it, areas you want to focus on. That should be discussed as part of your appraisal meetings'.
>
> (Dunja, Big-4 firm, UK, 39/2)

Her account is a good example of how career advancement is relatively institutionalized as something that is everybody's responsibility and part of being a good manager of people. Christiane and Anastasia, also partners at Big-4 firms, talk about similar processes that evolved around appraisal, feedback, and plans for the future. For example, Anastasia explains her experiences at the Big-4 firm which had taken over the small firm she previously worked in. She says:

> 'There is loads of process around promotions and things like that whereas in the small firm it was more, you know, "You've been doing the job for two years and you're doing a good job and so you get promoted to the next level"'.
>
> (Anastasia, Big-4 firm, UK, 36/1)

Even within this framework of procedures, however, there was some flexibility for her to position herself. Anastasia pointed out that much of what happened during one of the meetings was a product of ranks, bands, and scripts, as well as the management of other people's expectations of where one anticipated to fall in this system. She explains:

> 'You got spot rates at certain levels and things like that ... but it's not something that gets negotiated ... which is why I think the groundwork is more that you do beforehand: about managing expectations in terms of what you are expecting. Or you know ... like, I got headhunted for a job at another Big-4 firm and, you know, you kind of make it known that you're not just sitting around waiting to be promoted here and that you got other options. That you're aware of your market worth'.
>
> (Anastasia, Big-4 firm, UK, 36/1)

Anastasia describes how she understood that there was a system of internal structures with which she had to work in order to advance. While this was considered to be rigid in some ways, there were also opportunities for her to shape it in her own way by laying the 'groundwork'. This relates directly to Acker's (2006) discussion of the role of informal practices. While managerialist standardized procedures were in place, these are a little flexible and Anastasia understood this. She emphasizes her own market value as part of the reason for her advancement within the industry, noting 'spot rates' as well and thus drawing on capitalist terminology of rates and markets, commodifying herself and participating in the neoliberal conversion problematized by Rottenberg (2017) and discussed in Chapter 1.

What the interviews also highlight is the interaction of the women with a pool of senior executives at the firm rather than with just one manager. The partners responsible would change over time and the relationships were thought of more as part of the daily responsibilities involved in a job such as this, rather than predominantly a personal favour on the basis of sympathies and closer personal relationships. Individual relationships that were meaningful beyond their workplace function were seldom mentioned. They may well have existed, but they were not commented on as an aspect that helped the women in the UK advance in their careers. While trying to find out more about the relationships at work during later interviews, I asked Sharon directly whether she had considered someone to have been her mentor over the course of her career. She replied:

> 'You had a counsellor. You had a counsellor who was responsible for representing you actually in the performance management process and my counsellor happened also to be the lead of the business, so the human capital lead. So, I could get very clear guidance from him in terms of was I on track for promotion in the timing that I thought I should have'.
>
> **(Sharon, Big-4 firm, UK, 41/0)**

Sharon's response details a relationship that was entirely professional and was put in place for her by the firm. Everyone had to have a counsellor, and hers happened to be the head of her unit. While she felt that he did a very good job as a mentor, she also talked about it as if it was simply part of his job, which of course it was. In contrast to, for example, Anita or Elenor, her relationship with this individual was entirely bound by the limitations of her organization and, to some extent, time. If she moved units, she would be assigned a different counsellor and likely expect him or her to do an equally good job.

Making partnership in small and medium-sized firms in the UK and the role of ads and recruiters

This section focuses on advancement to partnership in small and medium-sized firms in the United Kingdom. Medium-sized firms in the UK are often very large, globally operating firms. They sometimes have more partners than Big-4 firms in Germany, for instance. Initially, I pondered shifting the cut-off point in my analysis in the UK to reflect this difference in size, but I decided not to as it is not my intention to argue that the women's experiences were radically different between the groups beyond this artificial cut-off point. Rather, I found that there were a range of experiences, but that these were not random but clustered with size and across borders, and I decided to use this as an opportunity to think about how this might make sense cross-nationally from a VoC and from a feminist perspective. I followed the respondents' definitions of the size of their firms. Therefore, while women's experiences in the larger medium-sized firms in the UK may well share many procedural details with those in Big-4 firms, this was less frequently the case in the smaller medium-sized firms. In the UK, the accounts showed that the women's career advancement in Big-4 firms was more about gaining a good understanding and making use of internal organizational structures, while the women's experiences of career advancement in smaller firms more frequently involved recruitment agents and headhunters. The latter is interesting in that it demonstrates a market for managers, senior managers, and partners in the UK in that specific segment of the industry that these individuals and firms cannot always navigate themselves.

Only two respondents in Germany had taken advantage of headhunters, although many of them had received cold calls from headhunters and talked about considering the possibilities before deciding against leaving their firms. These were mainly women in Big-4 firms while they were in middle-management positions. In the UK, on the other hand, the women who moved into smaller and medium-sized firms were more likely to take advantage of recruiters over the course of their careers. Denise, for example, enlisted the help of a recruiter when looking for a new position which would be closer to her hometown, as she did not enjoy working in London.

> 'I'd got (that position) through a recruitment agency. I saw this guy advertising. He advertised in *Accountancy Age*, which is the rag really, isn't it? So, I phoned him up about a different job and he said "I don't think you're suitable for that but I'll try and find you another one". So, he did the leg work' (laughs).
>
> **(Denise, small firm, UK, 39/2)**

She joined as a manager and became a partner in that firm a few years later. Similarly, for Tracy an advertisement in *Taxation Magazine* helped her escape a situation she found very frustrating. As a senior manager at one of the larger medium-sized firms, she felt she was going nowhere:

> 'During that time, it was suggested that I should go for partnership and ... in fact there were three women who were in a similar position (and) none of us seemed to be getting anywhere at all. I kept having the same conversation with HR. They said "Right we're at the beginning of the process" ... Well, hang on a minute: We had this conversation a year ago. We had this conversation two years ago. It can't still be at the beginning of the process! And we were just not getting anywhere'.
>
> 'Were other people progressing?'
>
> 'Yeah. Usually men (laughs). And so all three of us left and got partnership elsewhere ... I wasn't getting anywhere and so I happened to be looking at *Taxation Magazine* one day and saw two jobs which were offered: one was this one and one was another one of the other mid-tiers. I went for both and one was a director of tax and this one here as tax partner'.
>
> (Tracy, medium-sized firm, UK, 46/0)

Tracy suspected that herself and the other women she referred to were being discriminated against because of their sex. The supposedly gender-neutral and formalized structures were drawn upon by the firm in an almost passive aggressive way, frustrating her ability to progress (Acker, 2006; Castilla, 2008). Her account reminded me of Manuela's in Germany, who, failing to move ahead, made partnership after she proactively reached out to a variety of people at her firm. Yet, the situations are different: Manuela had no formal structures to work with and her situation resolved successfully—she did not have to leave the firm but made partner there. Tracy on the other hand felt held back by the structures that were in place. In her account, she describes it almost as hitting a wall. Every year she would be faced with the same review process, and she felt that there was nothing she could do about it. I also interpreted her account as an example of the more impersonal, market-orientated, and 'professional' ways in which career advancement is managed in the UK. Both Denise and Tracy talk about 'this guy', advertisements they saw in trade magazines, and 'HR', using detached descriptions. Indeed, many of the people who were involved in their career advancement over the years are not the same people that are in their lives now, and that is a key difference between the narratives of the very successful women in Germany as compared to the UK. Another key difference was the ways in which the German respondents talked about partnership as a long-term commitment. But in the

UK, 'divorce' was an option, and respondents noted, for example, the periodic removal of underperforming partners in bigger firms as well redundancy rounds in smaller firms in response to economic crises. These accounts are explored in depth in Chapter 6.

Managing Others and Developing Talent as Partners

While the interviews focused extensively on the discussion of the women's career histories, I was also interested in learning about their views and experiences in managing others, particularly women. In Germany, there was a sense that change was coming and that the introduction of standardized career structures was in principal a good development, but there was also ambivalence.

Managing others in Germany

During the interviews in Germany, respondents complained about the lack of management skills among accountants, noting 'quality assurance' guidelines implemented by the profession to encourage better human resource management, and to motivate firms to consider staff development. In smaller firms, this was often seen as a nuisance that did not reflect the day-to-day realities of the job. For instance, Andrea, a partner at a small firm, notes:

> 'Advancing their careers? Here? I am running after everyone, trying to talk them into training courses, so that they can advance or do something. I have this really good colleague here who is about my age and she worked her way up but now she reduced her hours because of the children. You can't do that everywhere. And it's also a financial problem, you know, in the past years, after we sent her to training courses all the time and seminars, she told me that she doesn't feel like doing those anymore, because now she has a young dog and so she rather walks the dog in the afternoon' (laughs).
>
> **(Andrea, small firm, Germany, 50/2)**

Andrea is frustrated. She feels she would like to help women advance in their careers but notes that the commitment of some of her team members to what constitutes ordinary family life, for example, looking after children and walking your dog, is not compatible with a career leading towards partnership that necessitates the prioritization of work. This is something the German respondents were quite insistent about, as I explore in more detail in Chapter 5. There were other details I was curious about. Small firms in

Germany often lacked traditional hierarchies as discussed above and were organized around a small group of partners. Career advancement implies that there is somewhere to advance to. From our conversation, I was left with the impression that there was nowhere to go for the employees. Andrea did not plan to expand the firm in the future and therefore was unable to provide promotions, for example. This was similar in Elisabeth's firm. Elisabeth was a partner at one of the well-known and nationally operating mid-sized firms. She said that there was simply nowhere for them to go after a certain point, because firm hierarchies were very flat or not every layered.

> 'How does career advancement work here now?'
> 'That's really not very attractive here. Our organization is very flat and so that means I have an assistant, then there is the tax consultant and then there is me next ... It's quite normal to progress from assistant to consultant of course, but to then progress to partner, that depends more on how we develop ... For a start you get a raise and when someone is unhappy with it then they will come and say so ... '
>
> **(Elisabeth, medium-sized firm, Germany, 55/0)**

Elisabeth's account resembled those of other female partners in mid-sized firms such as Hannah, Bettina, or Konstanze. The UK has significantly more qualified accountants as discussed in Chapter 2, and small firms are usually larger than what might count as a small firm in Germany.

Turning to Big-4 firms, the respondents were asked how they decided on promotions and developed talent in their own teams. Manuela, the partner who had to take the initiative in her career advancement due to the absence of both relationships and structures by contacting various people and offering her presentation to them, was very much in favour of a fixed protocol. When I asked her to reflect on her own involvement in people's development she noted: '*I make sure now to see that my team members get ahead and I do that without them having to approach me about it*', arguing that she understood that this was something she lacked in her own development. Meanwhile, Sabrina noted that she and four other partners were responsible for about eighty employees. While she felt that the partnership process was very formalized, promotions before that stage were a product of the meetings and discussions among the partners heading the team.

> 'I mean, let's say it this way, to be promoted from Associate to Senior is a relatively fluid process and depends solely on performance. Well, is someone able to lead a team? Yes or no? That is in fact the big question'.
>
> **(Sabrina, Big-4 firm, Germany, 42/0)**

She notes the fluidity of the process but simultaneously indicates that it is an objective one that '*depends solely on performance*'. Critical management scholars have drawn attention to the ways in which 'performance' can be measured in a variety of ways, many of which are gendered. Dalal (2005), for instance, notes that there are three broad performance domains: task performance, organizational citizenship behaviour (OCB), and counterproductive work behaviour. From a gender perspective, the first and the second dimension are of particular interest. Researchers such as Lyness and Heilman (2006) and Heilman, Wallen, Fuchs, and Tamkins (2004) have shown that performance evaluations at the task level are gendered (also see e.g. Rivera and Tilcsik, 2019). Studying archival organizational data of 448 upper-level managers and their performance evaluations, Lyness and Heilman (2006) show that women did not only receive lower performance evaluations, but those promoted to senior level scored, on average, higher than their male colleagues who were promoted to similar levels of authority. In addition, with respect to the second domain of organizational citizenship behaviour, men were shown to be rated more favourably when exhibiting OCB, which is defined as discretionary behaviour that is not formally recognized by organizational reward systems but may, in its aggregate, improve organizational effectiveness and customer satisfaction among other things (Podsakoff, MacKenzie, Paine, and Bachrach, 2000). But OCB is on average not only implicitly expected from women; women also experience a penalty if OCB is absent (Kidder, 2002). Men are less likely to exhibit OCB unless they feel obligated to do so (Thompson, Bergeron, and Bolino, 2020). Performance too, then, is gendered and what performance looks like can shift.

Julia, a tax partner in one of the Big-4 firms, felt that her staff had to show that they had the capacity to do the job of the next level already and complained about a sense of entitlement among their employees:

'I like that there isn't this sort of automatism. Just yesterday I talked to one of my colleagues who I was planning to promote to manager and she said she was going to ask me … about it because in the other departments there were no qualified accountants who had not been made manager yet and I said "Caution! This automatism doesn't exist here anymore! Like: I qualified now I become a manager" I said. "There are certain abilities a manager needs, certain characteristics. They need to be able to manage themselves and others. They need to be able to meet deadlines, win new clients" I said, and only when those conditions are all met, then I make someone a manager'.

(Julia, Big-4 firm, Germany, 41/0)

Julia appears to disapprove of her employee's query about promotion. This is interesting from a gender perspective, as much has been written about women losing out on promotions and salary hikes as they are less likely to ask for them (Bowles, Babcock, and Lai, 2007), but simultaneously women are expected to conform to gendered stereotypes along the lines of 'Nice girls don't ask' (Babcock, Laschever, Gelfand, and Small, 2003). Julia's description of what it would take to make the next grade in the hierarchy is to show that you already meet the criteria of the level you are seeking to be promoted to. In her own career history, Julia noted that the manager she had when she was an assistant was a 'supporter. You didn't have to beg with him'. He made sure to meet with her regularly and discuss her career advancement over time, but also noted that 'competency meetings weren't really on the agenda back then. That sort of thing only started about five years ago and at the time … it all really depended on your manager. How far you could get'. She was comfortable with having a manager who supported her. Her mentioning that she 'didn't have to beg with him' shows that she is aware that this kind of support was not universal and that things were moving towards standardization. At the same time, she argues that this 'automatism doesn't exist here anymore', which refers to a previous tendency to recognize seniority and experience and passing the Wirtschaftsprüfer qualification as a criterion for promotion. She conveyed to me that she wanted to promote her employee, but in contrast, she conveyed to the employee that it is out of her hands—that it all comes down to merit and showing certain abilities, meeting 'certain characteristics', and that it is ultimately in the hands of the employee herself. There was a sense in the accounts that it is a system in flux and that a move towards standardization of procedures akin to what their UK counterparts described was on its way and that there was some ambivalence around who is responsible for promotion; is it the individual herself who can determine their fate by meeting standardized barriers of meritocracy, or is it the manager who helps create the system and whose job it is with her peers to interpret what constitutes performance and merit?

Manuela, a partner in a Big-4 firm mentioned earlier, also talked about the introduction of clear progression structures and standardized appraisals at her firm when she had already made partnership, but noted that 'there were problems with it, especially here, the head of the department thought the idea was perverse and so he didn't really represent it enthusiastically'. Part of the problem was that this was seen as overstepping what was to be at a partners' discretion. The term Manuela uses to describe the department head's reaction is strong—he thought it was 'perverse', which according to

Merriam-Webster (2022) has a range of related meanings including 'turned away from what is right and good', or 'obstinate in opposing what is right, reasonable and accepted'. It is unknown whether he used this precise term or whether it is her interpretation of his reaction. But to what extent is the standardization of 'careers' problematic? The aim of standardization through the introduction of procedures and formal personnel systems is, after all, transparency and to partially address the ways in which organizations help maintain gender, race, and class inequalities endemic in wider society. On the other hand, as mentioned above, Acker (1990; 2006; also see Martin, 2006; Roth and Sonnert, 2010) demonstrated how these structures are routinely subverted. Further, Dobbin, Schrage, and Kalev (2015) note that their introduction is likely to result in managerial resistance precisely because they limit managerial autonomy. At the same time, they found that job posting systems and formal job ladders increase diversity. The findings here are in line with theirs. But 'perversion' goes perhaps beyond the loss of autonomy, and I wonder to what extent it is also a sign of resistance to being asked to potentially promote people one does not know well over people one does know, either professionally, privately, or both. Is this too a sign of what Stephens (2012) calls an 'upside down world' where things that used to be taken for granted as *good* (e.g. trust, friendships, relationships) have now been identified as a problem? Stephens (2012), drawing on Fraser and Gordon's (1994) seminal genealogy of the term 'dependency', for example, reminds us that historically those who came to a community or household unknown would have traditionally been treated with suspicion—independence was not always and in all contexts something to aspire to as a sign of freedom and autonomy but rather seen as a sign of potential for chaos and disorder (2012: 21). Perhaps this comes through in the uncomfortable laughter of Anita and Elenor, who relied heavily on friendships in their careers and in making partnership. For many of these women it was a key reason why they were able to advance to partnership relatively early. Both Elenor and Stephanie, for instance, noted that they were not established yet, that they had no clients of their own to bring to the firm, but that they were known well to the other partners and that this carried weight because when one makes a long-term commitment to share risks and liabilities, it was considered sensible to do so with people that one trusts and knows well. But with these sort of relationships less accessible to women, as discussed in Chapter 1, basing career structures around networks will also result in gendered (as well as racialized and classed) outcomes.

Managing others in the UK

The respondents in the UK were often assigned mentors in the larger firms and interacted with a larger group of people responsible for their development over the course of their careers, albeit on a less personal level. Sharon, one of the Big-4 partners, had been able to take advantage of mentorships in her own career. I asked her during our conversation whether she considered herself a mentor. She replied:

> 'I have lots of people I suppose I mentor because I lead this unit ... So, I would say to varying degrees I actually mentor all of them. Some of them will have more intense mentoring. So, for example if they sort of just returned to work following the birth of their child, or they have a promotion coming up, or they are a struggling high performer ... all of those reasons would cause me to up the amount of personal attention and guidance I might give'.
>
> **(Sharon, Big-4 firm, UK, 41/0)**

Sharon sees herself as a mentor to all those that are within her unit. It is part of her job, and the relationships then were bound by her position and her responsibility as a manager. This is also echoed in Dunja's comments, who noted that 'people do think about people's careers here' and added that career advancement in her Big-4 firm should be discussed as part of the formal process. Similarly, Marina talks about leading as mentoring. Asked how she decides on whom to promote in her team, she remarks:

> 'I mean, I think, that nowadays I mentor directors rather than actually below directors. But just like somebody mentored me, I now mentor two directors already ... It's just people who work with you, you know, on accounts'.
>
> **(Marina, Big-4 firm, UK, 59/2)**

Marina talks about her mentees in a non-emotive manner. Interestingly, they are not only non-emotive, the respondents also rarely mentioned whether their mentees were male or female. The relationships were often described as short-term and bound by a concrete task or project. Paris, a partner at a medium-sized firm in the UK noted that there was, and still is, a formal mentoring arrangement in place at her firm.

> 'When you're a member of staff, you'll have someone that you report to but I also had a mentor as part of the manager and the associate program. You were given a

mentor. So I had one partner who was my mentor who basically helped me push me into that direction'.

(Paris, medium-sized firm, UK, 49/0)

Mentorship was something everyone was 'given'. In her own experience of career advancement, this arrangement played a large part in her understanding of the structures in place and how she approached career progression. Madie, who only very recently made partnership at a medium-sized firm, also stressed the importance of mentoring as part of a wider career advancement structure. She noted that there was a two-step annual review system in place at her firm to ensure that the partners a) understand their staff's objectives and b) discuss together what skills are needed to achieve those objectives. On top of that, she had access to a mentor once she made partnership to help her meet expectations, which, given the possibility of partner removal in the UK, may well be more important than in Germany. The evidence on mentoring is mixed. In a meta-analytic review, Underhill (2006), for example, examining articles published to 2004, found that there was a significant albeit small advantage to being mentored than to not being mentored and that informal mentoring relationships were in fact more advantageous. On the other hand, Holt, Markova, Dhaenens, and Marler (2016) claimed that those who had informal mentors did not report significantly different performance ratings than those with formal mentors, however this was within a context where a formal mentoring system had been set up for all and the authors hypothesized why staffers would still look for informal mentoring (e.g. perceived lack of support from formal mentors). In a book assessing various diversity, equity, and inclusion (DEI) measures, Dobbin and Kalev (2022) note formalized and 'democratized' mentoring systems as particularly impactful, and indeed the degree of formalization is what differs across firm size and national borders, from very informal in the small German firms discussed, to very formalized in the UK-based Big-4 firms (see figure 3.1 in chapter conclusion below).

Within the small firms in the UK the process was less formalized than in the larger firms, but it was nevertheless seen as a common concern of the partner and there was a standardized approach. For instance, Summer, a partner at a five-partner firm, noted that she met with staff once a year to discuss performance and salaries. Denise, also a partner at a small firm, noted that promotion was not always an option, but unlike the small firms in Germany, this firm had also implemented a formal annual appraisal where career progression was also discussed. This was seen as best and common practice. A concern about retaining managers was notable among partners in the UK.

The accounts of the German respondents indicate how much they relied on the sympathies of a single person—their 'Vorgesetzte' or line manager—and how they were in some ways lost when this relationship did not develop in their favour. In contrast, the respondents' experiences in the UK were less personal, and while the respondents were on the one hand able to engage with the structures in place while negotiating their way to the top, how they talked about partnership also implied that it was not 'for life' and that they were in some ways more vulnerable than their German counterparts—a subject discussed in depth in Chapter Six.

Conclusion

This chapter sought to highlight differences in both the national as well as the organizational experiences of the respondents' career advancement and to demonstrate that both context and geography matter in how careers are organized and experienced by women. In particular, I have shown how in Germany women's experiences of career advancement were negotiated through relationships where those relationships were personal (or primary) relationships of trust in smaller firms and instrumental relationships that were maintained largely in the public sphere in larger firms. Meanwhile, in the UK, the women's experiences of career advancement were more frequently negotiated through structures and market-type mechanisms, where women in smaller firms often referred to recruiters and headhunters and women in larger firms pointed to the ways in which their experiences of career advancement were mainly facilitated by internal structures.

The Varieties of Capitalism framework can usefully inform the analysis because it encourages the researcher to think about how people interact with others within the structures of the firm, rather than focusing on what they talk about; which is also important and explored further in forthcoming chapters.

The focus on relationships vis-à-vis standardized career structures is explored graphically in Figure 3.1.

The diagram portrays a schematic non-linear representation of the relative significance of structures and relationships in the respondents' accounts of career advancement. On the left side are smaller firms in Germany and on the right side are larger firms in the UK. This graphic exploration highlights how both relationships and structures matter but there is always scope for discretion and, consequently, each curve will tend to lean towards the relationship model, away from the axes, and likely looking different for men and women as the discussion around homophily emphasized.

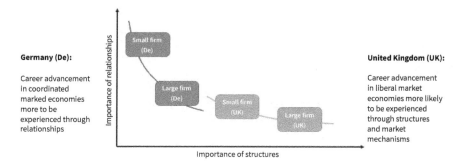

Figure 3.1 Comparison: career structures and women's experiences of career advancement in Germany and the UK

It is paradoxical to think of close, personal relationships as disadvantageous, which Sennett (2012) problematizes in his work. And, from a feminist perspective, we ought to be suspicious of the types of standardized career-structures encountered in the UK, which not only encouraged respondents to think about themselves as a portfolio of sorts, but also seek to mediate who one engages with, for how long, and to what purpose. Indeed, these sorts of market-like mechanisms appeared to be, in some ways, more gender-neutral over the years, perhaps acting as safety ropes or guide ropes for the respondents to a certain degree. But there was a sense that something was lost in the UK, and a fear and ambivalence over what was to come in some of the German accounts. And, as will be explored later in this book, neither the structures encountered nor the sort of fleeting relationships they encouraged functioned as safety nets, and the women partners interviewed in the UK frequently referred to the removal or 'redundancy' of partners which may have also been gendered decisions. On the other hand, the dependence on strong ties and friendships in the making to partnership in smaller firms is inevitably a process of gender, race, and class.

Decisions are never free of bias, and much has been written on homophily and our tendency to sociality with those who are like us (Burt, 1992; Kanter, 1977; Lamont and Lareau, 1988). This is likely to be more pronounced in smaller firms, where the respondents talked about primary relationships, than in larger firms, where instrumental ties were more commonly discussed. Ibarra (1992), in a seminal US-based paper, showed how men were more likely to develop homophilous (i.e. same-sex) ties at work, that these were usually stronger than women's ties, and that women were more likely to develop friendship ties with other women for social support and instrumental ties with men. These are points that Estevez-Abe (2002; 2005) for example also takes forward in her argument towards gendering the Varieties of Capitalism framework. Context also matters to the types, length, and quality of relationships people in any given place typically form. Burt, Hogarth, and Michaud (2000) found that one of the key differences between networks developed by French and American managers in their study was duration. The French managers would be embedded in long-standing personal relationships of trust to which they would add new relationships acquired through work. In contrast, Americans would be embedded in networks that spanned their careers, were mostly work-related, and within which they would develop personal friendships with more recent acquaintances. There are similarities to their findings in the interviews here. While France holds an ambiguous position from a VoC perspective, it is arguably closer to the CME side of the spectrum in terms of coordination. Hall and Soskice (2001) note its inclusion as part of a bigger Mediterranean pattern with capacity for non-market coordination, a history of state intervention but more liberal configurations with regards to labour market regulations, complicating an analogy.

Contemporary research is more mixed in its findings. Lutter (2015), for example, in an analysis of the US film industry over eighty years, found that the network context matters. For women there were network closure penalties in work involving cohesive teams, and disadvantages remained but were reduced in open network contexts. Interestingly, and also in a US study, Dahlander and McFarland (2013) found that those who were unfamiliar with one another would form ties on the basis of identifying matching traits, but that ties were more likely to last for those who have a shared history. Dahlander and McFarland (2013) also found that shared organizational foci did not necessarily help tie persistence, although they helped with tie formation. Status homophily variables such as sex were insignificant in tie persistence, but they did matter with regards to tie formation.

Standardized career processes such as the ones encountered in the UK and particularly in large firms can help facilitate and contain the making of relationships and in this way support tie formation across ascribed status variables (e.g. sex, race, class, disability). Market-like mechanisms such as the recruitment agents, headhunters, and job advertisements described by the UK respondents in smaller firms help make ties across firms. The UK respondents were more likely to draw on market-type mechanisms, but they were also more likely to talk about themselves as part of this market, as a commodified self with a value and a spot rate. The commodification of the self helps sustain hierarchies on the basis of fleeting relationships where trust or loyalty are only ever situational or mediated by the firm and agents. The gendered implications of these differences will be explored in more depth in the following three chapters in relation to sexism, discrimination, and difference at work (Chapter 4), in relation to motherhood (Chapter 5), and with respect to work centrality and job security (Chapter 6). This is the central focus of the Gendered Hierarchies of Dependency frame: hierarchies were negotiated in different ways across borders; relationship-based hierarchies are biased and make it more difficult to advance for women, but market-based standardized career structures, while more gender neutral in terms of facilitating advancement, are less reliable and women are more vulnerable to redundancy. The outcomes are thus always gendered, as Chapters 4 to 6 will draw out.

4
Sexism at Work

The accounting profession remains marred by employment tribunals and lawsuits in relation to sex discrimination, as outlined in Chapter 2, and this remains an issue in the wider world of financial services and consultancy. Yet, within the accounting and wider organization studies literature, there is a reluctance to talk about sex discrimination with respondents directly, especially more recently. The 'post-modern turn' (Walby, 2007) saw a move from understanding the role of the researcher as observer to interpreter, and a shift from analysing what is said, to interrogating what is meant by what is said, and what it does in the context in which it is said. Asking someone whether or not she had experienced sexism at work, therefore, leaves us open to at least two types of critique. First, put simply, it is a closed question, although by allowing the possibility of replying 'no', closed questions may provide a safe haven to respondents when discussing subject matters that could be perceived to be uncomfortable. Second, in which ways can the question render useful information to the researcher, as one reviewer of my work enquired. Sexism and discrimination at work will range from bias in recruitment, work allocation, and promotion, to violence and harassment in the workplace—and all such behaviours remain rampant at work today and many of these are gendered or sex-based (Fernando and Prasad, 2018; Grosser and Tyler, 2021). Asking women about their experiences of sexism and discrimination at work is useful not because it tells us precisely the rate of incidents, or precisely the ways in which women at work are discriminated against, but because it can tell us about perceived inequity which has been shown to affect job satisfaction, job commitment, and turnover intentions (see Dalton, Cohen, Harp, et al., 2014).

What, then, is sexism? Glick and Fiske (1996) posit that sexism is a 'multidimensional construct that encompasses two sets of sexist attitudes: hostile and benevolent sexism' (1996: 491). Hostile sexism includes behaviours that signal open dislike of and prejudice against women. Benevolent sexism, on the other hand, is defined 'as a set of interrelated attitudes toward women that are sexist in terms of viewing women stereotypically and in restricted roles but that are subjectively positive in feeling (for the perceiver) and also tend to elicit behaviours typically categorized as prosocial (e.g. helping) or intimacy-seeking (e.g. self-disclosure)' (1996: 491). In 1977, Kanter pointed to both when discussing women's entry into top management positions. She called the former 'testing behaviour' (1977: 42) and referred to the latter as old-fashioned and chivalrous mannerisms, which were frequently adopted by men who had often no experience in interacting with women who were 'anything but a secretary or a wife' (1977: 42). Kanter (1977) further noted how instances of sexism or discrimination were often dismissed by women.

Linda McDowell (1997; 2010) has written about this extensively in relation to the work culture in the City of London—the (former) home to many of the world's largest financial institutions (many of which have now moved to Canary Wharf)—noting the ways in which a particular hyper-sexualized masculinity dominated working culture and the significance of class. Over a decade after the publication of her book *Capital Culture*, she reviewed whether things changed leading up the financial crisis of 2007/2008 and beyond, arguing that financial services as a sector remains a gendered and masculinized arena. Women, according to McDowell (2010), are either expected to maintain boundaries and police men's behaviour or to participate, more or less reluctantly, in banter and sexualized 'horse play'.

This ties in with debates surrounding the repudiation of feminism (McRobbie, 2007; Scharff, 2012), and, more recently, the rise of a 'popular' feminism (Banet-Weiser, 2018) and 'confidence culture' (Orgad and Gill, 2021). In McRobbie's work on young femininities, she demonstrates how the 'new female subject is, despite her freedom called upon to be silent, to withhold critique in order to count as a modern, sophisticated girl' (McRobbie, 2007: 9). McRobbie (2007: 718), as well as other researchers such as Scharff (2012), draws attention to the contemporary establishment of a 'new sexual contract' in the labour market in post-industrial nations, where 'young women are ... understood to be ideal subjects of female success, exemplars of the new competitive meritocracy'. This is particularly relevant in the context of this research where the respondents had not only successfully negotiated their way to the ranks of partnership, but furthermore, in most cases, came of age during what some refer to as 'second-wave feminism', but made their careers during the 'cultural space of post-feminism' (McRobbie, 2004). McRobbie (2004: 256) notes that the year '1990 (or thereabouts) marks a turning point, the moment of definitive self-critique in feminist theory' as noted in Chapter 1. She examines the change in rhetoric through a cultural analysis of the media, focusing in particular on notions of 'success' and '"female individualism", ... which seems to be based on the invitation to young women by various governments that they might now consider themselves free to compete in education and in work as privileged subjects of the new meritocracy' (McRobbie, 2004b: 258). Meritocracy, here, is subject to scrutiny, and McRobbie's analysis ties in with critiques by, for example, Broadbridge (2010), whose work on women executives, and critical analysis of the 'choice' versus 'constraint' debate, highlights how women's 'choices' in her research were constrained in ways in which men's were not by, among other things, organizational cultures and heteronormative stereotypes (Crompton and Lyonette, 2008a, b; Gammie and Gammie, 2007; Leahy and Doughney, 2006). Yet, such constraints were not consistently challenged, but rather frequently rationalized through a rhetoric of preferences and choice. This individualist rhetoric is problematic as it shifts the burden of unequal collective outcomes onto the shoulders of individual women, thereby neglecting to challenge persistent social and structural constraints (Broadbridge, 2010; Fleetwood, 2007) and leaving the tensions experienced by women at work unacknowledged.

The literature on postfeminism has evolved rapidly over the last decade, with competing notions of postfeminism, neoliberal feminism, or popular feminism (Banet-Weiser, Gill, and Rottenberg, 2020) emerging and being brought in as a broader variety of analytical tools to make sense of women's disaffection and more recent return to feminism, but a type of feminism that focuses uncritically on personal choice and oneself as an entrepreneurial self and which is as a result devoid of a clear critique of capitalism and its role in perpetuating and maintaining women's sex-based oppression. Again from a Foucauldian perspective drawing on the idea of governmentality (see Chapter 1), Gill and Orgad (2017; 2022) have written about what they term 'confidence culture', arguing that confidence is drawn upon as a technology of self—shaping one's expectations of oneself and locating and attributing issues or a lack of confidence to something at fault within the individual. Importantly, this is gendered and, Gill and Orgad (2017) argue, particularly directed at young women who are given to understand that 'they are being held back not by patriarchal capitalism or institutionalized sexism, but by their own lack of confidence—a lack that ... is presented as being entirely an individual and personal matter, unconnected to structural inequalities or cultural forces' (2017: 6). This is also applied to becoming a mother. Chapter 1 talked about Rottenberg's contributions here, who introduces the term neoliberal feminism (with a focus on the US) in relation also to the formation and maintenance of family life and work-life balance, arguing that women are not only responsibilized for their own health, well-being and their careers, but also for crafting what she calls a 'felicitous work-life balance'—turning inward in this quest. Similarly, Gill and Orgad (2017) trace a move from postfeminism where feminism was disavowed as no longer necessary—despite the evidence—towards a 'popular' feminism, a feminism that is for 'everyone' and mostly toothless as a critique of capitalism. Poignantly, Gill and Orgad conclude that 'confidence is sexy because it does not challenge the patriarchal gaze and asymmetric power relations; its value is partly that it is attractive to—and requires no change on the part of—men' (2017: 17). The effects of bias and harassment on women's lives and careers are undeniable, as discussed in Chapters 1 and 2. This chapter considers how the elite women interviewed for this research project felt about equal opportunities in the industry, whether they felt they had been discriminated against, whether they felt they had experienced sexism in their careers, and the extent to which gender intersected with other categories of difference in shaping their experiences at work. I am interested in thinking about differences in the women's talk across borders and considering how their narratives make sense or not within this particular literature on post-, neoliberal, or popular feminism, and the extent to which context here also matters.

'We are all equal, but women need to make a choice'

In Germany, seventeen of the participants thought that equal opportunities had been largely achieved in the profession, and several claimed that they had never been discriminated against or experienced sexist comments or behaviours. Given the small number of women in partnership ranks in German firms, this is an interesting assertion that deserves further attention. One example here is Elenor, a partner at a medium-sized firm. She notes:

> 'Well, I must say it (gender inequality) is often lamented and just this morning there was some sort of news item that said women only hold every fourth leadership position. But talking from my personal experiences, I have never experienced such disadvantages. In fact, I sometimes felt it was an advantage. Of course, there are a few fossils running around. I once had this situation where I went to a client's on my own and the client said "When your boss said you were coming I thought—a woman?—but then I called myself to order and said, well, why not!"'
>
> **(Elenor, medium-sized firm, Germany, 51/0)**

Indeed, Elenor likes to think of the accounting industry as a 'meritocratic' environment where being a woman is, if anything, an advantage, a way of standing out, and where discrimination or sexism are only ever isolated incidents. Curiously, Elenor had pointed out earlier in the interview that her very first position had only been given to her as the result of drunken, sexist 'banter' at a Christmas party:

> 'I was invited to an interview and later on learned that this was one of the sparkly wine moods of my boss. I was the only woman and there were twenty men at that shop and the secretaries were female, of course, and well, our boss was of the opinion that women can't do this sort of thing. He compared the intelligence of his own woman[1] (wife) with all other women and came to a bad conclusion. And my colleagues told me later that he said "Can you imagine? A woman applied!" along the lines of "never heard of such a thing" and of course they had all been drinking at the Christmas party and so they said "well, wouldn't that be a fun idea?" Yes. So, he invited me along for an interview and gave me the job'.
>
> **(Elenor, medium-sized firm, Germany, 51/0)**

Although she had worked in an environment where women were openly considered to be less intelligent than, and thus inferior to, men, she felt that she personally had never been disadvantaged or discriminated against. In addition, Elenor had also worked with clients who informed her that their wives do 'not need to work'—clearly a sexist remark, which implied that a) her husband was evidently not earning enough and b) she should ideally be at home. Nonetheless, Elenor insisted that she had never encountered discrimination or sexism in her twenty-five years working in the industry. Her account ties in with those of sixteen other respondents who described situations during follow-up discussions that were clearly sexist or misogynist, yet claimed that equal opportunities had largely been achieved and simultaneously dismissed sexist moments as something they 'could take'.

Johanna's account highlights this tension. She says:

> 'The problem in the profession as a woman: when they see a man coming, they presume he can do it (the job), and when they see a woman, they say "Well, let's see whether she can do it!" You are constantly doubted and have to prove that you can. All the time … What can I do? I go and show them that I can. Of course, that is exhausting. It takes a very long time until you get there. It costs a lot of money as well. But it costs the men the same'.
>
> **(Johanna, small firm, Germany, 53/1)**

---

[1] The term 'wife' is 'Frau' in Germany, which also means 'woman'. In order to convey that the meaning 'wife' is referred to, one says 'meine Frau' (my woman). Similarly, for husband, one would say 'mein Mann' (my man).

68 Sexism at Work

Her account first points to a collective issue, yet the solution is individualized. *'What can I do? I go and show them that I can'*. And further, she notes:

> 'I live it (gender equality)! I never wasted any time discussing it. And I never ran about in dungarees. I remember the time when those women's rights people wore their purple dungarees and drank Jasmine tea … that was too silly for me, I just went and did it'.
>
> **(Johanna, small firm, Germany, 53/1)**

Here, feminism is 'unpopular' (McRobbie, 2005), it is a silly waste of time. Possibly then, Johanna is rejecting the victimization associated with feminism (Kelan, 2009a; 2009b). The term 'feminism' was mentioned twice across all interviews in Germany and both times rejected as something of a waste of time. Just like Elenor, Johanna dismisses activism and the idea that there are still barriers for women in the profession, yet paradoxically then moves on to provide examples of such barriers. It is an excellent example of what Gill and Scharff term as the third way of defining post-feminism—'a backlash against feminism' (2011: 3), which, as they note, often comes in contradictory terms. At the end of the paragraph, Johanna seems uncomfortable to acknowledge that there may be barriers that are specific to women and is quick to point out that men and women pay the same price—almost correcting herself. Like Elenor, she too distanced herself from those 'people', presumably women, in silly purple dungarees and instead identified as an individual, rather than a woman, with agency and choices, who just got on with it.

The accounts were also frequently linked to motherhood in Germany. Nina, a partner at one of the Big-4 firms, believes that the absence of women in higher positions in the profession is largely due to their 'personal' decisions in favour of a family.

> 'I believe it is much better now. I believe that, if you look at the statistics that there are still fewer women than men, and there is a significant difference. But nonetheless, I believe, that it (women working) is widely accepted in practice. Nonetheless, there are barriers, which are internal, and I do ask how it happens that there are so few women in partnership positions. It's not that they can't make it, but it is also certainly a question of personal decision-making that one says, ok, I don't want that, because of me, my partner, so my husband, raises the kids, if we had any. Then of course I have to think about how will I manage? Do I not want to have children, or do I want that somehow a nanny or my parents do it, or whatever? I believe that it is still a life decision that many women eventually, no matter what

chances or what career progression prospects they could or might have, make. To say: "Alright, so then I will stay at home"'.

(Nina, Big-4 firm, Germany, 39/0)

Like Elenor and Johanna, Nina dismissed gender inequalities in the workplace and instead referred to individual 'decision-making' as the main reason behind the (very) low number of women in partnership positions in the profession. This individual decision-making, however, is only required of half the population. In line with Gill's notion of a postfeminist regime (also see Gill, Kelan, and Scharff, 2017; Gill and Orgad, 2022; also see employed in e.g Adamson and Kelan, 2019), Nina's talk focuses on autonomy and choice. At the same time, she is clear about the fact that small children need looking after and suggests that who cares might matter. There is an assumption of sex difference, of dependence and of the limits of time—that one cannot be primary carer and work the vast majority of one's waking hours. This differs from what Rottenberg (2017) observed in the US where outsourcing one's care responsibilities was acceptable and perceived to be a common way of managing the care of dependents from afar. In Nina's talk, motherhood is constructed as a choice with consequences for a woman's career, not a right. This is not a 'choice' men have to make. In her narrative, Nina reveals the normalization of parenting as synonymous with mothering (Johnston and Swanson, 2006; O'Reilly, 2016), which is further explored in Chapter 5 and a consistent theme in the German accounts.

Freja, also a partner in a Big-4 firm, shared a similar viewpoint.

'Of course, everyone should have the same chances and opportunities. Yes. But as a woman, I think, you cannot fool yourself into believing that if you insist on having a career, that consciously or unconsciously, at some point you will need to make a decision, because you cannot have everything. That is impossible. It is naïve to think that if you have two colleagues, whether male or female, and one is there and extremely committed and the other one goes home every time because, he has to, because he is already somewhere else in his mind, because he thinks of children and stuff like that, then automatically you will not treat them the same. And objectively, that wouldn't be fair anyways'.

(Freja, Big-4 firm, Germany, 44/0)

The above two accounts are interesting because the respondents appeal to fairness and equity in different ways, noting that if women want equality, they will need to pull their weight at work, which comes at a price. Besides evidence of continuous bias against women in recruitment, hiring, and promotion, as discussed in Chapter 2, Freja holds on to the idea that it is a question of commitment and not one of being male or female. Freja uses 'er'/'der' when talking about a person who 'goes home every time, because he has to' referring to the childcare responsibilities of this hypothetical other who may not necessarily be male, as the way she uses er/der here is in relation to the term 'jemand' and meant in a gender-neutral way. Her point is that it does not matter whether one is female or male; what matters is whether or not one is at work. But holding on to this sort of idea of a meritocracy at work is only sustainable if one disavows gendered practices in the private sphere, ignoring the fact that most of the unpaid care around the world is provided by women, propping up the ability of mostly men and some women to participate in the labour market as if they were independent (O'Reilly, 2016). This is precisely why ethics of care feminists note that the artificial divide of public and private life and the valorization of paid over unpaid work is inherent in capitalism and a key reason for the inequalities women encounter in both spheres. At the same time, Freja is aware that it is women's reproductive capacity and declining fertility after the age of 35 (Harper, Bolvin, O'Neill et al., 2017) that means that, for women, 'at some point, you will need to make a decision, because you cannot have everything'. Interestingly, the possibility that the hypothetical partner, who appears to be almost exclusively male, could stay at home is dismissed, it seems, as undesirable in Nina's account, and left unacknowledged in Freja's narrative. Indeed, Freja uses the term 'insist' as if having a career as a mother was a rather 'atypical' occurrence—despite the fact that three quarters of mothers in Germany are working mothers.

These accounts are markedly different from the accounts encountered in the UK, where eleven out of the thirty women, and nine out of the eighteen mothers I interviewed, had partners who worked part-time or were full-time homemakers, as I further explore in Chapter 5. In Germany, meanwhile, there was not a single case where the partner was at home or working part-time.

Only nine of the thirty participants in Germany believed that there were any barriers to women's career advancement. Two of them pointed to the 'burdens' of motherhood as an explanation, one simply referred to the statistics ('*the statistics speak for themselves*', Katrin, 44, Big-4 firm), and only one woman pointed to gendered internal structures and processes. This respondent, Manuela, referred to male bonding rituals as one problem.

'What do you think about gender equality in the profession?'
'There is no such thing, it really does not exist. There is only equality to a certain degree. In my opinion, my male colleagues have rituals, which unconsciously

exclude women. When we talk about careers then it is comparable to a certain point. I would almost say up to Manager. When we talk about Partner-level then it becomes relatively evident that men really make partner sooner. And with qualifications that, in my very objective opinion (laughs), a woman would never make partner with. Now we have to ask ourselves why that is. Um ... and I think that it is mainly personal relationships. And especially those personal relationships that are easier to attain as part of those male rituals than with a woman. So, in terms of equality, that is an illusion, there is no such thing'.

(Manuela, Big-4 firm, Germany, 47/0)

Manuela had worked in the UK at the same Big-4 firm for a few years, and I felt that this was one key reason that she was conscious of a more rights-based way of thinking about inclusion and exclusion, about bias, and the role of organizations in maintaining and perpetuating inequality endemic in wider society (Acker, 2006; Hayes, Introna, et al., 2018). Her observations about relationships are also in line with findings by Morgan and Martin (2006) who argue that these relationships are indeed of importance and easier to attain in homosocial situations. This was already discussed in the last chapter—in Germany, relationships were very important for the women's advancement. Yet, Manuela, as the only one who had worked in the UK, questioned whether this was one practice holding women back.

Equal Opportunities in the Accounts in the United Kingdom

In the UK, the respondents were less certain about the extent to which they encountered equal opportunities at work. Among the thirty respondents, eighteen took the view that women were still disadvantaged and that equal opportunities had not been achieved. Of course, not all of the women I interviewed held the same stance, indeed demonstrating the tensions involved: some believed that more needed to be done actively to promote women's advancement, others thought it was not the employers' responsibility or that positive discrimination needed to be avoided at all costs.

Sharon, for example, similarly to Manuela in Germany, argues that the requirements for men to move ahead are less stringent than those for women and that this is unfair. She says:

'Basically, what I have observed is that if you're good, you'll get through. You'll get what you want. If you're average and you're a man you might still get through. If you're average and a woman you won't get through. So, there are more average men in senior roles than there are average women in senior roles. And, of course, there are more men—good men—in senior roles than senior women, but most of the women in senior positions will be really good at what they're doing. So, that for me is the disparity. If you're average and you're female, you don't have an equal chance of success as your average man'.

(Sharon, Big-4 firm, UK, 41/0)

Sharon was happy in her position and did not feel that she had been discriminated against, but she stressed that she had been very good at her job, working very long hours and spending many years abroad. But she acknowledged that, on average, persistent problems remained.

Leslie, also a partner at a large firm, shared similar insights. In addition to feeling quite strongly about the lack of equal opportunities, she also felt that what she observed as the 'empowered' talk of the younger generation did nothing to alleviate the situation. She notes:

'When I started, everyone said "Oh, it's all changing!", "Don't worry your pretty little head about it, there is plenty of opportunity for women blah blah blah" and undoubtedly there are now more women around than there were 25, 30 years ago. But I am not convinced that we've actually made any real breakthrough and I think it's too easy for particularly the younger women at the moment. They always say "Oohoo! We get promoted!" etc. I feel that undoubtedly, when you're a small minority, there is a bias against you and that we actually need to do more to compensate for the biases that there are in society generally. And if that's positive discrimination, so be it. But I think we need to do more than we have done ... otherwise it's gonna be another 100 years before we pick up to, you know, an acceptable 45 per cent female partners'.

(Leslie, Big-4 firm, UK, 52/0)

Leslie was very outspoken about women at work. Unlike some of her German counterparts, she was undisturbed by the idea of positive discrimination (which is unlawful; positive action, however, is legal) and she saw no reason why the objective should not be almost the same number of male and female partners. She is critical of what she sees as young women's unwarranted optimism.

For Lauren, a partner in a medium-sized firm, the question I posited was confusing. While she noted that the number of women in partnership positions at her firm was 'rubbish', she had personally had a very good experience of working at the firm and appeared to be worried about blaming someone.

According to her estimates, women represented about 50 per cent of the initial intake at trainee level, which then dropped to '60/40 through the manager grades and the junior manager grades, 70/30 between senior manager grades and then, you get to partner—it's rubbish. It's just, you know, very, very few women'. Yet, personally she felt that her experiences at the firm had exceeded her own expectations, noting that she had been able to 'be herself' in every way and to combine partnership with having a family. She suspected the low number of women in the profession may be related to a false perception of who could be a partner. She explains:

> 'We do get them drop out as we go through. I know I've heard from, you know, friends who are still managers and people who are coming through that there is a perception that you have to be of a certain type of person to be a partner ... And one of my biggest challenges is to say "Actually, you don't have to be that sort of person—you can just be yourself". Because I don't play by their rules. I play by my rules'.
>
> **(Lauren, medium-sized firm, UK, 36/1)**

Lauren here talks about 'being oneself', which appears to be about breaking free from stereotypes of what a partner might look like, including but not necessarily restricted to gender stereotypes. But it is also an unthreatening way of looking at things—just be yourself—it does not necessitate changes based on collective grievance. Lauren's politics are different to Leslie's above, who is sixteen years Lauren's senior and who felt that '*we ... need to do more*'.

Lauren's accounts were partially echoed by Marina, a partner at one of the Big-4 firms with two grown-up children. She was promoted quite quickly, but acknowledged that it may have been more difficult for other women:

> 'I never had personally any ... I've never experienced discrimination in terms of being a woman, because I happened to be the best person from all the men. So, I am sure some women feel like that, because it's still that kind of men's club. So, I think that still exists and you do have situations where men, without thinking, make comments not only about women, but also about diversity in general. Whether there are differences or different kinds of lifestyle ... So, that, you know, still exists because you cannot wipe it out totally regardless how good the firm is. But the matter is actually how you deal with it and how we try to kind of eradicate it'.
>
> **(Marina, Big-4 firm, UK, 59/2)**

While she too felt that she 'personally' experienced equal opportunities, she also acknowledges, in similar ways to Lauren, that the profession is still male-dominated. Both simultaneously stress that they had been fine as 'individuals', yet unlike their German counterparts they did not dismiss the existence of constraints. Interestingly, Marina also talks about potentially sexist remarks and notes that the onus is on the firm to 'deal' with it. This is particularly in contrast to the ways in which some of the German respondents talked about 'responsibility' and 'choice' when it comes to addressing sexism at work.

'Taking it with a bit of humour': Dismissing or Problematizing Sexism at Work

There were not only differences in the accounts on equality, but also in the ways in which the interviewees made sense of sexism and harassment at work. While respondents in Germany were reluctant to talk about moments of sexism or sexual harassment, or claimed to have experienced neither, the majority of women in the UK had at least one tale to tell and acknowledged that it persisted as a problem. The analysis of the accounts unveiled how women in the UK also had a much wider definition of what constitutes sexism—thus further demonstrating the vague nature of the term itself. The respondents in Germany appeared to have a perception of it only as bordering on sexual harassment, in which case it was casually dismissed as banter and something that was best approached with a 'bit of humour' or a witty repartee. While they only rarely and reluctantly pointed to instances of hostile sexism, experiences of benevolent sexism were largely absent in their accounts (Glick and Fiske, 1996). In contrast, the interviewees in the UK alluded to both.

Of the few respondents in Germany who acknowledged sexism, Susanne describes a situation where a client refused to work with her because she was a woman, yet she felt that humour was the appropriate response:

'Yes, there was a lot of that (sexist comments). There were clients who were refusing to show me certain things. Like, I remember this one CEO who did not want to tell me what his income was. He said I should send over my colleague, but my "colleague" was my assistant. So yeah, those things happened, and in particular with men'.

'How did you deal with that?'

'Oh, I was capable of taking it with a bit of humour'.

(Susanne, medium-sized firm, Germany, 53/2)

Her client refused to talk to her and presumed that the man who was present with her was equally, or even more, qualified than she was, yet she did not take the time to correct his assumptions or challenge his behaviour. It is noteworthy that she uses the word 'capable', suggesting that ability to dismiss the client's behaviour was a skill or something that she mastered—implying that to challenge the situation would be a sign of weakness; it is almost beneath her to challenge it. Indeed, the narratives of women in both countries were frequently rejecting what they presumably perceived to be victimization, and emphasized their individual 'strength' and 'choice', thereby neglecting the ways in which such choices are gendered, and also classed and racialized and constrained on various individual and institutional levels (Bradley and Healy, 2008; England, 1989; Healy, 1999; Kirton and Greene, 2005; Kirton and Robertson, 2018; McDowell, Ray, Perrons, et al., 2005).

In a similar vein to Brigitte, Freja, a partner at a Big-4 firm in Germany, also said she had never encountered sexism or sexist remarks but that she presented herself in a 'callous'[2] way, which, she felt, prevented such behaviours from occurring. Nina, also a partner at a Big-4 firm, noted that she too had never been subjected to sexism, but that she did not think she was the type to receive such comments, as she would respond straight away. She elaborates somewhat:

> 'But, um, if I were to talk about discrimination then this concerns perhaps usually women who do not shoot back straight away and that is problematic enough as well ... '
>
> **(Nina, Big-4 firm, Germany, 39/0)**

Nina was one of the few women who believed that equal opportunities had not yet been realized and felt that something needed to be done. Yet, she dismissed sexism as something that only happened to weak people or indeed weak women; despite later talking about stereotypes of women, she did not feel that there was still a problem of sexism. In her view, sexism only encompassed intentionally malicious actions by men.

Brigitte, a partner at one of the Big-4 firms in Germany, was part of the majority who claimed that she had never encountered sexism in her career:

> (Laughs) 'No. No, no. I think, well let's say, I don't want to rule out that it would be possible, but I am relatively sure that it has a lot to do with nobody daring to say something like that to me, because they could not live with the reaction. And also,

---

[2] She said 'unempfindlich' in German.

whether such jokes are made or not, usually depends on how you present yourself as a person'.

(Brigitte, Big-4 firm, Germany, 41/0)

Brigitte highlights her own strength and her position among her peers. She stresses her ability to take care of herself in situations such as these and alludes to the responsibility of the potentially offended to prevent such occurrences through the way they present themselves. The onus is thus on the woman to present herself in a way that does not elicit sexist remarks. This corresponds in many ways to US findings by Kanter (1977) and UK findings by Collinson and Collinson (1996), almost fifty and thirty years ago respectively. In an analysis of the UK assurance industry, Collinson and Collinson (1996: 44), for instance, described a 'vicious circle of sexual harassment' where women's complaints were not only not taken seriously, but also reinterpreted in ways that justified their subsequent exclusion, thus maintaining and 'reinforcing rather than transforming the prevailing masculine culture'. However, the discussion here adds a cross-national dimension and shows how while this 'vicious circle' appears to be paradoxically maintained in Germany through the employ of individualist narratives, it is frequently challenged by the UK partners.

Why sexism is an issue and must remain a concern is demonstrated by Pauline's account. In our interview, Pauline remembered the time she went on the interviewing circuit as one of the phases in her career in which sexism was quite openly practiced. She recalls how the interviewing partner had left her briefly alone in the room, and upon his return expressed concern that she may have read a note that he had attached to her application. She replied that she had not, but he insisted on talking to her about it, noting:

'He said to me "You know what it says?" You see my first name is Pauline and he said (the post-it says) "I'd rather have a Paul". Yes. That's what he read out. That is what he had written down'.

(Pauline, small firm, Germany, 41/2)

Asked how she reacted to this incident, she says:

'Well, maybe the job might be interesting to me, so I am not going to say "that is unacceptable and I am gonna go", so yeah that is simply how it goes'.

(Pauline, small firm, Germany, 41/2)

She considered a job, even though it would mean working for someone who openly dis-preferred women in the workforce. In her view, the best approach to the situation was to sit it out. At the same time, she noted it was in her interest to hear what the job was about.

This is different to the situation encountered in the UK. All respondents had at least one tale to tell. This ranged from moments where sexist language was used in their presence, to the respondents filing a complaint to the firm's board about sexual harassment.

Like numerous other respondents in the UK, Sharon shared an experience about what she felt was inappropriate male behaviour towards her.

> 'I had it with clients. It wasn't intended as harassment, it was meant as a friendly thing. But I found it to be a sign of disrespect, where it kind of just puts you down. It was just a client, you know, putting an arm around you inappropriately, just being too chummy and physical and it wasn't even the way, you know, men would be physical by barging. So, I just had a quiet word and he stopped (laughed). I just said I feel uncomfortable with this. Yeah, this is not normal client-consultant behaviour'.
>
> **(Sharon, Big-4 firm, UK, 41/0)**

For Sharon this behaviour was a sign of disrespect, which she felt was unacceptable and thus confronted.

Henrietta was physically harassed by a client once but noted that her employer at the time 'actually clamped down very hard and told him this was not acceptable'. She felt reassured by that but remained concerned about sexist beliefs as a barrier to women's career advancement.

She recalls the partnership interview she had at one of the Big-4 firms where she had previously been a partner:

> '15 minutes into the interview, one of the partners said "And your husband is happy with it, is he?" ... and I just burst out laughing, because I could see the other men on the panel with their heads in their hands. I said: "You know what?" I said "If you don't make me up to partner now, you do realize you got a major problem, right? I don't have to answer that comment, because I believe that what I have been doing already demonstrates that I can do this job" to which one of the other guys sort of said "No, no, we do too and we're gonna shoot him afterwards"'.
>
> **(Henrietta, medium-sized firm, UK, 49/2)**

Henrietta's case shows how seriously a question, which could be construed as sexist, was taken during the interview. Three out of the four people in the room were immediately aware that the question was inappropriate and could have consequences for the firm. This is quite different from the accounts in

Germany, where such remarks were dismissed or laughed at. Henrietta also laughed but made it quite clear that she was aware of her rights.

A few of the respondents talked about sexist daily practices, particularly during their earlier years in the profession. Paris remembers a similar encounter to the one reported by Susanne. She too was mistaken as being one of the juniors in the team. She recalls:

> 'When I was at the medium-sized firm there, I was obviously quite young, I had a young man who was a junior and we were on site and the client came in and he went and addressed the man straight away. And the guy said "I'm sorry but this is Paris, she's my manager ... " and the chap was very embarrassed'.
>
> **(Paris, medium-sized firm, UK, 49/0)**

This account differs from Susanne's in that Paris' colleague immediately pointed out the mistake. Neither Paris nor her colleague were worried enough about embarrassing the client to continue with the role reversal. It is another demonstration of how the women I interviewed in the UK thought somewhat differently about sexism than the participants in Germany. As the German respondents took it 'in their stride', dismissed and laughed at it, while insisting that equal opportunities existed, the UK partners were more likely to note that sexism was something that was still encountered and needed to be confronted, that it was in their rights to do so. It resembles the discussion on equal opportunities, as it was again paradoxically the German women partners who more frequently drew on individualist narratives of 'strength' despite the more collectivist context, according to the VoC. But of course, there is also a sense of a duty to the collective to endure rather than to threaten the status quo.

Time and Age

Some of the respondents talked about time, how things have changed and the progress that has been made. They also talked about the ways in which gender interacts with age. Asked about her thoughts on equal opportunities in the profession, Sarah, a partner, notes that things have changed for the better over time. She says:

> 'I do notice how things have changed over the years. I have been here over twenty years so I've probably gone through ... there are people who are working here still when they first started. There weren't really any women at all. At most, they were secretaries. I think things have changed, if you look at it critically,

phenomenally over the last 30 years. Well, I don't know if you watched this TV programme: It was called *Life on Mars*[3]?'

'No I did not'.

'It's actually quite interesting ... because it was based on somebody from today, a man from today, who ended up going back into the early 70s. And just seeing, I mean I was what? 10 at the time? And you just realize, because you live through it, you don't realize how much things have changed. When you watch that, it was really illuminating because you just thought I can't believe I lived through all of that ... and I don't quite know—I really don't—because, you know, for quite some time now women are going into the profession as compared with men. It's pretty even I think at the trainee stage?'

(Sarah, medium-sized firm, UK, 45/0)

Her account is reflective and optimistic. Looking back she notices things have changed and that there are now more women in the profession. It is interesting that she draws on *Life on Mars*. Alice employed a similar strategy, pointing to the TV series *Ashes to Ashes*, which was a sequel to *Life on Mars*. Alice, a partner in a mid-sized firm, recalled her earlier years in the profession and also concluded that things had notably changed over the years with regards to what was now deemed unacceptable behaviour. She says:

'Do you ever watch that program Ashes to Ashes[4]?'

'Once, yeah'.

'Yeah? It's quite funny, because that is actually quite an accurate reflection of what 1980s culture was like. Which was quite sexist, quite unreconstructed. I would be an audit senior and out on site. Walking across a factory floor was an awful experience, yeah? You know past the girly calendars past the "Oi darling" (changes voice) and "woohooo" and I was there to do my job. So, you know you dreaded moments like that. And that wouldn't happen these days. But within the practice in which I worked, sure, there were inappropriate statements, you know, joshing down the pub, which now you'd be "huuuuu (sucks air in loudly)". But then, society was so accepting of it, you kind of thought "tsk, oh you idiot". But that was all you thought. You didn't think "I'm going to take you to a tribunal for inappropriate comments in the workplace". Whereas now if I heard one of my managers or partners talking to a female member of staff like that I'd go "eeep eeep—no (shakes fist), in here, now!" So, yeah. I am a bit older now so people assume I must be in some position of vague seniority, but when I was a lot younger, people permanently or

---

[3] *Life on Mars* was a TV series broadcasted on the BBC. For a discussion of it, see, for instance, Chapman (2009).

[4] *Ashes to Ashes* was a BBC TV Series and a sequel to *Life on Mars*. The series' main character is a police officer with the Metropolitan Police in London who, after being shot in 2008, wakes up in 1981.

consistently thought that I was my boss' secretary as opposed to a professional member of staff. You know, nothing wrong with being a secretary, but there was just a natural assumption and I've been asked to go out and get tuna sandwiches for people before. Now I think (both laugh), alright'.

(Alice, medium-sized firm, UK, 47/2)

Like Sarah, Alice is optimistic and feels encouraged when thinking back in time. She feels that things have changed and that people are more alert as to what constitutes inappropriate behaviour. Here, Alice reflects on her own passivity when she was a young professional, lacking hierarchical power, and at the same time notices that she is now ready to police others instantly if she witnesses discriminating or sexist behaviour among her staff and colleagues. She also noted how age has provided her with a cloak of 'vague seniority'. She is old enough, even as a woman. Authors such as Moore (2009) argue that age can impact on women's experiences at work: both as being too young for some things and too old for others. I drew on Paris' account in the previous section to demonstrate how sexist situations at work were encountered. In her discussion, Paris partly defended the offending client by noting that she was not only a woman at the time but a young woman as well. I wanted to learn more about this and asked:

'When did that change? Where were you not young anymore in their eyes?'

'I'm always young! I'm always young but at that point I felt when I was very young, it was people in business don't see that many women in charge so soon and so as they go in a room, the women weren't in charge the man in the room was in charge. That's my training years. It was a very unusual environment, but it's made me very resourceful now. It's made me quite strong'.

(Paris, medium-sized firm, UK, 49/0)

She was, at the time, seen as too young to have authority. This was also reported by the German respondents. Chloe, for example, when talking about her frustrations about not being able to move ahead, noted the importance of age in her discussion with her superiors. When trying to make partner, she met with several of the existing partners at her firm in order to discuss her chances of progression. She recalls:

' … and then he told me I shouldn't be so impatient. And I said "That's what you tell me now and in three years you'll tell me I'm too old for it (partnership). I cannot accept this"'.

(Chloe, Big-4 firm, Germany, 52/1)

Chloe had a suspicion that the partners were using age as a trap. In her case, she confronted the situation straight away and made partner relatively soon after.

There is a small but growing set of literature on age and gender, which suggests that Chloe's suspicion was justified. Granleese and Sayer (2006: 500) call this 'the double jeopardy of gendered ageism', and Duncan and Loretto (2004) note that women are never the right age and more often encounter ageism at work. Women in the UK were slightly younger (31–55) than the women in Germany (34–59), however this can be explained by the relatively longer time spent in education and training. In addition, women in Germany talked more about being too old or it being too late for further progression than their UK counterparts. For example, Bettina and Anita in Germany thought that the time had now passed for them to fight their way up the hierarchy within the partnership ranks. They both indicated that they were content with their role as partners. Part of the hierarchy negotiation at that level included the amount of shares held, responsibilities, and whether partners were salaried or full equity partners.

In both countries, women felt that they were deemed to be incompetent and lacking authority in younger years. Denise, now in her late thirties, summarizes it well:

> 'I am still quite young, so they also look at me like "Ohhh, I don't know if you got enough experience to tell me what I need to know". Sometimes. You know? But there we are. When I have grey hair, I'll be alright (laughs)'.
>
> **(Denise, small firm, UK, 39/2)**

Age is also tied to reproduction, especially in Germany where women were frequently reminded of their own reproductive capacity and aware of that of other women. This was less the case in the UK, as will be discussed in depth in the next chapter.

Being Different at Work

Gender inequalities were not the only form of structural inequalities discussed in the interviews. While the group of respondents was relatively homogeneous, the women's understandings of diversity and difference also arose as a topic of discussion, in relation to class, race, and ethnicity. Two of the women interviewed in Germany had parents with migration backgrounds, one in Scandinavia and the other in Eastern Europe. In the UK, the group of respondents was only slightly more diverse. One participant identified as British with a white-Indo-Caribbean background, one as Indian, one as Italian, and one as Japanese/Australian. In addition, one of the respondents was from Ireland.

In Germany, the two women with migration backgrounds reflected on it in a positive way in the sense that their language skills aided them in their career advancement. For Freja, her ability to speak Czech was an asset to her boss, she said, and in the case of Sabrina, the fact that her mother was Norwegian meant that she was able to work in Norway for a while. Both women worked in Big-4 firms. I was interested in learning more about Freja's experience throughout her career. In Germany, surnames can be seen to signal heritage and those with surnames that are not explicitly Germanic may find that they are asked where they are from—at times repeatedly, with a view to this being an inquiry not about where one grew up, but where one's parents and grandparents are from. This sort of 'nachbohren', or probing, has been problematized in the media; for example, Klasen (2014), writing for the daily die Sueddeutsche Zeitung, argues that such lines of questioning may be motivated by xenophobia, and, similarly, Henry (2003) draws connections to how this is may be related to power also (also see Edeh, Riley, and Kokot-Blamey, 2021).

Interestingly, Freja, now in her forties, explained that people tended to assume that it was not her name in the first place. She recalls:

'No, generally people just always assumed that I married a foreigner (laughs) so I never had a problem like that. I think I had the advantage growing up that we moved a lot and I grew up in smaller towns and it was also the title again, the hierarchy. Mummy was a GP, so it was "Oh Dr. so and so" and "the children of the Dr". You don't get nasty foreigners-should-leave-type comments then. So, in that way I never had a problem. The only thing like that is when I am in situations where someone makes a joke about foreigners in my presence and is then surprised that I am not joining in the laughter'.

(Freja, Big-4 firm, Germany, 44/0)

In this account Freja's experiences of identity as a second-generation migrant intersected with class and gender. Being a white woman 'protects' her from the suspicion of being foreign because she is cast in the role of a wife in the imagination of others, and being upper-class 'protected' her from the suspicion of being some sort of burden on the collective. This resonates with Gruner (2010), who notes that discourses of racism in Germany (and potentially elsewhere) often construct working-class migrants as 'associated with disorder, chaos, immorality, criminality and illness' (2010: 283), whereas upper-class migrants may escape such negative associations.

Sarah's account in the UK was quite similar to that of Freja's in Germany. Although she identifies as white-Indo-Caribbean and, growing up, her family was working class, neither her name nor the colour of her skin made her identifiable her as 'different' to others. She says:

> 'I remember when I was at university, one of the guys that I was good friends with was going out with a Sri Lankan girl and I said something to him about mixed marriages. And he looked at me (pulls face) and said "Mixed marriages? What on earth would you know about a mixed marriage?" And I said "Have you ever looked at the colour of my skin?" And he goes "Well, you are a little bit dark skinned" and I said "That's because of my parents. I got an English parent and a ... " And he said "I'd just assumed you were English (high pitched voice)!" And most people always said to me "Well you're just so English" that it's never really come up'.
>
> **(Sarah, medium-sized firm, UK, 45/0)**

Sarah did not think that her class or ethnic background had interfered with her ability to advance in her career, because she felt she was not perceived as 'different' i.e. non-white. She suggested that it was more of an issue at home as her father, who had quite traditional views, had always expected her to marry and was quite set on it, rather than being invested in her career. Sarah, however, felt very strongly that she did not wish to rely on a man 'to set her a budget', as she felt that this was what she witnessed happening to her mother. Her story resonates with recent writing by Netto, Noon, Hudson, Kamenou-Aigbekaen, and Sosenko (2020) who argue that, as a research community, we are not paying enough attention to understanding the context of our respondents within the private sphere and how power dynamics within the home environment affect the capacity of those with migration backgrounds to advance at work or in their careers.

It is also noteworthy how Sarah's friend said he thought she was 'English' instead of, for instance, 'British'; an indication perhaps of the ways which Englishness too is racialized and conflated with whiteness (Leddy-Owen, 2014). But Englishness also has class and gender dimensions and was a factor in other respondents' accounts. Martha described herself as a working-class Scottish woman and noted that she had felt somewhat different over the course of her career. Although she did not look different, she sounded different:

> 'When I was at the Big-4 firm, I was very aware of the class system in England, because there was me with my working-class accent. I still kept it, you know, on purpose. Not so much on purpose, but I'm not ashamed of it. It's just like "I take a size five shoe and I've got a Scottish accent". Same thing nearly, you know, not gonna give it up ... I was very aware that some of my contemporaries had been to Eton for example, so I was very aware of the differences and there I was Scottish working class and I was female and I also had a friend there and she'd been

to University with me and she was Scottish. A bit less working class than me, but nevertheless from a working-class background. And she was female. So, we were aware that we were considered to be different a) because we did stand out more because we were female but also, I think, because we were Scottish'.

(Martha, medium-sized firm, UK, 54/0)

Martha was very reflective of her own background, and in her account, gender, 'nationality', and class intersect. She felt different in multiple ways, and later also talked about moments where she encountered open hostility once she had moved out of the very structured and urban environment and became partner at a smaller firm in the Cornish countryside. For example, one of the other partners in her firm would mock her accent openly during meetings, mobilizing her accent to produce her as different (Edeh, Riley, and Kokot-Blamey, 2021).

'I get comments here from one or two of my partners mocking my accent. Ay. Which I never had in London, you know? I guess it's the only thing. Women never do it. It's only men. I don't remember a woman ever making comments about my accent. It's men that do it. They want to put you down. It's the one thing that, because they can't really get you on intellect or ability, so they go for accent'.

(Martha, medium-sized firm, UK, 54/0)

Like Sarah, Martha worked in a small firm when I interviewed her, however she also had experience of working for one of the Big-4 firms and noted that while she perceived herself to be different to the other people she worked with there, she only encountered and endured openly hostile behaviour at a small firm and outside of London. This too points to the ways in which sex, class, and race/ethnicity intersect and shape experiences of difference in complex ways and the ways in which geography and context can matter.

Apoorva, whose parents had migrated from South Asia, also felt that it was more of an issue in her private life. She said she had had a working-class upbringing in the UK, noting that both her mother and father worked in factories at the beginning and that she grew up in council houses with her siblings. As a family they were very socially mobile and improved financially over time. Now Apoorva was a partner at a small firm, where the other partners included members of her family. She recalls:

'We went from living in a council house, to my dad buying a house, to sending us to school here. Yeah, it was fine. This is what you grow up with, you know? And you respected your parents for what they've been through. I didn't feel that (discriminated against). I mean because my parents, they faced racism here I suppose, you know. And they always said, you know, if someone treats you badly or doesn't treat you well, then just ignore it. Rise above it. We were always taught to rise above it, but I never did experience racism'.

(Apoorva, small firm, UK, 37/2)

I return to discuss Apoorva's experiences in Chapter 6, sharing how difficult it was for her to secure a training contract after graduating; how she had to write many applications and start her working life working for free in a small accounting firm. I also return to Apoorva's account in the next chapter where she shares the difficulties of having a baby as a partner when no provisions for maternity are made in the deeds. Yet, despite the difficulties she experienced in her career, she did not attribute these to structural inequalities per se.

Conclusion

The first part of this chapter explored how the women partners talk about equal opportunities and sexism at work. In Germany, the respondents described what they conceived to be a mostly meritocratic working environment and one that they claimed was free of sexism, despite evidence to the contrary—both statistically and through their own experiences. The subject of children and becoming a mother arose consistently, but it was a matter to be taken into account by only half the population who were assumed to have to make a choice between their careers and motherhood. Similarly, the women's discussion of sexism placed the onus firmly upon the shoulders of individual women, emphasizing 'strength' and confidence and frequently dismissing instances of sexism. These observed patterns, tensions, and contradictions in the talk of the German respondents highlight the importance of critiques of cultural theorists in this context. Gill (2007: 74) notes that one 'of the problems with this focus on autonomous choices is that it remains complicit with, rather than critical of, postfeminist and neoliberal discourses that see individuals as entrepreneurial actors who are rational, calculating and self-regulating'. This neoliberal subject, Gill argues, must 'bear full responsibility for their life biography no matter how severe the constraints upon their action' (ibid.).

Gill's argument, while introduced in a very different context, resonates with some of the conflicting accounts produced by the respondents, particularly in Germany: where the accountancy profession is both represented as egalitarian yet a space where women need to make a 'choice'; where feminism is rejected or left unmentioned while moments of sexism are briefly recited then dismissed and only ever problematized at the individual level (' ... whether such jokes are made or not, usually depends on how you present yourself as a person', Brigitte, 41, Big-4 firm, Germany). Scharff's (2012) work on the repudiation of feminism—the act of simultaneously taking feminism for granted and fiercely rejecting it—sheds light on both. It highlights the interrelation between postfeminism and neoliberalism, enabling an uncritical rhetoric of choice and a firm placing of responsibilities upon the shoulders of the individual: to be in charge of one's career ('I just went and did it', Johanna, 53, small firm, Germany), to present oneself in such a way as to prevent sexism or sexist remarks from occurring, and, finally, to make a 'choice' in relation to motherhood. In Germany, the discussion of motherhood, and its presumably career-destroying powers, in particular points to problematic assumptions with regards to differences between the sexes (Gill and Scharff, 2011): while men can be fathers and have a career, women, according to a number of respondents, need to choose and live with the consequences. Biologically determined differences, while acknowledged, are a justified constraint only for half the population.

It does not, however, explain why this was less of an issue in the UK. There, participants, while also unveiling tensions in their talk, were more inclined to acknowledge continuing structural constraints and the costs of sexism and discrimination to women. A majority of the respondents noted that women remained disadvantaged and that equal opportunities had not yet been achieved. In addition, all the women I interviewed in the UK shared at least one tale where they had encountered and often challenged sexism at work, and their understanding of what constitutes sexism was a more comprehensive one. The point of tension here was less whether or not discrimination exists, but rather, as Marina notes, 'how you deal with it and how we try to kind of eradicate it'. Indeed, when it came to 'dealing' with sexism, the narratives of the respondents focused more on how sexist behaviour by clients, colleagues, and employers was defied. Sharon described how she dealt with a client's 'intimacy-seeking' behaviour (Glick and Fiske, 1996: 491) by noting its inappropriateness and rejecting it. Here, gender is deemed relevant: even if the respondents felt they had not experienced sexism or discrimination at the 'individual' level, they were more likely to acknowledge and problematize gender or sex-based discrimination at work at the collective level.

This contrast in how the women talked about discrimination, sexism, feminism, and equal opportunities from a cross-national perspective could also relate to the different feminist legacies as explored in Chapter 1. As Offen (1988) argued, the focus of the feminist movement in the UK, and also in the US, was much more rights-based than in Germany. Bisiada (2021), for example, exploring social media discourses on Twitter (on a relatively small scale) around #MeToo, showed how in the English-speaking as well as Spanish-speaking Twitterverse, #MeToo was seen to be a movement or an important moment in time, whereas it was more frequently referred to as a debate or hysteria in German-speaking media discourses. Bisiada argues that the German negative connotations of 'hysteria' were unique, and that her comparison unveils a reluctance to see it as anything other than a blip. There are complications here because Germany, at the same time, was grappling with a new policy for those seeking asylum from Syria. But I think that beyond the variegated feminist histories, or perhaps alongside it, we might consider how the sort of embeddedness the respondents talked about also has implications for how they might approach situations that may lead to conflict. Being part of a much smaller, much more embedded group of professionals within a context that scores more highly on collectivism, where coordination and cooperation are more highly valued, might make direct complaints or confrontations riskier. Women in positions of power here are not only conflicted through the minority yet elite juxtaposition, which is much more pronounced in Germany, but are also co-owners of the firm they represent, thus likely further complicating their allegiances. This embeddedness is reflected in their dependency on superiors while advancing in their careers, which, as shown in Chapter 3, as a mechanism for negotiating organizational hierarchies, is more liable to bias. This embeddedness and the complications that arise from it for women thus may come at a cost. This is also explored in the next chapter.

5
Mothering in Accounting

The analysis in this chapter focuses on how the female partners interviewed talked about mothering and motherhood. It is a contribution to the accounting and the wider organization literature, which, as outlined and explored in Chapters 1 and 2, has mostly side-lined the study of motherhood. Beyond the literature on cross-national variations and the Varieties of Capitalism to which I return in the conclusion, I draw on two specific feminist literatures in order to explore these accounts from a cross-national perspective. First, the feminist ethics of care literature introduced in Chapter 1. I count O'Reilly's significant contributions to maternal studies here as well as Stephens' (2012) work on postmaternal thinking. Secondly, I draw on the contributions of organization and management studies scholars Gatrell, Cooper, and Kossek (2017), who utilize the work of late anthropologist Mary Douglas to explore the extent to which the maternal body is othered and treated as a social pollutant at work. The analysis shows that the women in Germany seldom challenged the institution of motherhood, which juxtaposes the maternal body with professionalism and establishes one's becoming a mother as incompatible with audit work at partnership level. Becoming a mother was discussed as an irreversible point of difference, with mothers expected to work part-time and continuously described or implied to be a cumbersome burden on others—the firm, clients, and even third parties, thereby resonating with Gatrell, Cooper, and Kossek's (2017) Douglasian notion of the maternal body as a social pollutant. In contrast, in the UK, motherhood was not seen to be special or a status of womanhood, and a 'sameness' approach was shared, which at times however made women's transition back to work following birth challenging. In addition, while the mothers in the UK talked more frequently from a perspective that aligns with O'Reilly's notion of empowered mothering—that is, mothering from a position of authority, agency, authenticity, and autonomy—there were hints that, while they were less likely to be expected to engage in intensive mothering, they were instead constrained as organizational elites and breadwinners to give up motherwork for the economic good of the household.

Matricentric Feminism and Experiences of Difference

O'Reilly (2016) draws heavily on the work of Adrienne Rich (1986), who famously coined the distinction between motherhood as institution and mothering as experience and practice. This was a 'breakthrough' (O'Reilly, 2016), as it enabled feminists to both critique motherhood as an institution 'as defined and restricted under patriarchy' (Rich, 1986: 14) and value mothering as a 'site of empowerment' (O'Reilly, 2016: 20). Nonetheless, as outlined in the introduction to this book (Chapter 1), motherhood remains troublesome for feminism because to talk about motherhood means to talk about sex difference and a key strategy of liberal feminism was, and is, to challenge biological determinism and to argue against essentialist (and thus biologically determinist) perspectives of sex and gender (Jeremiah, 2006; O'Reilly, 2016; Stephens, 2012). O'Reilly acknowledges this dilemma and critique of maternal studies and proposes a 'matricentric' feminism to navigate around it—a feminism that is centred on mothers with an understanding that motherwork may, at times, be carried out by people other than the biological mother and comprises three broad tasks (Ruddick, 1995: the preservation of children, their nurturance, and finally their introduction to society and social acceptability. She argued that becoming a mother, for many of us, disrupts our sense of self and our idea of who we identify with (1) at work, (2) at home, and (3) across the generations. Oakley (1981: 1) described this poignantly, noting that 'becoming a mother is a crisis in the life of a woman, a point of no return … and it is the moment when she becomes a mother that a woman first confronts the full reality of what it means to be a woman in our society'. Acknowledging experiences of difference is therefore at the heart of O'Reilly's framework. Firstly, becoming a mother 'encumbers' us as workers, producing a sense of difference at work. This is also the case for those working in professions, where, as long as we mould into the underlying gendered organizing systems and remain unencumbered 'with or from children' (O'Reilly, 2016a: 43), women may experience working lives that are to a large extent similar to that of men. This is evident in the works of Haynes (2008b) and Anderson-Gough, Grey, and Robson (2005), where mothers working in accounting were conflicted about, and in some instances resistant to, being expected to work to the unencumbered norm and where they felt that they ought to hide the fact that they had parental responsibilities at home (see Chapter 2). Secondly, becoming a mother frequently results in a sudden sense of difference in the household. Even in egalitarian relationships, the arrival of an infant will often radically redefine the relationship and responsibilities in the household. Besides the initial phases of breastfeeding and the infant's dependency on the mother, two terms have come to represent this experience of difference in the work-related literature in later stages of the parenting journey also: *the second shift* (Hochschild and Machung, 1989) and *the mental load* (Robertson, Anderson, Hall, and Kim, 2019). The former describes the fact that despite the majority of women now working in the labour force, most remain also primarily responsible for household chores, thus returning to their home after a day's work to carry out a second shift (ONS, 2016). The mental load (Robertson, Anderson, Hall, and Kim, 2019) describes how working mothers remain responsible for researching and planning family life (children's hobbies, childcare providers, signing children up to doctors, and so forth), even when both partners work equal hours. Both the second shift and the mental load represent the disruption of a sense of sameness in the household. Thirdly, as our pre-maternal ambitions and working lives appear more similar to those of our fathers than those of our mothers, (possibly temporarily), we have lost what Lowinsky (1992) refers to as the *Motherline*: a sense of a shared and collective experience between mothers and daughters across the generations. The search for the Motherline to bridge this sense of difference is echoed in recent research by Lupu, Spence, and Empson (2018), where respondents described the challenges of matching their mothers' involvement in their children's lives but while holding down demanding full-time careers. It also comes through in Haynes' (2008b) work, where respondents were caught between the expectations of their workplaces and looking towards their own childhoods and experiences of having been mothered to construct for themselves an appropriate identity. This identity work dramatizes the isolation with which the institution of contemporary motherhood burdens mothers. Stephens (2012) views this cultural anxiety of the maternal, among other things, as a by-product of globalization and the rise in neoliberalism and, drawing on Sennett's work (1998), highlights the resulting 'illusion of self-sufficiency and the related fantasy of motherlessness' (Stephens, 2012: 59) as key features of what she refers to as 'postmaternal thinking'.

Professional women today thus experience three dramatic shifts to their sense of self upon becoming a mother: the recognition that they are different to men and childless women at work, being different to their partners at home, and being different to their fathers and often failing to find a common experience with their mothers. O'Reilly (2016: 145) formulates precisely some of the ways in which motherhood as institution oppresses, which include the idea that children need the biological mother to be the primary carer; that the children's needs are more important than the mother's; that mothers must lavish children with time and attention as well as money; that the mother has full responsibility but no power from which to mother; and that mothering is to be a private undertaking. These concerns resonate with a traditional German 'Mutterbild' (Ruckdeschel, 2009), which imagines that a woman *consciously* sacrifices her career when deciding in favour of having children, relinquishing work for the sake of her child as she is considered indispensable for his or her wellbeing (also see Dienel, 2003). But with more women working, the pressures become more complex. Hays (1998) coined the resulting conundrum as intensive mothering, where working mothers are expected to give themselves fully and selflessly to mothering on the one hand, and, on the other hand, are asked to compete in the labour market as if they had no children at all. The latter is an important part of Hays' coinage, but one that is, unfortunately, often dropped in the usage of the term 'intensive mothering' (Stephens, 2012). Bueskens examines the capacity of matricentric feminism as a framework, noting that the context matters when determining what constitutes empowered mothering. She notes:

> 'O'Reilly opens the doors of possibility and through this, we can see the variegated landscapes of empowered mothering beyond the prevailing model of intensive motherhood or its polar opposite – the neoliberal model of self-sufficiency, which denies the centrality of care ... Importantly, different strategies may work at different times in our lives and in different social and cultural locales. Staying at home, for example, can be radical in a context that demands all women, including mothers of young dependent children, enter the paid labour force. On the other hand, extricating ourselves from the strictures of economic dependence in patriarchal marriages and providing for ourselves is also fundamentally empowering'.
>
> **(Bueskens, 2016: xiii and xiv)**

From this perspective, then, different approaches to mothering can be radical depending on the context presented. There is an acknowledgement here that a sameness approach to workplace organization, which denies the dependencies of, for example, little children, too can be oppressive as it conceals inequalities, pushing them to the margins—a point very close to the one feminist philosopher Kittay (1999) makes and which I introduced at the start of the book. As this chapter will show, how the female partners interviewed for this book in Germany and the UK talk about motherhood is notably constrained in both contexts, but differently so.

The Maternal Body as Taboo at Work

When focusing more specifically on the world of office-based work, further dilemmas come to the fore. Notably, this relates to an implied juxtaposition between the maternal body on the one hand and professionalism on the other hand. Haynes (2008a), drawing attention to the historical exclusion of women in the accountancy profession in the UK, points out that the price for women who wanted to be promoted would historically be a willingness to forgo marriage and children. Her work highlights the persistent notion that motherhood contrasts with professionalism, something that women may first experience during pregnancy. Both Haynes (2008a) and Lightbody (2009) make similar observations with reference to the accounting profession, pointing to the ways in which pregnancy often functions as the first point in time where women lose control over their bodies. The pregnant body, unlike the menstruating, menopausal body, will not be concealed. Citing Warren and Brewis (2004), Haynes (2008a: 337) explains that '[p]regnancy can represent an intrusion of the female sexual and fertile body into the context of the masculine professional world of employment', demonstrating how her respondents were not only suddenly aware of their pregnant bodies, their size, their ability to reproduce, lactate, and feed, but also at times physically exhausted, thus belying 'the modern Western conviction that we have and possess our bodies and are able to mould them accordingly' (2008a: 329). But the marginalization of mothers and pregnant bodies as different and alien in regimented and constricted workplaces is also often practiced by others at work. Lupu (2013), in a working paper on accountants in France, similarly found that a perceived contradiction between motherhood and professionalism in accountancy remains and that women internalize this conflict and address it through complex identity and boundary work. Gatrell, Cooper, and Kossek (2017) argue that this juxtaposition between women's bodies and professionalism is not new. Drawing on the work of anthropologist Mary Douglas, they invoke her notion of women as 'social pollutant(s)' to also apply in contemporary organizations and particularly at the top of the hierarchy. Douglas describes how pregnant women, for example, were excluded from sites of business and business-related decision-making and regarded as a danger to the business of production in the tribal populations she observed during fieldwork conducted between 1949–1953. Picking up this idea, Gatrell, Cooper, and Kossek (2017) argue that the maternal body at work is subjected to a comparable kind of marginalization, and they further demonstrate how the ways in which women's health has become medicalized means that the maternal body (i.e. the body with reproductive capacity) is seen as unstable and considered to be less likely to be productive in the labour market.

This is interesting, because it returns us to feminism's dilemma with the subject of motherhood and biological difference as discussed in Chapter 1 and above. Menstruation, pregnancy, birth, and menopause are, of course, all physical experiences, some of which can be challenging, and which do not apply to all those who carry out motherwork, and which do not apply to men, but to the majority of women. Here, a matricentric feminist perspective falls short of capturing the maternal body as defined by Gatrell, Cooper, and Kossek (2017). It is not clear, though, whether matricentric feminism is defined too narrowly, or whether Gatrell, Cooper, and Kossek's (2017) definition is too all-encompassing. I would argue for the latter in the case of the specific group interviewed, where equality in terms of access to the profession has improved dramatically since the Second World War, at least in the UK, but progression to partnership has only made slow progress. This suggests that it is motherhood that disrupts rather than women's reproductive capacity per se—again, at least in the UK. Women have been successfully hiding menstruation and menopause from men and business for decades, but it is pregnancy that blows our cover and motherhood that disrupts our sense of self and carries a penalty in the labour market. In Germany, in contrast, access to the profession remains a significant problem (see Chapter 2).

Mothering and Motherhood in Accounting

Mothering and motherhood was discussed with all respondents; at times as mothers, as daughters of mothers, but also as those responsible for managing mothers and women planning to have children. The focus of the interviews in relation to both mothering and motherhood differed cross-nationally, emphasizing different tensions.

There were three main themes running through the narratives in Germany:

1. As mothers and children burden the firm with additional costs and labour, the women I interviewed felt that it was their duty to keep firms informed when planning a family;
2. Furthermore, as children need their mothers, they were expected to return to work part-time after maternity leave;
3. Finally, as partnership is a full-time commitment, women with children cannot be firm partners.

Table 5.1 Marital Status and childcare arrangements among the respondents

Country		UK	Germany
Marital Status	Married	25	16
	Single	4	4
	Partnership	1	7
	Divorced		3
	Women with children	18	13
	'Househusband'	11	0
Childcare	Herself±	3	4
	Nanny	12(4)*	8
	Husband	9	0
	Nursery	2(1)**	2(1)**
	Total interviews	30	30

Numbers in brackets indicate that this was not the first childcare organization named.
* In nine cases the husband was not working professionally or working part-time, but in four of these cases a nanny had also been employed at some point in time.
** In two cases, the respondents indicated that they relied on a nursery, but one of them had previously indicated that she was the main caretaker.
± In two cases, one in Germany and one in the UK, the respondents mentioned the regular involvement of grandmothers in the upbringing of the children but noted that they felt they were the primary caretaker.

In the UK, the women's accounts were concerned with:

1. Their access and rights to maternity leave, with their experiences varying with firm size;
2. Their decision on whether or not to be the main carer being based on various cost-benefit analyses, with the women frequently relinquishing motherwork to their husbands.

The ways in which the women organized childcare was perhaps one of the most striking differences between the two countries (Table 5.1).

Among the thirty women I interviewed in each country, more of the UK partners (18) were mothers than their German counterparts (13). Interestingly, while eight out of the eighteen mothers in the UK reported that their husbands had taken full responsibility for childcare, with eleven of the women married to 'househusbands', this was not once the case among the German respondents. Indeed, it was the absence of fathers in their talk that was striking. In both countries, the respondents relied on nannies and childminders (Tagesmütter), with only a small number enrolling their children in nurseries.

Germany: the maternal body as social pollutant

The first recurring theme in Germany was a concern about being fair and honest with the firm and its partners about plans to become a mother, given its assumed economic implications. Anita, for example, talked about planning to adopt a child as a decision she felt she ought to discuss with the other firm partners first. She recalled:

> 'I discussed it with them (the other partners) beforehand, whether it (adopting a child) would be possible, when I was made partner, because I think that is only fair—to discuss this beforehand, if you are planning a family (laughs)'.
> **(Anita, medium-sized firm, Germany, 45/1)**

Anita's account highlights tensions between formal processes and informal practices, which are inherently gendered in nature (Acker, 2006). While the law protects women from gendered conversations of this kind, it is Anita who seeks it. I was initially surprised by her account. It was my first interview in Germany, and although I understood that as a business partner and therefore a co-owner she would want to inform her fellow partners, I was intrigued by her terminology ('*whether it would be possible*'). I enquired why she felt that she had to include the firm in this decision and whether she thought that men who wanted children would do the same. Anita argued that a man would not be working part-time as he would likely be married to a stay-at-home-mother or a part-time worker, revealing, first, a clear sense of foreboding that becoming a mother would be the moment where her life was to become different from that of her male colleagues (O'Reilly, 2016a); second, an understanding that she was diverting from normative expectations (Edlund and Oeun, 2016; Pfau-Effinger and Smidt, 2011; Ruckdeschel, 2009); as well as third, a sense that her decision to become a mother would have a detrimental impact on the firm, thus evoking a 'social pollutant' stance in line with Gatrell, Cooper, and Kossek's (2017) Douglasian thesis. In a similar vein, Pauline talked about planning her family earlier in her career. She said:

> 'I never made it a secret that I wanted children and so then of course I wasn't made partner (at that firm). I mean that only makes sense! Being a partner or on the

exec team always requires you to be working full-time. There you go. Obviously, I wouldn't be once I had kids'.

(Pauline, small firm, Germany, 41/2)

At the time, Pauline worked for a medium-sized employer. Her account also incorporates a presumption that becoming a mother means working part-time and that the latter is incompatible with partnership. It is telling and perhaps ironic how Pauline relayed the experience as one 'that only makes sense' as she is now both: a mother and a firm partner. Like Anita, Pauline too shared her desire for children with her employer, or, in her own words, she never made it a 'secret'. From a matricentric feminist perspective, both Anita's and Pauline's accounts emphasized sex difference and suggested that one's becoming a mother is in its effects consequential for others, in line with a Douglasian notion of the mother and her child as social pollutants. The two themes—being fair with your colleagues, clients, and the firm as a mother on the one hand, and working part-time as a mother on the other hand—were frequently encountered in Germany in varying forms and narrated to me by mothers as well as childless women. The boundaries between public and private were much more fluid than in the UK.

A mother of two children, Susanne, also emphasized the 'costs' to both the employer and co-workers involved in one's becoming a mother. She explained:

'It's interesting to look at this from the other side. I run a business here and I already had several colleagues who had babies ... This is how it is: if I have 12 employees and someone is gone for three years, you see, then I have to employ someone else because the work has to be done ... and so I employ another young woman and I have to tell her after three years 'now you have to go because the other one is coming back, so you have to go home'. So, I have to give her a temporary contract from the beginning, which I think is unfair. And I don't even know whether the other one is in fact coming back'.

(Susanne, small firm, Germany, 53/2)

Here, Susanne argued that becoming a mother is unfair to at least one other woman. In addition, she implied that it was unfair to her as an employer due to the uncertainty it causes. Becoming a mother disrupts the business of production and is constructed as a matter that involves not only the mother to be, but also employers, colleagues, and, ultimately, even yet unknown potential third parties who would need to be recruited as cover. It illuminates the empirical context-specific applicability of Gatrell, Cooper, and Kossek's

(2017) theory on the maternal body as a social pollutant, disrupting those trying to go about their tribal, or firm, business of production. Specifically, it is the long-lasting threat of the uncertainty surrounding the mother's return to work that irks Susanne. Susanne partially blamed the German welfare system at the time for this dilemma and argued that it was much more difficult for smaller and medium-sized firms, as they did not have the means to overcome staffing shortages appropriately. This was a point that was also often made in relation to the supposedly stronger client-partner relationship in medium-sized and smaller firms, which would, it was claimed, not survive a separation or part-time availability. In some ways, then, the auditor finds herself already in the role of mother, whom this client is fantasized to be dependent upon. This is in line with Anderson-Gough, Grey, and Robson's (2000) work, which shows how the client takes a central position in the socialization of trainee accountants and shaping their expectations on themselves as 'professionals'. Much like in the works of Lightbody (2009) and Haynes (2008b, c), here too becoming a mother is incompatible with a notion of professionalism that holds the ubiquitous client and their needs at the heart of its imagination.

The case of Barbara highlights how this can then translate into a systemic problem of statistical discrimination in practice. Barbara left a firm after she felt that she was repeatedly side-lined in the allocation of projects. She recalled:

> 'We were talking about future projects and ... I was wondering why I didn't ever get a whole project assigned ... My supervisor at the time said "you are in your early 30s and you can see how it goes. If we give you a project now and then you have children and you're not here and then we again have to send in someone new and that's how it is"'.
>
> **(Barbara, small firm, Germany, 38/0)**

Barbara was not just an auditor, but a maternal body at the height of her reproductive capacity of which her employer was hyper aware. Barbara's experience too supports Gatrell, Cooper, and Kossek's Douglasian framework and suggests that it is not only becoming a mother that is a burden to the firm, but it is their reproductive capacity that is perceived to be a risk to business in Germany. Barbara's employer notes that if she had a child, she would be absent from business—a perhaps very ordinary conclusion, yet interestingly one that is not encountered in the UK narratives. Therefore, one overarching concern displayed in the accounts on becoming a mother is its effects on others: clients, colleagues, and the firm, which resonates with Gatrell, Cooper, and Kossek's (2017) theory that women's reproductive capacity is feared as having the potential to disrupt productivity at work and that this treatment of the reproductive body as a social pollutant is experienced by potential mothers and mothers alike, and crucially acquiesced with by the women themselves, at least in theory.

Yet, while many of the women I interviewed in Germany did not actively resist the ideological constraints of motherhood in their speech, by, for instance, insisting that they ought to have a right to be both a firm partner as well as a mother, they embodied their resistance through their simultaneous claims to maternity and partnership in practice. It resonates with Bueskens' argument that 'empowered mothering and women's empowerment as mothers is a complex and varied landscape' (2016: xv) and that what constitutes resistance to motherhood as a patriarchal institution depends on context.

Germany: childcare as mother's care

When it came to discussing childcare arrangements, the women too felt that children were a mother's responsibility and that children need their mothers, with fathers mostly absent from their talk. Interestingly, of the thirteen women who had children in Germany, just over half of them (8) employed what is called a 'Tagesmutter' (childminder). Four women out of thirteen indicated they were the main caretakers, in two cases because the children were very little and the women were still on maternity leave and in one case because the respondent was working part-time for half days and able to go home when the child returned from school. In two cases, the respondents relied on private or state-funded institutions such as all-day schools, which usually operate from 8 a.m. until 3 p.m., with the possibility of adding further wrap-around care.

Melanie was one example where childcare had been provided almost entirely by external services. Both Melanie and her husband worked full-time and when asked how they organized childcare, she said:

'With a lot of staff. I had two shifts of staff. I had someone who covered the morning shift and domestic chores and took care of the little children and then I had someone who was there until 8 pm. I organized it so that I was very close by and … I would break for dinner with the children … '.

'And who was responsible when the school called and things like that?'

'My daughter insists that I always forgot her at school (laughs) although usually I did not pick them up myself but they were being picked up. Maybe at different times. But yes, I was the one responsible. They would call me'.

(Melanie, small firm, Germany, 58/2)

Asked how 'they' organized childcare, Melanie responded 'I had two shifts of staff', perhaps indicating that she was the one planning and managing these staff and thus carrying the associated mental load. Her husband did not feature in her recollection of this experience and neither was he present when she explained how she would break to have dinner with her children. In Melanie's case, her experience of difference is located in the private sphere (O'Reilly, 2016a), and she communicated this by first describing to me how both herself and her husband had demanding careers, before separating herself from him in her talk about the organization of childcare: she organized the staff, she had dinner with the children, and the school called her.

Besides being responsible for the mental load (Robertson, Anderson, Hall, and Kim, 2019), Melanie's account also hints at more complicated concerns with respect to feelings of guilt (Elvin-Nowak, 1999; Sutherland, 2010), perhaps indicating her awareness how her mothering practice is not aligned with historically constituted German Mutterbild. Melanie did not have to tell me that her daughter thought she was forgotten at the school gate, but she was prompted to mention it in the context of the question.

Melanie was one of the mothers in my research who already had grown-up children. Many were mothers of younger children, in kindergarten or school. Guilt was often evoked by comments made by their children. They would, for example, share anecdotes where the children would enquire whether the mother had to work because the father did not earn enough money. A very similar comment had been made to one of the respondents by a colleague as discussed in Chapter 4, indicating that the view that women should ideally look after children if this was financially possible for the family was relatively widely held. The ideology of motherhood is context-specific (Bueskens, 2016), and even young children absorb and hold their mothers accountable to it. In addition, others attempted to police respondents' mothering to be more in-line with the dominant motherhood ideology in Germany. As a single mother, for example, Hannah faced resistance to her return to work from her ex-partner's parents:

> 'Well, at the beginning my mother-in-law said "Now you go and rent a studio and take care of your child. You're a Rabenmutter[1]". So then we didn't speak for six months. But I contacted her again and said I think it would be sad. I said the child already doesn't have a father (who had moved away and did not seek to stay in touch with the child), at least he should have a granny. And she came straight

---

[1] The literal translation of Rabenmutter is Raven Mother. Drawing on news articles and legislation, Slotkin (2007) notes how the term 'refers to mothers (raven) "who leave their children in an empty nest while they fly away to pursue a career"' (Slotkin, 2007: 287).

away with all her luggage and we made up. But there was hostility, you know, sometimes'.

(Hannah, medium-sized firm, Germany, 48/1)

Hannah's account was the only one where a respondent shared a moment of conflict where she consciously and actively resisted the expectations placed upon her by others and in ways that may more readily bring to mind O'Reilly's notion of empowered mothering. Perhaps it was her class position, or her position as a fully qualified auditor, that enabled her to do so, or perhaps it was the fact that she was a single mother. Motherhood, and its expectations as portrayed in this encounter, is closely aligned with Ruckdeschel's (2009) description of what constitutes an ideal Mutterbild. Men have no such expectations placed upon them. Mostly absent throughout the accounts by the German mothers, in this particular case the father was not involved and certainly not expected to give up his career to help carry out motherwork.

But while Hannah resisted the constraints of motherhood, others subscribed to it. In fact, it was predominantly the women who did not have children, and those working part-time, who constructed childcare as something that needed to be carried out by mothers, while simultaneously constructing firm partnership as something that needed to be done full-time. Meanwhile, mothers who worked full-time subscribed fully to the latter. Therefore, in Germany, the majority of respondents agreed that the firms need partners to work full-time, and the majority also agreed that children need mothers to be there with them in the early years and to work part-time, if at all—thereby effectively making it impossible for mothers to meet expectations when pursuing partnership.

This is reflected in Anita's account. Anita, who worked part-time herself and had the help of her mother and a network of friends to draw on, noted:

'I work thirty hours a week and she (daughter) goes to an all-day school. That works out well … I work until around 3 pm and … my mother lives next door … I try to avoid (working at home)'. (Anita, medium-sized firm, Germany, 45/1)

She elaborated:

'Well, if a woman decides in favour of children, then, I think, she doesn't do it because she wants children but because she wants to spend time with the children and that's simply not as uncomplicated in a profession like audit as in other occupations or professions that are structured around part-time work. That's just how it is. If you fly to the moon you can't just get out of your cabin in the middle of things and take care of your child either'.

(Anita, medium-sized firm, Germany, 45/1)

This is an interesting account. Motherhood in Anita's words echoes Ruckdeschel's (2009) description, which imagines children as a woman's choice with the underlying assumption being that children need their mothers and that, if women *choose* to become mothers, they should thus sacrifice their careers to meet this need. It is also interesting how Anita employed a metaphor that projects the accountancy industry in a light that the wider public would perhaps not immediately share, curiously drawing an analogy to astronauts. In line with this analogy, then, working while mothering puts others at risk.

Even more explicitly, according to Konstanze, mothers working in a profession that often requires travel may damage their children. Having decided against children herself, Konstanze felt very strongly about working mothers in the industry:

'When your mother is permanently travelling, I think, you can't raise any children … You can see it with the younger employees whether they come from a stable family. You just notice it'.

'How do you notice it?'

'The people aren't as resilient … You'll only notice when you get to know them a bit better and get more access to people … but I think they are less resilient'.

(Konstanze, small firm, Germany, 42/0)

For Konstanze, a stable family is one where the mother is present and reliably available to the child. In both Anita's and Konstanze's accounts, men are entirely absent, resonating with O'Reilly's (2016) arguments that becoming a mother is, for many of us, an experience of difference at work and at home and, as Anita's and Hannah's accounts emphasized, often also intergenerationally.

Yet, while in Germany mothers were seen as different to childless women and men, they were also seen as special in the mind of the child. In some, very selected cases, when mothers were not discussed as burdens to others, this special status would bear small privileges. Andrea, a partner in a small firm who I interviewed in the afternoon, for instance, noted that 'it's pretty empty down there (on the office floor) in the afternoons as you can see' and pointed out that the women she employed in her firm, many of whom were mothers, were usually 'Halbtagskräfte' or 'half-day workers'. That was also the case in Elisabeth's firm, a mid-tier partnership. When asked about flexible working, she pointed out that there are 'core hours' between 9 a.m. and 5 p.m. where employees are expected to be present, but that there are some women who work 'part-time'. She said:

> 'In my team there are, for example, two women, mothers, who only work half days and I am one of few people here that does this. But there are no problems at all. For the two women it works great and there is no reason to complain'.
>
> **(Elisabeth, medium-sized firm, Germany, 55/0)**

She was also the only female partner at her firm, which may suggest that the presence of women at partnership level may have an influence on the acceptability and availability of 'half-time part-time' work for mothers—something observed by a range of researchers, including Kanter (1977), Konrad, Kramer, and Erkut (2008) and Eagly and Carli (2007). Half-time/part-time work here is defined as something that mothers can do if they have an understanding manager. Few other reasons were deemed acceptable in the interviews, and mothers were constructed as different from others in this regard. Hannah, a partner at a medium-sized firm, who is a mother as well, noted:

> 'Well, as long as they don't have children and aren't married, we'd actually want them to work 40 hours a week. We have a few in tax who are mothers and then we are very flexible … the male colleagues sometimes resist, but then I put my foot down and say that I want it this way and when they return to work then it's a good experience … We have one exception. But someone would have to be very good for us to make an exception … if you're mediocre or less than mediocre then there are only 40-hour weeks'.
>
> **(Hannah, medium-sized firm, Germany, 48/1)**

In Hannah's team, to work part-time, one had to be either exceptional in terms of performance or be a mother. Mothers warrant a different and special status, because they are seen as important for the well-being of the child, yet this status does not align easily with partnership ambitions.

Becoming a mother in these accounts was frequently presented as a woman's 'choice', necessitating sacrifice for the sake of children and at the same time thought to result in a negative impact on the firm and its clients, as well as yet unknown women—those who will need to provide maternity leave cover. From a career perspective, it resonates with Gatrell, Cooper, and Kossek's (2017) social pollutant concept, which was problematically practiced and reinforced by many of the women I talked to in Germany. But from a matricentric feminist perspective, drawing conclusions about these accounts is more complex. In practice, their presence at partnership level embodies their resistance to an ideology which imagines them instead entangled in a mother-child dyad and tucked away in the private sphere. It may, however, help explain why women's representation in the profession in Germany is lagging far behind the UK.

The UK: contracts and household economics

In Britain, the themes that emerged from the analysis had a different focus. In the interviews, becoming a mother was experienced as a private concern and the women I interviewed were not expecting to share their family planning or childcare consideration with the firm. On first glance, the women's talk appeared less weighted by the institution of motherhood from an intensive mothering perspective. But their experiences too were shaped by institutions around them and were deeply entrenched with problematic language of the free-market economy and cost-benefit analyses. In line with a rights-based and arm's-length approach discussed in Chapter 3 and Chapter 4, when the respondents discussed starting a family, they talked about contracts. And when they talked about childcare, this too was a choice resembling simple economics. It was not always a financial decision, but the talk was laced with notions of which (household) partner was most appropriately skilled for their division of labour. Becoming and being a mother was talked about in a way that suggested that they were inhabiting no special status at all, at least not one that was different from that of fathers.

The respondents' experiences of family planning were mediated by the organizational context. In Big-4 firms, the existence of comprehensive policies on pregnancy and maternity meant that women felt that they were able to be flexible in terms of how much leave they wanted to take, for example. Anastasia, who was pregnant when I interviewed her, noted:

' ... I am trying to keep it flexible and it's pretty flexible here. So, I've said I don't know how long I want (to take maternity leave for). I want to see how it goes. But it's been pretty, yeah, pretty open, pretty flexible'.

(Anastasia, Big-4 firm, UK, 36/1)

Another Big-4 partner, Dunja, noted that her return to work following maternity was actually easier when she was a partner. She said:

'My first child I had a few years into director ... When I came back it was incredibly difficult to come back and settle back into the career in that it felt like, because

I'd given all my clients away, I started back with a blank sheet. And it was as if I had started my career all over again … As partner, they are my clients. It's different when you are a director because you are an employee of the firm and you have to do what's best by the client'.

(Dunja, Big-4 firm, UK, 39/2)

In smaller firms, the reverse appeared to be the case. In small firms, while others would be able to take maternity leave as an employment right, those rising to partnership ranks needed to negotiate as they were due to become self-employed and often found themselves to be the first female partners with no arrangements in place to account for the sex-based realities of reproduction. Alice, a partner in a smaller medium-sized firm, with two children, said:

'Well, I knew I wanted to have children and I've got a solicitor to look through the (partnership) contract and went back and said what I would like to see in there and so I had a side agreement for that and then with the next alteration—and the whole rewrite of the partnership deed—that went in … I wanted to be able to take up to a year if I wanted to'.

(Alice, medium-sized firm, UK, 47/2)

Planning a family with work in mind is here reduced to a contractual issue and one that needed to be negotiated individually, with varying outcomes for women. After Summer, who had planned to have children, became a partner at a small firm, the partnership agreement for the firm was reviewed twice. She recalled:

'Yeah (the old partnership agreement was) quite amusing, because it had different conditions depending on the number of children I had (laughs) and he (managing partner) said "I feel like I am controlling how many kids you're allowed". In this one (the new partnership agreement), there isn't anything and I explicitly said "Hey why not?" and said "I want something in there!" And he said because the way it's worded I am allowed to come and go as I please, we're all allowed to come and go as we please … '

(Summer, small firm, UK, 44/0)

In the Big-4 firms, the respondents had an experience of difference at work, but one that was contained through the existence of organizational policies that acknowledged that women's experiences of reproduction, and their associated needs, are different from that of men. For Alice, in a medium-sized firm, her own clarity of what she thought was appropriate helped. But in Summer's case the firm had initially set up a number of conditions attached to regulate maternity, perhaps trying to control the risk associated with women's reproductive capacity, before oscillating radically to taking a sameness stand where everyone could 'come and go as we please', despite the fact that the managing partner himself was never going to give birth to a baby. Summer did not interrogate this further in her account to me, and neither did I probe further; instead, I remember feeling excited about this account at the time, thinking that it was a perfect example of gender-neutral policies. But pregnancy, birth, and breastfeeding are, of course, not gender-neutral (or rather unisex) events, and the consequences for women of firms pretending that they are were made more evident by Apoorva's case.

Apoorva had her first child when she was a partner at a small firm. She questioned the absence of maternity leave arrangements in her contract at the time of negotiation, however, she noted that the partnership agreement for the firm was 'very old' and had been under review for a few years but had never been finalized. She recalled:

> 'I am self-employed and not an employee. So, I don't have employee rights. So, I questioned that … and they said to me that " … what you can do, if you have a baby, you will … um … as only you currently work with your portfolio whether it's from home or the office and whether [other people] undertake the work load, you will still get paid". So, to me, that just meant: You just carry on working! So, I said: "You're happy for me to work from home?" and I said "Ok. Fair enough". Self-employed people didn't have any rights at that time so I just thought that's fine, that's what it is. When I did have my child in the early 2000s that's why … from the second week he was born, I was working from home ad hoc'.
>
> **(Apoorva, small firm, UK, 37/2)**

In stark contrast to the accounts in Germany, here, becoming a mother did not make her special at all—biological difference was almost deemed irrelevant as if the carrying, bearing of, and caring for young children had no material implications for the mother's ability to be present at work.

Apoorva's description of this experience was a stressful one, where she was trying to see to her newborn child while also answering emails and keeping a foot in the door at the firm. In her account to me she also evoked notions of 'fairness'—she said she concluded the policy was 'fair enough', followed by contextualizing this assessment for me in light of the absence of 'any rights' for self-employed people at the time. While the firm ascribed to a sameness dogma, her subsequent experiences were arguably that of difference—but a difference that was hidden in the private sphere. Apoorva's case demonstrates how important a formal written arrangement would have been here and stresses the vulnerable position female partners can be in. From a matricentric feminist perspective, the agreement stresses agency through an illusion of sameness, but this is not how it is subsequently experienced. Both Apoorva and Summer had their concerns about the absence of special arrangements for mothers rendered impotent through claims to sameness which, within the liberal feminist space of the UK, is frequently conflated with equality.

Apoorva perfectly met the ideology of motherhood in the UK, juggling childcare with her responsibilities as a firm partner and doing so quietly, privately, and without affecting anyone at work (Johnston and Swanson, 2006). It resonates with liberal market economy dynamics and current thinking on the effects of neoliberalism, where 'choice' is emphasized while the effects of the choices presented are pushed upon the individual (Bauman, 2000; Care Collective, 2020; Scharff, 2012; 2016). While in Germany everyone had an opinion on what constitutes good motherhood, in the UK the practice of mothering and the centrality of care—the dependency of the infant on mothering—was peculiarly absent.

The UK: reversing gender roles as good household economics

In the UK, among the thirty elite women, and of the eighteen mothers, nine were married to men who were focused on looking after the home or working part-time, and who were considered the primary caretakers of present children. While it was the absence of fathers in the accounts of the German firm partners that was particularly striking, in the UK, half the mothers I interviewed had relinquished the day-to-day motherwork to their husbands.

One case, where the husband was solely responsible for childcare, was that of Christiane. She recalled:

> 'It just wasn't possible. It wasn't financially possible to have longer (maternity leave) and when I had my first child, my husband gave up work. So that suits us … He looks after the children and then we share everything else pretty much … It was kind of a joint idea I think. I was worried if I stopped work I'd find it really hard to get back in the work market and my husband never really cared, you know, he wasn't career focused. And I think it worked out really well. He is calmer than I am. He is less driven than I am um so …'
>
>   'That's how you organize childcare'.
>   'Yeah. I don't do it (laughs)'.
>
> **(Christiane, Big-4 firm, UK, 43/2)**

It was interesting to talk to Christiane about the decision. She was proud of her own work achievements and the way they made it work as a family in the private sphere. But at other times she appeared defensive, perhaps reflecting on her breadwinner role. It is a conflicting account, particularly as it starts with reference to a lack of resources and thus with a lack of autonomy and agency implied. Beyond the economic factor of the household's decision-making here, Christiane also noted their different motivations. Perhaps both were ways for her to justify the role reversal in her household, yet she jokingly added that she does not do childcare, which is almost certainly an exaggeration as she engages in family life on the weekends, evenings, and indeed emotionally. It is also noteworthy that she and her husband shared the remaining domestic chores such as cleaning and shopping equally, according to her account. As the 'breadwinner-wife', she did not expect her husband to take on domestic labour beyond childcare. She also mentioned that she was concerned about her return to work, a sign that her mothering here is constrained by employment practices which penalize mothers who fail to return unencumbered (Acker, 2006; O'Reilly, 2016a).

Christiane mimics normative expectations of fathering, only complying with some aspects of the expected juggling in relation to household chores. Her account marked her as vulnerable too, and there are indications that she may, at times, have experienced tensions. She noted, for instance, that her husband was calmer, a compliment, before negating it to some extent by noting that he was less driven. Meisenbach (2010), who interviewed fifteen 'female breadwinners', found that common aspects in the narratives were feelings of pressure on the one hand and feelings of guilt and resentment on the other hand, while valuing the supporting contributions by partners, having control, and their own career progress.

In the case of Martine, the financial aspect was also at the forefront of the couple's decision-making.

> 'Well, I didn't really have a choice. I was always gonna have to work because my husband earns a lot less than me so it was always gonna be that way round. So, yeah, I took maternity leaves and some extra with both of them. So, then he worked part-time to look after our youngest daughter ... A lot of days it's a lot easier to come into work than to (laughs) stay at home with (laughs) two teenage girls'.
> **(Martine, medium-sized firm, UK, 53/2)**

Martine presented the decision of the husband being the main carer as a financial one, and argues that she did not have a choice. Here, too, Martine's talk lacked agency and autonomy, and her account, much like Christiane's, pointed to a conflicting frame. As an organizational elite, she is not expected to give up her job, but instead there was economic pressure to give up motherwork for the good of the household. And, indeed, to give it up in a way that a normative father might have done.

While the German firm partners were firmly arguing that mothers needed to work part-time for the sake of the child, and that such a working pattern was incompatible with partnership, in the UK, for many of the respondents, partnership involved a gendered role reversal rather than, for example, a shared responsibility for both productive and reproductive labour. And like for many normative fathers, this meant not only perhaps understanding that caring for two teenagers may be difficult, as Martine suggested, but also being aware that one misses out on experiences together.

Marina, who had her children relatively early, was aware of the cost for her of this gender reversal. Her children were now grown up. Asked how she felt about not being the main carer at the time, she replied:

> 'Absolutely. I missed. I missed some. But that is the price you have to pay. In my days you had no option. In my days, it was the 80s and the early 1990s and in those days you had to kind of be there like a man and the men always had wives at home. So for us, it was reversed roles. And this is the right answer for me, for the children and for my family'.
>
> **(Marina, Big-4 firm, UK, 59/2)**

Marina's account too lacks agency, although she seemed to be referring perhaps to her wanting to sustain her career after having children. She had to 'pay the price', she 'had no option', and she 'had to be there like a man'. What is often cited in the literature as an advantage for men married to a housewife is not only the childcare aspect, but also the emotional support in their careers (Dempsey, 2002). Interestingly, that is also something Marina discussed in our interview.

> '(My husband) was fantastic. He is the one who actually encouraged me to progress and assisted me initially when I was kind of really, you know, not confident enough … So, it's a testament that it worked for us. It just clicked'.
>
> **(Marina, Big-4 firm, UK, 59/2)**

Financial concerns were not always reported to be the main factor. In two cases the husband's career had previously been prioritized. Nonetheless, decision-making strategies frequently revolved around ideas of wanting to optimize the division of labour within the household, given each partner's strengths and weaknesses, mimicking market rationales. It shows how deeply neoliberalism is entrenched within the psychic life of individuals in the UK, running all aspects of their lives as if they were a business (Scharff, 2016), and to such an extent that even mothers who are arguably top earners in the country feel that they have no choice but to align themselves to the ideal or unencumbered worker norm (Acker, 2006).[2]

The findings echo what Stephens (2012: page x in foreword) termed 'post-maternal thinking', which 'refers to a process where the ideals intimately bound up with the practices of mothering are disavowed in the public sphere, and conflicted in the private' sphere. Stephens links the term postmaternalism to Orloff's work (1996; 2006), who described the ways in which policy in the 1990s stopped supporting mothers' care-giving and instead focused on gender neutrality, but mostly for those in the labour market. Postmaternalism, Stephens notes (2012: 3), is 'a process where women's claims as *mothers* have lost their political authority' with their route to legitimacy framed only through their status as '*workers* or *citizens*' (Orloff, 2006). In her own thesis, Stephens (2012) argues that postmaternal thinking today is intricately linked to neoliberalism, which, through its valuing of individualism, gives rise to a space dominated by a 'fantasy of self-sufficiency' and thus a denial of the centrality of care, as Bueskens (2016) asserts. It links back to O'Reilly's (2016a) argument that motherhood remains troublesome in particular for liberal feminism, as its traditional emphasis on independence presents a dilemma. The respondents in this study offered little resistance to an employment space marked by postmaternalism and neoliberalism, aligning themselves to the unencumbered norm, albeit often hinting at the tensions that the disavowal of centrality of care brought to the fore for them.

Conclusion

The subject of motherhood in accountancy and beyond remains a neglected site of research, as this chapter has reiterated. In Germany, becoming a mother was often seen as a burden to the firm and its clients, with part-time work described as available to mothers but incompatible with partnership, and full-time work considered inappropriate for the raising of children. The parallels between the talk of the women in my research in Germany and the thesis proposed by Gatrell, Cooper, and Kossek (2017) to explain

[2] I use the term 'unencumbered' instead of 'ideal' throughout. As Acker (2006: 450) remarked, although 'work is organized on the model of the unencumbered (white) man, and both women and men are expected to perform according to this model, men are not necessarily the ideal workers for all jobs'.

the underrepresentation of women in executive positions was striking, and indeed it was women's reproductive capacity too that was treated with suspicion. The accounts were gendered, with fathers entirely absent from the women's talk. In the UK accounts, interestingly, recurring themes the respondents raised were accessing maternity leave, either as an employee or as a partner, and their experiences of returning to work. More than half of the respondents with children in the UK were married to 'househusbands', and while they frequently displayed a contentment with this arrangement, there were also tensions in their talk, with some respondents noting a lack of 'choice' because of household financing, despite representing organizational and economic elites.

Making sense of these findings from a cross-national perspective, here too I wonder to what extent the sort of embeddedness in relationships the women recounted in Germany also encouraged the blurring of the public and the private spheres, where women are met not just as workers, but are always also considered as potential mothers and where one's involvement in caring for others in the private sphere is also subject to scrutiny in the public sphere. From a Gendered Hierarchies of Dependency perspective, the women here were more dependent on others, making them also more vulnerable to a narrative that positioned the maternal body as taboo and as a potential burden to the firm. Yet, they were also able to resist this in practice, as will be explored in the next section.

Between a rock and a hard place: motherhood as institution and the unencumbered norm

In their talk, respondents showed awareness of the ways in which the institution of motherhood (O'Reilly, 2016a; Rich, 1986) restricted them, and, to varying degrees—although at times fortuitously—they were able to resist them. This came to the fore, for example, in cases where fathers were doing the bulk of childcare, thus challenging the norm that children *need* the mother to be the primary carer. There were frequently tensions in their talk. For example, Christiane felt financially restricted in her ability to take longer maternity leave ('It just wasn't possible'), but, on the other hand, also showed that she had been keen to return to her career ('I was worried if I stopped work, I'd find it really hard to get back'). Martine and Marina mooted conflicts in their portrayal of family life and working motherhood (e.g. 'I missed some, but that is the price you have to pay'), while in Germany Melanie also worked through these tensions in our interview, sharing her daughter's accusation that she felt forgotten at the school gates, before rejecting this account as implausible ('usually I did not pick them up myself but they were being picked up'). It serves as a reminder of the ambivalent feelings that the subject of motherhood brings with it: on the one hand a fear of losing one's self (Chapman and Gubi, 2019; O'Reilly, 2016a) and on the other hand the psychological effects, the cognitive dissonance and anxiety associated with the transgression of norms. These tensions are representative of the ambivalence (Lowy, 2021) that 'characterizes all human relationships' (O'Reilly, 2016b: 70), but in the case of the mother-child relationship is problematic because of the feelings of guilt and anxiety that motherhood as institution evokes precisely due to its essentialization and naturalization, or, in other words, the assumption that all women ought to be mothers and that all women naturally enjoy and know how to mother (O'Reilly, 2016b: 65). Some of the respondents were in a better position to address these conflicts internally and externally than others. For example, Barbara was relatively junior when she was told that she would not be allocated a whole project due to the possibility of her falling pregnant. Her lack of seniority and age mattered. Similarly, Dunja described having to give up her clients when going on maternity leave as a director, but then being able to keep them during her second maternity leave as a partner, making her return easier. Anita, as a firm partner and therefore co-owner, negotiated a part-time status for herself which meant that she could better accommodate her status as a working mother while continuing to hold on to more traditional motherhood norms herself.

Interestingly, Anita was one of few women who felt more comfortable to challenge the unencumbered norm in this way. One recurring theme in the accounts in Germany was an insistence that making partnership in accounting requires full-time working patterns. In contrast, in the UK, respondents who had agreed a gender role reversal with their partners were often working like normative fathers. There was little room here for compromise, for shared domestic and shared economic labour, for example, while progressing to partnership, leaving the unencumbered norm mostly intact and unchallenged. There were moments of uncertainty around this. For example, when Summer, hoping for maternity leave, was told that, as partners, 'we are all allowed to come and go as we please' or when Apoorva was being given to understand that, as a firm partner, she could just continue working after having a baby or arrange a cover in private, denying the embodied experience that becoming a mother is for many women and, as Bunting (2020) puts it, relegating mothering to the status of a hobby.

In this case of elite women in professional service and accounting firms, the respondents were in a privileged position and thus had varying pathways available to them to meet the unencumbered norm by, for example, a gender reversal in the household, by employing nannies, relying on institutionalized childcare, but also by not having children. Among the respondents, twenty-nine out of sixty did not have children. Partly this very high rate of childlessness (48 per cent) will arguably reflect an increase in the rate among the general population (Bunting, 2020), which, for women, is known to negatively correlate with income (Barthold, Myrskyla, and Jones, 2012). But in some ways, it is also likely a representation of the fact that the unencumbered norm does not budge for motherhood and that, rather than challenging the ways we work, working mothers are invited to deny the significance of care and dependency work in and on our lives at the organizational and the political level. The finding that women working at the top of the organizational hierarchy in accountancy are less likely to have children is not new; indeed, as noted earlier in this chapter and in Chapter 2, this was traditionally the price women had to pay (Haynes, 2008a) in accountancy and beyond (see e.g. Wajcman, 1998). However, childlessness too constitutes a digression of norms (Peterson, 2015; Wager, 2000), albeit one that does not disturb the prevailing culture at work. But with four out of five women in the general population becoming mothers in their lifetime, it is also perhaps unsurprising that the number of women at partnership level has failed to significantly increase over the past two decades.

Centring mothers in accountancy

Motherhood as institution constrains women in varying ways, as the analysis and discussion has shown. The women I interviewed were at times aware of these constraints and developed strategies to resist or manage them internally and/or externally. The unencumbered norm, on the other hand, was mostly left unchallenged, with the task of managing and hiding one's care responsibilities left for individual women to work out in private, with the primary beneficiary of this concealment being the firm and its clients. This abjection of the maternal body within spaces of business is historically constituted, as Gatrell, Cooper, and Kossek (2017) demonstrated so brilliantly by going back to the work of Mary Douglas (1966) and applying it to the context of executive women. What is different today is that women *are* now allowed in sites of business, but under the condition that they successfully and convincingly split off the maternal. If they 'choose' to be mothers, they are either lured to join their child in the private sphere or, alternatively, required to present themselves as a 'postmaternal self, paradoxically ungendered and thoroughly instilled with the market ideal that it is possible to be the "owner" of one's own person' (Stephens, 2012: 60). This is evidenced in the accounts through i.e. the many complicated ways in which respondents such as Pauline or Anita juxtaposed becoming a mother with making partnership in accountancy, or when Apoorva and Summer felt unable to protest the absence of maternity leave in the firm deeds on the arguably quite reasonable basis that becoming a mother is, for the majority of women, an embodied experience. There is a sense of fear of speaking as a mother, perhaps reflecting a knowledge that care is not socially valued but that children demand it. It is also echoed in the tensions in the accounts of the women who worked more like normative fathers and the fact that a disproportionate amount of the respondents did not have children. It is representative of what Stephens (2012: 60) refers to as postmaternal thinking, an ungendering of policy and politics, where women are left unable to make claims as mothers and as carers of dependents, where children are seen as a burden and dependency as 'shameful', rather than an unavoidable part of everyone's life's cycle.

O'Reilly's matricentric feminism is clear about the damage this does to women specifically, who, after all, continue to perform most of the unpaid care work as discussed in Chapter 1 and returned to in Chapter 4 as well. Her primary focus is on restoring motherhood to a central place within feminism, and echoing and leading critiques that feminism has abandoned motherhood (Bunting, 2020). Stephens (2012), making links to neoliberalism and globalization, presents this as a wider process of cultural forgetting, noting instead the many efforts of early second-wave feminists to address concerns impacting the lives of young children and their mothers and asking instead why this 'maternalist ethos ... has been forgotten or hidden in many contemporary renderings of feminism's complex legacy' (2012: 88). She calls for an active remembering of the maternal, nurture and care, and for us to challenge 'political structures of forgetting that have led to "dependency" as a deviant condition, or as a failure of will' in order to 'enable both women and men to arrange their lives around care, not only care for children and other dependents but also allowing themselves to be cared for at times of vulnerability and need' (2012: 144). For this to occur, we must be able to talk about care and dependency and to claim rights on the basis of our commitments because they are socially valuable and necessary. This will be a particularly urgent demand in the wake of the COVID-19 pandemic, which, for many parents but especially mothers, will have inevitably collapsed any illusion of unencumberedness previously sustained by access to grandparents, schools, and childcare providers. The gendered effect of this is already starting to crystallize: in a study of US working hours following the start of the pandemic, Collins, Landivar, Ruppanner, et al. (2020: 110) found that 'mothers with young children reduced their hours over four times as much as fathers', and similarly shocking first findings about the inequitable division of household and economic labour in the pandemic are reported in Germany (Suhr, 2020) and the UK (ONS, 2020), leading the UK campaign group *Pregnant Then Screwed* to describe women as the 'sacrificial lamb of the crisis' (Topping, 2020). In accountancy, the effect of the crisis on mothers and women more broadly is not yet clear, although it will likely, in many ways, reflect wider gendered patterns in the distribution of caregiving responsibilities. With the vast majority of women now in the labour market, motherhood straddles the private-public sphere as outlined in the introduction to this book in Chapter 1, and in often uncomfortable ways this exposes the extent to which organizations remain designed without women and their bodies in mind.

6
Job In/security and Work Centrality

This chapter examines two interrelated themes. First, the notion of job in/security and the extent to which the elite women interviewed here felt secure in their positions comparatively, and, second, work centrality and related issues of health, leisure, and making space for non-work related parts of one's life. Job insecurity is a perceived and as such a subjective variable and distinct from, for example, labour market insecurity, although Manning and Mazeine (2020: 8) found that 'job insecurity today is strongly associated with job loss or job change tomorrow'. Understanding job insecurity matters because it is a key stressor (Jiang and Lavaysse, 2018) and is related to various psychological and other health outcomes, as well as work-related variables such as job commitment, job satisfaction, and turnover intentions (Debus, Probst, Koenig, and Kleinmann, 2012). It is also related to work centrality discussed in section two in this chapter. Interestingly, while there has been a significant rise in scholarly attention on the subject of precarity, as evidenced by Manning and Mazeine (2020) and a steep rise in related publications, the authors found that while perceived job insecurity is affected by changes in the economy and therefore cyclical, the level of perceived insecurity has over the past four decades to the start of the pandemic not significantly increased and was at historically low levels in 2018. In a comparative analysis of data in the US, UK, and Germany, Manning and Mazeine (2020) found that workers in 2018 felt significantly less insecure than in the mid-2000s, for example. Context thus matters here as well, although the relationship between welfare provision, employer sanctions, and job insecurity is not linear. For example, Debus, Probst, Koenig, and Kleinmann (2012) demonstrate that job insecurity is related to the social safety net within a country, as might be expected, but that what they call enacted uncertainty avoidance, as a cultural characteristic, too is a moderator and uncertainty avoidance is, as Hofstede (2001) argued originally, significantly higher in Germany than in the UK. The authors claim that within countries with more rules and norms to address high levels of uncertainty avoidance, workers will have a better idea of the impact of job insecurity, which will thus result in a less pronounced negative reaction, than in countries with low enacted uncertainty avoidance such as the UK. There are also demographic properties. Historically (see e.g. Cheng and Chan, 2008), under a traditional male breadwinner model, the view was that men experienced lower job insecurity than women due to higher occupational mobility, but that men reacted more strongly to job insecurity because they were more likely to be the breadwinners. This is interesting within this context of this book, because many of the UK partners interviewed here had negotiated a role reversal in the household, often earning more than their partners and husbands and, in just over a third of the cases, being the sole breadwinner. In addition, unlike Germany where job insecurity has been shown to decrease with an increase in education, the results are more mixed in the UK where this is not always the case (Manning and Mazeine, 2020), meaning that the elite status of these women may not necessarily and consistently act as a buffer in times of economic change, for example.

There is surprisingly little research to be found on the subject of job insecurity and networks more broadly, for example, the extent to which networks and one's embeddedness within them can moderate both perceived job insecurity and one's reaction to it. There is a relatively recent study by Mehreen, Hui, and Ali (2019) on teachers in Pakistan, which argues that careers have become more 'agentic'. This is in line with the literature on the responsibilitization of the individual under neoliberalism, with the latter seen by some as a political project (Harvey, 2007). Mehreen, Hui, and Ali (2019) investigate the extent to which social ties moderate job insecurity and perceived employability. High perceived employability was positively related to job performance and information sharing, as might be expected. They found that strong ties support perceived employability and are strongly negatively related to job insecurity. The findings for weak ties were mixed and not always consistent with previous research (e.g. Granovetter, 1973; 1974). However, finding that weak ties were positively related to job insecurity follows logically, that is, if we think that those with many but less close relations may be less able to draw on emotional support and reassurance but better able to benefit from information sharing. I have already talked about the research on networks among accountants specifically in Chapter 2, for example, the work by Sellers and Fogarty (2010), which shows the embeddedness of accountants in social networks through their training firm and also their exposure to clients. The Big-4 firms, especially in the UK, train the largest number of chartered accountants, and it is built into the system that many of these trainees will leave upon completion of training, thus creating extensive networks across potential and existing clients and in competing firms.

But part of the growing interest in perceived job insecurity that Manning and Mazeine (2020) problematize may also be related to a broader interest in the subject of precarity from a sociological perspective in the 1990s and around the turn of the century. Here, a focus was brought upon the tracing of, first, individualization, which Bauman, in his foreword to Beck and Beck-Gernsheim's book (2002: xv) on the subject defines pointedly as consisting in 'transforming human "identity" from a "given" into a "task"—charging the actors with the responsibility for performing that task and for the consequences (also the side-effects) of their performance'—very similar thus to what Rottenberg (2014, see Chapter 1) writes about neoliberalism turning 'human beings into human capital', but with the latter having a distinct focus on markets and the marketization of everything, including the self. Neoliberalism then is also understood as a political project (Harvey, 2007) with an emphasis on markets and 'freedom', and opposed to welfare and collectivism, thus representing a 'divorcing of economic activity from its wide social consequences' (Bone, 2012: 653). This literature also brings to the fore the role of accountants and accounting 'as a primary enabler of neoliberal logic' (Brown and Dillard, 2015: 248), interestingly explored in various contributions by accounting scholars, which as a discipline has always been mindful of the role of accounting in society (see e.g. the points made by Tinker (1985) discussed in Chapter 1 in this regard). This shift towards accelerated capitalism under neoliberalism and its corrosive effects are a key concern for Sennett (2012). Women are especially implicated, because they are more likely to be subject to a derivative dependency, performing and taking on the vast majority of dependent care around the world (Kittay, 1999; Bunting, 2020), and thus entering the market place not as equals with men who *can* enter under the illusion of independence which is propped up precisely by the care work, on average, more likely to be performed by women.

It connects to the Varieties of Capitalism literature because scholars like Weishaupt (2021) have shown that neoliberalism is played out differently across borders, therefore noting the significance of geography, the political economy, and welfare regimes in providing a buffer effect. Some see this pessimistically, claiming a continuous convergence towards liberalization (see Thelen (2012) for a discussion of these debates). But for many the literature around welfare regimes and the Varieties of Capitalism still holds meaning, pointing towards the robustness of the described differences (see Chapter 1). Manning and Mazeine argue that insecurity has not changed in any significant way over the past forty years. But what has changed, as Sennett observes, is that individuals, especially within the Anglo-Saxon context, are now less socially connected within their community and more isolated within their daily lives at home and at work. This isolatory effect will be more sweeping in the UK, where job tenures are lower than in Germany and employee turnover higher (Chen and Hou, 2019). Within this chapter, I explore how such differences might play out within the accounts when talking about the economy, exploring first the respondents' recollections of entering the profession and their motivations for doing so, and second the extent to which they were exposed to job insecurity themselves, or not. Accountancy is often considered a 'safe' career, with accountants needed in times of growth as well as during, for example, liquidations, prompting Tieman (2010), for the *Financial Times*, to note that 'Accountancy may not be a recession-proof profession, but it is surely the next-best thing'. But to what extent did the respondents' accounts mirror this sense of job security, and are there differences between the accounts in the two countries? These questions will motivate the next three sections.

Recessions and Reunification

Job in/security was not a subject discussed specifically with respondents, but it emerged from the analysis with an interesting contrast in how a significant number of the respondents in each country talked about the economy and the extent to which they worried about it—or not. The respondents talked about the past differently, with the UK respondents placing more emphasis on the state of the economy than their German counterparts. In total, thirteen out of the thirty respondents in the UK referred to recessions or economic downturns as significant factors in their career development. While this is not a majority, it is interesting when considering the contrast in Germany, where only one respondent made that connection, and secondly, when bearing in mind that the respondents are all women who have made it to the very top of their profession, and hence professionally 'survived' these events. Table 6.1 summarizes this.

However, the state of the economy was not entirely absent in Germany, and eight of the respondents referred to the reunification and its positive impact on the economy as a factor that aided in their career progression, whereas only one of them, Chloe, was born and raised in the former German Democratic Republic. Two more respondents pointed to the internet boom as a positive factor in their career development (Table 6.2).

These contrasting ways of talking about the state of the economy, one pointing to the impact of economic downturns and one pointing to impact of economic upturns, are explored in more depth in the next two sections.

Table 6.1 Respondents who referred to recession/economic downturn as a factor in their career advancement

Name	Age	Firm Size	Country
Martine	53	M	UK
Martha	54	M	UK
Tracy	46	M	UK
Alice	47	M	UK
Claire	43	M	UK
Abbie	46	M	UK
Kelly	49	M	UK
Christiane	43	L	UK
Sharon	41	L	UK
Apoorva	37	S	UK
Kerry	38	M	UK
Denise	39	S	UK
Dunja	39	L	UK
Katrin	44	L	Germany

Table 6.2 Respondents who referred to the German reunification and the internet boom as a factor in their career advancement

Name	Age	Firm Size	Referred to
Melanie	58	S	Reunification
Chloe	52	L	Reunification
Nadine	46	S	Reunification
Katrin	44	L	Reunification
Anita	45	M	Reunification
Pauline	41	S	Reunification
Katja	40	L	Internet boom
Stephanie	39	S	Internet boom

The economy and entering the profession

Asked why they decided to become accountants or join the profession, respondents in the UK frequently referred to the state of the economy at the time in a way that implied that they became accountants because it was a certain path in uncertain times. As a partner in a medium-size firm, Martine exemplifies this:

'Ugh! (sighs). Well, when I graduated from university in the early 1980s, we were in the middle of a recession then. Not quite as bad as I think we're going through at the moment, but pretty … well you know. I had a degree in economics and everyone in my year … we must have applied to 50, 60, 70 jobs. I mean, I was hoping to go into banking or possibly law, but, obviously it was better to have a job than no job so that's how I got into accountancy'.

(Martine, medium-sized firm, UK, 53/2)

During the interview, Martine indicated that she was content with how things turned out: while she would have made more money in banking early on, partnership in accountancy meant she was more flexible than she would have been otherwise. Despite the recession, she was able to stay within the wider boundaries of the financial services sector. Now, as a partner responsible for a team, she proceeded to question female colleagues' wisdom to leave the profession in favour of possibly quite well-paid appointments in industry and the financial sector, noting that in the 'long-term, it's better (in public accountancy, since) it's a lot more flexible as well, you know. You can work from home you're not … if you're in industry you're tied to deadlines and so on for whoever you are working for'. By pointing out to me that she was having these conversations with her female charges, she also reveals her views on the gendered nature of parenting. Interestingly, this is despite the fact that, while she took time off work after having children, her husband had taken on the role of primary carer, as noted in Chapter 5. However, the way Martine highlights the flexibility she attained through partnership, and therefore ownership, draws attention to how accounting here is constructed almost as a second-best safe option with respect to both recessions and childcare.

The account of Kerry, a partner in a medium-size firm, entails a similar history to Martine's:

'I became a chartered accountant because, um, I am a failed engineer basically. I left school wanting to go to university to study engineering, but at the time, it was a recession in the UK and things like Marconi were collapsing, Ford wasn't taking on students and I thought at that stage it possibly wasn't the best career movement. But I still wanted to do something professional and quite liked business so I rather fell into accountancy. Yeah, but a recession was on and all firms were doing was cutting their graduate intake or cutting any intake so I started life with a small local practice near where I lived'.

(Kerry, medium-sized firm, UK, 38/2)

In similar ways to Martine, the recession meant Kerry had to consider a change of direction, make a compromise and a good, responsible choice. Apoorva had a different experience. Now a partner in a small firm, she always wanted to be an accountant, but the economic circumstances at the time meant that she could not find a training contract. Instead, she started working without remuneration for a 'one-man band', also close to her hometown. She recalls:

> 'Well, actually when I graduated, which was in the early 1990s, it was a very terrible time. We had a bad recession .... There were no jobs around, no training contracts for graduates. It was really dismal. It was very dismal. So, what I did was I approached small practices and just offered to do work for free as a volunteer basically, just so I could gain some experience. I rather did that then to sit at home and so I worked for a small practice. A one-man band who had about three staff for six months'.
>
> **(Apoorva, small firm, UK, 37/2)**

Apoorva took her professional tax exams and only several years later proceeded to sit the professional accountancy exams; albeit, as she indicated, largely due to pressure from others at work. Her account also indicates that recessions were perceived as a defining element at the point of the respondents' entrance to the profession and strongly impacted on their ability to secure employment, which they sought by drawing on market mechanisms—working with recruitment agents and applying to advertisements. Unlike their German counterparts, as discussed in Chapter 3, they only very rarely relied on personal relationships to secure employment. In contrast, the German respondents talked about the same period in their lives, at least to some extent, differently, often related to the reunification of Germany. Like Markus (1996, 2021) notes and as outlined in Chapter 2, public or chartered accountancy did not exist in the GDR. At the point of reunification, previously state-sponsored companies in the GDR needed to be evaluated and audited to formally exist within a capitalist tax system and financial market.

Kellermann (2021: 1) writes: 'On July 1, 1990 the *Treuhandanstalt* (*Trust Agency*) started its difficult task to privatize about 12,000 East German companies with the declared aims of making the GDR economy fit for the free market and preserving as many jobs as possible'. This was not a straightforward economic moment in Germany's history, as the reunification saw a breakdown in manufacturing in the former East Germany, a sharp fall in employment, and mass migration within the new united Germany (Rothschild, 1993). It was also a moment where Germany flexed the muscles of its social democracy. For Wirtschaftsprüfer, it resulted in a steep increase in demand for its services. Accountants were needed to enable the transition which reinforced the undersupply of the 'Wirtschaftsprüfer'. Katrin recalls:

'I studied business and economics. That's what it was called. Because of the GDR, well that means there was no accountancy profession in that sense. I studied business and economics. Then in 1990, I didn't know what to do and so I applied to an accountancy firm because at Uni everyone was talking about it like it was something like what we studied. So, I really didn't know what it was'.

(Katrin, Big-4 firm, Germany, 44/1)

Similarly, Pauline felt that the demand created for accountants by the reunification aided in her career development. Pauline remembers:

'When I graduated that was just a year after the wall came down. Everyone was desperately looking for audit assistants. I could have, with pleasure, gotten a job at any of the big firms but I wanted to work at a mid-tier firm'.

(Pauline, small firm, Germany, 41/2)

And Anita says:

'I finished (university) in the early 1990s, so that was like a really good time because it was still due to the wall coming down and the redevelopment in the East that there was still lots and lots of demand and, well, I really could have had any job I wanted. It was that extreme. But I had already worked here (at the family friend's firm) and I thought it was nice and so then I stayed'.

(Anita, medium-sized firm, Germany, 45/1)

Unlike Apoorva, Martine, and Kerry, in Germany Pauline, Anita, and Katrin did not need to write '50, 60 or 70' applications to secure a job. They all actively chose accountancy as a career—although Katrin was not entirely sure what this might entail—and they felt confident in their ability to secure a position. The ways in which accountancy was constructed as second-best in the UK and actively chosen as a career in Germany may reflect a difference in status—in Germany, the exam to become an auditor is touted as one of the most difficult exams in the country and the profession's membership is small (see chapter 2).

Elisabeth's career history was an interesting exception, in that she framed her entrance into the profession in similar ways to those encountered in the United Kingdom, yet not referring to national developments, but sectoral ones. Originally, Elisabeth wanted to become a teacher, but at the time of her graduation from secondary school the market for teachers was 'flooded', and she therefore decided to pursue a career in accountancy and tax instead.

She notes however that,

> 'it was possible to train as a teacher, but I didn't do it in the end because too many wanted to do it and I didn't want to be unemployed when I graduated and so I studied business administration but already with the goal of becoming a (Steuerberater) tax adviser'.
>
> **(Elisabeth, medium-sized firm, Germany, 55/0)**

Most fully qualified chartered accountants in Germany are also tax adviser. Despite 'abandoning' her original plan of becoming a teacher, Elisabeth 'kept control' over her choice of career, by pursuing a PhD and then teaching part-time at a university. This meant that she spent most of her time either working for her firm or teaching at university. Asked why she chose to do so many things at once she says:

> 'Yes, yes. Well (laughs) let's put it like this: the lecturer position kind of means that I am at least partially doing what I originally wanted to do. When I wanted to become a teacher back then that was really affinity, so pursuing a degree in business administration and tax was a rational decision that I found hard, but I had to move away from my original plan and today I am glad that I did, but I didn't know that then'.
>
> **(Elisabeth, medium-sized firm, Germany, 55/0)**

Her account is more in line with those of Melanie or Pauline, as she highlights her ability to redirect her career development in the way that she initially envisioned. Her choices are active, her narrative is one emphasizing agency and her capacity to shape her working life. In contrast, respondents in the UK largely 'fell' (Summer) into the profession by 'accident' (Tracy), because another plan 'didn't pan out' (Lauren). In fact, fifteen of the thirty respondents in the UK said their entry to the profession was largely accidental and that they had originally planned to do something different or studied entirely unrelated subjects when they had graduated from university.

While the emphasis in liberalism may well be on choice, the individual must also be seen to be responsible. The women's entry into chartered accountancy in the UK was frequently experienced as a compromise, a Plan B, while participants in Germany framed their motivation more often in terms of opportunities. In the UK, this is not entirely unexpected, as Gill too found in his analysis of interviews with male accountants working in Big-4 firms in London, where accountancy was seen to be 'a very sensible thing to do in the absence of a strong desire to do anything else' (2009: 12).

For his respondents, accountancy was instrumental, bringing the potential for status and money and a recognized qualification. This too was the case for many UK respondents in my study. In Germany, however, accountancy was usually closely related to what the respondents had initially hoped to pursue as a career path, and only three of the respondents who had studied law had changed careers. It may reflect the less generalist and more specialized skill formation often described as being predominant in Coordinated Market Economies. Training is arguably more intensive in Germany, the likelihood of failure is higher, and the qualification is more specialized, making it a more significant investment in Germany which has around fifteen times less chartered accountants (even when including Vereidigte Buchführer) and a considerably lower rate of women in the profession (around 18 per cent versus between 29 (ICAEW) and 48 (ACCA) per cent in the UK, as shown in Chapter 2). It is one of the reasons, according to Hall and Soskice (2001), why labour markets in CMEs are less flexible: workers are only motivated to invest time and resources into the acquisition of specific skills if these skills are reasonably protected from unemployment. Estevez-Abe (2002) extended this argument, arguing that as women face more frequent interruptions in the labour market, it would be more costly for women to acquire such professional qualifications, helping make sense of the lower rate of women in Germany. But indeed this inflexibility is also protective, as discussed in the next section.

The economy, redundancies, and pay freezes

The economic climate, downturns in particular, was also more present in the accounts of the UK respondents than those in Germany when talking about the later stages of their careers. Nine out of the thirty respondents in the UK mentioned redundancies in the profession, either with regards to being involved in internal redundancy rounds, being affected themselves, or experiencing it from afar. This is in contrast to Germany, where no redundancies were mentioned, although some of the partners did talk about resigning. An interesting contrast emerged where it was the German women who relayed choice and agency in their talk, supported by having gained access to a profession that is more exclusionary and in high demand due to the low number of qualified individuals in the country, strong ties within their networks, and, arguably, a context where there *is* a negative relationship between job insecurity and education.

Table 6.3 Respondents who referred to redundancy rounds

Name	Age	Firm Size
Kerry	38	M
Denise	39	S
Christiane	43	L
Summer	44	S
Tracy	46	M
Claire	43	M
Martha	54	M
Mary	52	M
Marina	59	L

While none of the respondents in Germany referred to redundancy rounds, two said that their firms had initiated so-called 'Nullrunden' (salary freezes) in the past—although in one of these cases it was her place in the hierarchy that meant that her salary would be considered for adjustment only every second year. It was therefore not in response to external conditions, for example. One of the respondents described that there was some chaos because of a merger that resulted in a halt to promotions while integration took place, which she found unacceptable.

Tracy, a partner at a UK medium-sized firm, was leaving a firm as I interviewed her. She had joined the firm a few years earlier as the first female partner. She told me that she was let go. It was one of my earlier interviews in the UK, and I was surprised. I said:

'I didn't know partners could be made redundant'.
'Well, I am not technically being made redundant because I am self-employed, but they sort of said that they need to reduce the number of partners because of the current climate, so … '
'Did this come out of the blue for you?'
'Yes, absolutely'.
'When did that happen?'
'End of last year.'
'And when do you have to go?'
'Well, I am actually finishing next week (laughs). But, it's a bit of a bizarre situation because although I am finishing I am coming back to finish some projects because

I get paid for a few more months. But then they said they want me to come back and do some consultancy work (laughs)!'

'How do you feel about that?'

'Well, it gives me some money (laughs). Basically, at the moment, I've got nothing to do'.

'Why do you think that was? Were you last in?'

'No, I wasn't last in. There is another partner who has been here only a few months'.

'And he also has to go?'

'No, he is not going'.

'You're going'.

'Uhuh'.

'Why do you think you were selected?'

'The explanation I've been given, because obviously I asked the same question, the explanation I've been given is that he is well known in the industry and they wanted to stick with the man that was known within the industry … Equity partners weren't going to go anyway. I am self-employed but I am sort of salaried fixed profit and the two of us who have been made redundant are both fixed profit'.

'What was your reaction to this?'

'I didn't react actually. I thought it was a joke, actually. Because it came so much out of the blue and the way it went down: they just kind of called me down! I had literally no idea. They called me down and said: "Oh, have you got 5 minutes?" and it happens quite frequently that people will say "Have you got 5 minutes" to go through something. So, it wasn't anything out of the ordinary. They just sat me down and basically said "We're gonna have to let you go" and that was almost the first words they said to me'.

'Was there everyone there?'

'No, it was just the two senior partners'.

'Isn't it difficult working here now?'

'That's why I am finishing soon. Just coming in from time to time. I wasn't able to say anything. It was only announced last week that we were going. Up until then none of the staff knew. So, it was really difficult'.

'Did you have a reaction from the staff?'

'Yeah. Shock, and some of them were really upset'.

'Do they have to go as well?'

'No, they are not going anywhere. No'.

'Oh'.

'(Laughs) I wouldn't try and work it out. I can't'.

(Tracy, medium-sized firm, UK, 46/0)

Tracy said she avoided an 'emotional' reaction to the situation at all costs. The partners told her about the decision during a half hour conversation that was initiated on an ad hoc basis—unannounced and inconspicuous. Tracy stressed that she 'just wanted to be civil and all the rest of it'. Her account and recollection of her experience resonates with Sennett's writing, where he notes that workers under accelerated capitalism are discouraged from showing emotions, from connecting with one another, and from taking responsibility for one another. But her reaction is also an excellent example of what he calls 'repair work'. Tracy manages to contain herself and to resist 'economically induced withdrawal ... withdrawal of the sort described by Max Weber, being the negative side of the work ethic, an isolation which increases anxiety as the person focuses ever more on his or her insufficient self. The point of the repair is staying socially connected to others—a task that, paradoxically, requires lowering the emotional temperature' (Sennett, 2012: 227). Sennett, thinking about the trauma of unemployment among different groups of workers in the US, notes that, in the short-term, white-collar workers will react to unemployment with a focus on doing 'whatever is necessary to pay the bills' and indeed Tracy was doing so also, agreeing to consultancy projects. But Sennett's work is also relevant in making sense of the callousness with which Tracy was let go. The indifference she encountered and the expectations upon her to keep quiet, to remain contained, and to continue as usual without sharing the news with her team until it was announced at a later point—convenient for the firm. Sennett (2012: 176–178) argues that the financial elite that he observed in New York City—including auditors—had become a silo. That while the financial elites used to be firmly embedded within civic society, i.e. as governors at art institutions, schools, and so forth, and thus taking responsibility for life around them, they had now become a globalized elite, a social island, always going somewhere else, not rooted anywhere and governed by a short-term focus on profits and shareholders, superficial teamwork, and an absence of trust in those around them. This absence of trust comes with an absence of 'earned authority' (2012: 206). He argues: 'The new capitalism permits power to detach itself from authority, the elite living in global detachment from responsibilities to others on the ground, especially during times of economic crisis' (2012: 279). Tracy's laughter throughout our conversation betrays her lack of trust in the sincerity of the partners' decision, noting that she failed to 'work it out' and make sense of it.

Within the UK, some of the partners I talked to had witnessed redundancies and noted the chilling effect these had on their feelings about their job. Claire, for instance, recalls how her time as a partner in one of the Big-4 firms was affected by the economic downturn that followed the burst of the IT bubble in 2003:

> 'They started making partners redundant, so one of the women, you know we all went to a meeting, and suddenly she'd lost her job. And then 6 months later suddenly another one lost her job. And, so, there'd been a sort of trickle of people ... They were not all women, no. But given the very small proportions of women in the partnership it was a disproportionate effect.
>
> And when I got back to work, after maternity leave, we had three rounds of redundancies and you know, we had too many partners so when they said "Oh how about a deal?" (I said) "Oh, yes please!"(laughs)'.
>
> **(Claire, medium-sized firm, UK, 43/2)**

Claire had been actively involved in preceding redundancy rounds, which she experienced as very stressful. As a junior partner at the time, Claire was also responsible for communicating redundancies to her staff. The redundancy rounds were initially set up to follow a strict 'merit-based' protocol. Nonetheless, she felt that those processes were gendered—among the partnership and more junior grades. Talking about the negotiations of who would be asked to leave in her team, she recalls:

> 'So, this girl had been on the list on the second round of redundancies and somebody rung me up and said "Oh, so and so is you know—she is on the list" and I said "Oh that's very interesting. Every time somebody talks to me about that person, all they tell me is she works part-time, she's got three children—so if you test the criteria we set up and you come back and tell me she's actually the worst performing: absolutely fine. But if not, get lost". So, they then looked at the criteria compared with the peer group and she was the best performing, so she stayed'.
>
> **(Claire, medium-sized firm, UK, 43/2)**

Claire draws attention to her observations that redundancies had a gendered element to them, and eventually this colleague did not survive the third redundancy round. It is a good example of how informal practices can subvert organizational structures (Acker, 2006). It was Claire's intervention that meant the redundancy decision was taken on the basis of previously agreed criteria and within the formal structures in place—at least during two rounds. It had ground her down, and she was ready to leave herself upon returning from maternity leave.

Similarly, Mary, a partner at a mid-tier international firm who was leaving, was disillusioned by how the work had changed over time, and recent redundancy rounds at the time of interview had convinced her that it was time for her to do something else.

'Me and another female partner in the firm are leaving. When we made partner redundancies in the summer we made four female partners redundant. We used to have 10 per cent female partners here and I think it's now 6 per cent. And it's very disappointing'.

(Mary, Medium-sized firm, 54/0)

Reflecting on the change in work ethic and culture over time, she says:

'Most of my career happened in the 80s. The 80s was a hedonistic time. We went for long boozy lunches and then went back to work. We worked very long hours. You did everything. You didn't say "Oh I am a senior manager, I am not doing that". We just all chipped in. It was a much different firm. Much smaller. Much friendlier. Much more fun. I was fortunate'.

(Mary, Medium-sized firm, 54/0)

In her critique, Mary's reflections echo some of Sennett's observations of a change towards less integration, less friendly encounters, and the detachment of those in positions of authority from everyday working life and 'chipping in' where necessary. For both Mary and Tracy, the sudden realization of their disposability despite their status initiated a period of reflection. Tracy, after her terrible experience of redundancy at her firm, told me that she had other interests and, if it were financially possible, that she would like to do something else. However, as she was the main breadwinner, and with her husband out of the labour market for a significant amount of time to support her work, this was not very likely. And this too echoed the stories Sennett shares from his interview with the financial elites in New York.

Job security and work centrality are intimately connected, and the realization of the lack of the former prompts a reconsideration of the latter—importantly this is played out within a broader socio-political arena. Unlike Sennett's US elites and my UK elites, the narratives shared within the more welfare-orientated ordoliberal German context were different in focus. Here, recessions and redundancies were simply not something the German respondents worried about. Only Katrin noted that the state of the economy played a role in her making partnership a little bit later. She recalls:

'I worked here as a manager and was supposed to make partner that year but then I somehow fell off the nomination list three weeks beforehand. It happens every year like shortly beforehand. It's a numbers game. Can we afford this? What is the economy like and so forth. So, I fell off the list that year and then made partner the year after'.

(Katrin, Big-4 firm, Germany, 44/1)

Katrin was one of the German respondents to refer to the reunification as a crucial factor in her career development upon entering the profession, as discussed earlier.

More broadly, the German partners were often recounting protracted and emotive battles over power and respect. They were secure and confident in their ability to keep in position or sustain themselves outside their firm should this be necessary, and several resigned when things did not go their way or if they felt uncomfortable or disrespected.

Freja, for example, was unhappy with the way one of her superiors talked to her one day. At the time, members of her team had asked her repeatedly when they would be notified about the annual salary increases that year, and she finally decided to talk to her line manager about it. She recalls:

> 'I asked him one night: "Well, where are those (letters indicating the annual raises for the staff)?" and this leadership-competent gentleman had nothing better to do … than to question me—"Well what are you asking for? You won't get one anyway. You got a pay freeze … Prokurists[1] (often level before partner) only get a raise every two years". So, then I turned around, walked out, and the next day I started making phone calls'.
>
> 'Wasn't there a recession at the time?'
>
> 'Yeah. Anyway, so I talked to three of them (other firms) and had made appointments for the beginning of January and, you see, I am not someone to make appointments while others had a bit of a snooze and then walk away again afterwards—so I did the interviews and then the offers were simply too interesting'.
>
> **(Freja, Big-4 firm, Germany, 44/0)**

Freja felt that the way she was spoken to was disrespectful, and she felt strongly enough about it to immediately start the process of departure while her narrative indicates that she was seeking revenge by leaving. It is an interesting contrast to the discussions in Chapter 2, where the UK respondents talked about their 'worth' and moving through the career ladder within their firms, but this worth appears to fluctuate with the market and the economy. In Germany, in contradistinction, many of the partners I interviewed had drawn on relationships with others in the profession to secure positions and move up the hierarchy. Their 'value' did not fluctuate, but relationships with others, colleagues, at work did and could turn tricky as the above extract shows. Unlike the UK respondents, who referred to going through formal recruitment processes and competing with others in the market, for example

---

[1] Technically, a Prokurist may or may not be a Gesellschafter (partner) with the firm. The partnership will grant a Prokurist the right to sign on behalf of the firm.

by calling recruitment agents, Freja called people she knew and framed her decision to leave as the result of a personal affront. The fact that Germany was going through a recession at the time did not, according to Freja's account, have a notable impact on her decision-making. And Freja was not the only one to do this.

Manuela resigned twice in her career, and in both instances it was because she was unhappy with a male colleague or manager and their conduct. One time she resigned, she felt that she was being bullied by her new senior partner. She was taking her exams at the time. Under time pressure she needed some materials that were locked in another office. She ran into a group of colleagues, including the partner leading the tax department. As she was so under pressure, she recalled:

'I said hello into the group and said "Quick, I need the keys to get into this office to get the paperwork and make it to the notary in time". And so we ran off. And later, I returned from my exam, and the managing partner for tax called me into his office and he said I shouldn't be surprised if he puts his feet on the desk if I don't even greet him when I run into him on the road! (both laugh). It was so crass. And I thought—what is happening? And then, what happened was that another partner very carefully suggested to me that they were considering taking over a firm in another city and whether I could imagine leading it? And I said well, we need to talk about this more, have I got enough experience? and so forth. They explained I would have support there. They told me to keep it confidential. But somehow this managing partner got wind of it. And he came to my office and said "What did they want from you anyway?" and I said "Well this is difficult because they asked me to treat this confidentially, but we could go to the partner I had talked to and discuss this together". And he said "If you think anything goes on here that I don't know". And I said well, we can go together? And then he came towards me, and I mean I am not tiny, but I thought he was going to hook me on the chin or something like that (laughs). It was so verbally aggressive! I've never been approached by a man like that before. Well, then he left and came back in the afternoon and sat across from me and said I shouldn't think he didn't know about what was going on and I wasn't suitable for the position anyway. Hm. And then I applied elsewhere and resigned pretty quickly after that'.

(Manuela, Big-4, 47/0)

In the UK, there was a lack of emotions and there were few heated verbal altercations. As discussed in Chapter 4, there were incidents of inappropriate behaviour and sexism and these were handled quickly, often at arm's length and from a rights-based perspective. But in Germany, emotions were at times running high, as the encounters and hostilities recalled in the accounts of Manuela and Freja demonstrate.

The professionalization of work and the standardization of careers as seen in the UK examples is a double-edged sword here—on the one hand, it keeps the workplace free of this sort of aggression, but it also disavows emotive responses where these might be appropriate, such as when facing redundancy.

The next account from Stephanie gives a sense of how small the industry in Germany is, how short of chartered accountants it is, and what that means in practice:

> 'Well, you know, there weren't very many left of those I started with. I am actually wondering if there was any of them left where I was? No, we were 5 and of those there was no one left. The majority didn't pass the exams. So, many fail the tax exam already (Steuerberater) and then, maybe they have one more go, but then enough is enough. And then they might, maybe even after the first try, go to a client's and work in their accounting or controlling department and you know many with great success. Even if you do not manage to become a Wirtschaftsprüfer it is good to be able to have some time with a chartered accounting firm on your CV.
>
> Many left after some fluctuations and the managing partner at the time was focusing on restructuring. It was in his blood. And for two years I worked on restructuring mandates. It just wasn't fun. You get there with a big team but the only one who has any kind of fun is the person at the very top. Everyone else is doing support work for that. Planning calculations. For half a year, really, that was all I did and it really got very boring. Some people started to associate loosely and approached me. And, of course, it is risky to go it alone but then I didn't have a child or a husband and I thought "If not now, when?" And then we started this. And I jumped into the cold water ... It was so worth it. It is mentally a totally different way of working. At the old firm I had so much stress. Now I have a lot of work on, but I know what for. No, I would never go back and I never regretted the decision (to leave)'.
>
> **(Stephanie, Germany, small firm, 34/1)**

She became a partner in this new firm at a very young age, having passed exams six months earlier. She left the larger firm she trained with because she did not enjoy the work and she was approached by people she knew well to become part of a new entity.

Another partner in Germany quit because she did not enjoy the commute of approximately forty-five minutes by car or train, which could take twice as long in the morning, and she did not want to move. She moved to a medium-sized firm in her hometown and explained how her resignation was received:

> 'It wasn't very comfortable and my manager was very angry about me resigning. I had a six months' notice period and so that wasn't that nice. He had simply thought I would stay longer and I didn't really have any objective reasons in that sense. It was just personal reasons; I just didn't fancy this commute anymore and I didn't want to move to this town and so then the only solution was to do this. He didn't think that was very good and at the beginning I thought "Oh dear, this will be awful!" but then it settled down. Of course, they didn't send me to training and so forth. That is normal ... I didn't write applications everywhere or anything. It was clear I was going to come here (mid-tier firm she is a partner at now)'.
>
> **(Elisabeth, medium-sized firm, Germany, 55/0)**

None of the respondents in Germany had ever been made redundant. Nevertheless, turnover in professional service firms in Germany was reported to be high. According to the respondents, this was however not due to redundancies, but rather down to personal and firm-related circumstances, as well as generally flatter hierarchies. Elisabeth above, for example, noted that associates would leave the medium-sized firm she was a partner at now, because the hierarchical structures in place were simply too flat. She argued that it was hard for the firm to offer them reasons to stay (see Chapter 3). Julia, like Stephanie above, mentioned that the failure to pass a professional exam would be considered a reason for associates to leave or be asked to leave, but she also noted that she was able to stay despite failing her own exams repeatedly, as her supervisors thought her highly capable. Julia too mitigated her evaluation by stressing that such 'leavers' would still have very prestigious career prospects in industry, as professional service firms were considered to be stepping stones. The respondents also conceded that it was possible that professional employees were unable to meet expectations in other areas, in which case 'it would be time to think about whether we should go our separate ways', according to Freja. The German respondents talked frequently about being able to 'retrain' instead. Sabrina mentioned that it was very rare for directors who did not make it through to partnership to stay on without the potential to progress further. The partners therefore acknowledged high turnover rates but not in relation to economic conditions such as recessions. Redundancies were thought to be exceptional and individually negotiated between supervisor and employee. The accounts relay that the respondents in Germany felt less insecure in their jobs, which is in line with wider cross-national trends. While it was more straightforward for the UK partners to climb the career ladder within the more liberalized, standardized, and professionalized context of the British accounting industry, they were also more insecure in their positions, and the anxieties this produces are likely exacerbated by the fact that a significant proportion of them were sole breadwinners. In contrast, the comparatively more cumbersome and chaotic relationship-based hierarchies described in Germany were a little bit more robust, but at the same time the women also relayed more unprofessional encounters which caused them to seek out a change.

Work Centrality and Work-life Balance

The subject of work centrality has been tackled from various perspectives and is significantly related to job in/security (Jiang and Lavaysse, 2018). It can tell us about someone's job involvement and commitment, and is thus related to job and organizational performance as well (Hattrup, Ghorpade, and Lackritz, 2007; Sharabi and Harpaz, 2010). There is evidence that work centrality increases with one's hierarchical status (or vice versa), and that this is a consistent pattern for both men and women (Sharabi, 2017). In line with these, all of the respondents in this study worked long days, averaging fifty to fifty-five hours a week, noting that they would put in extra hours during peak times. A number reported working more than seventy hours and one, in a large firm, noted that she regularly worked between seventy and ninety hours a week. In the UK, more women referenced being disillusioned and, as a result, maintaining stricter boundaries between work and home. In the UK, as discussed in the previous chapter, more respondents had children than their German counterparts, and they therefore talked more frequently about how they managed to fit in their hours and see their families.

High work centrality is problematic where it produces conflict, stress, or ill health. Critiques here often focus on the extent to which work can or fails to provide meaning under neoliberal capitalism, noting a downward trend as marketization and financialization intensifies. These debates are closely linked to, but not synonymous with, Weber's critical work on the Protestant work ethic—the idea that a good citizen is a good worker, thus linking one's sense of one's worth to one's work (Sennett, 2012: 223). This has changed over time. A much-cited study by Morse and Weiss (1955), where the authors asked over 400 men if they would continue to work even if they came into large inheritance, has been revisited a number of times. While in the original study 80 per cent of respondents said they would continue working in such a scenario, this dropped to 72 per cent in a study by Vecchio in 1980 and to

68 per cent for those answering between 1994 and 2006 (Highhouse, Zickar, and Yankelevich, 2010; in this study the hypothetical scenario was winning the lottery). Clearly, this *is* a trend in decline. However, while we know that we have become more alienated from our work than we used to be—at the same time, and paradoxically, work has become synonymous with one's sense of self-worth (Sennett, 2012: 223; Scharff, 2012). Sennett, writing within a predominately Anglo-Saxon context, links this to the rise of unrestrained capitalism, which encourages and rewards competition and assertiveness. He says '[i]ndividuals are driving themselves because they are competing against themselves. Just as you are, you aren't good enough; you strive constantly to prove yourself by success, but no achievement ever feels like solid proof of adequacy. Invidious comparison is turned against the self' (2012: 193).

Our focus on competition, he argues, has meant that we lost the skill of cooperation and are no longer able to communicate in a way that allows for moments of tension to remain unresolved. Here, cooperation does not mean to capitulate into compromise, but to accept difference and to see moments of disagreement as an opportunity to learn about and clarify one's own position. He refers to this kind of cooperation as dialogic encounters, referencing the work of late Russian philosopher and sociolinguistic scholar Mikhail Bakhtin, arguing that competition and cooperation need to be balanced within a functioning society, but that our current pre-occupation with work, to salvage our sense of self-worth, is resulting in increasing withdrawal and isolation of individuals—first by denying ourselves social pleasures which may interfere with our commitment to work, and second by fearing others, particularly those unknown to us who may come across as threats with demands that are not our own or different from ours.[2]

Women's reproductive capacity is one factor that genders and complicates the debates Sennett problematizes, as outlined in Chapter 1 and relayed again above. Rottenberg (2014), drawing on an analysis of executive women's autobiographical writing, notes that for young women today just focusing on work or just focusing on family life is not good enough. Rather, women must craft a 'felicitous work-family balance … as the ideal for progressive contemporary womanhood' (2014: 146; also see Adamson, 2017; Gill, Kelan, and Scharff, 2017; Lewis, Benschop, and Simpson; 2017a, 2017b; Orgad and de Benedictis, 2015; Rottenberg, 2017 on postfeminism and neoliberalism or neoliberal

---

[2] Interestingly, he observes that there are two mechanisms to deal with the anxieties this produces: narcissism and complacency. Here, Sennett likens Weber's work to that of Trilling (1972), who argued that being encouraged to be 'authentic' too is an invitation to turn inward that is unlikely to have the desired results, writing: 'Authenticity is not concerned with making oneself precise and clear; instead, it is an inner search to find out what one "really" feels, and contains a strong narcissistic trace. But this search is elusive; one never arrives at really knowing one's authentic feelings' (Sennett, 2012: 195).

feminism). At the same time, as Chapter 5 showed, half of the women I interviewed were childless, which is common among senior executive women, but which further complicates this paradox of one's alienation from work and the simultaneous conflation of work with one's sense of self-worth, from a gender perspective.

There are cross-national differences in work centrality, and a range of authors working at the intersection of cross-cultural and organization studies argue that work centrality—i.e. the extent to which one focuses on work in one's life—is higher in collectivist societies such as Germany, and less important in individualist societies such as the UK and the US (Hattrup, Ghorpade, and Lackritz, 2007; Hofstede, 2001). There are several reasons why this might be. From a Varieties of Capitalism perspective, CMEs encourage workers to invest in specific rather than general and more easily transferrable skills (Hall and Soskice, 2001): to become an expert—arguably this is more likely to enable workers to take pride in their work, with work centrality consistently linked to one's perception of one's work as meaningful (Jiang and Johnson, 2017). This is where job security comes in which can be directly affected by policy. For example, in Germany workers enjoy higher job and economic security with stronger unions, higher employment protections, and better welfare provisions under an ordoliberal rather than a neoliberal policy focus (Kalleberg, 2018), as outlined in Chapter 1 and section 1 of this chapter.

Short-termism corrodes our character and society, Sennett argued (1998). Hochschild also beautifully illustrates the effects of markets on our most private and intimate parts of life (Hochschild, 2003; 2012). Alienation here is relevant both in the classic Marxist sense, through the split of labour from capital which turns workers into commodities and removes the extent to which workers can take pride in skill and end products (see e.g. Marx, 1844), as well as through an accelerating pattern of short-terminism under (neo)liberal capitalism, which has transformed our workplaces. For Sennett, short-terminism is a serious issue, because it weakens relationships and commitments to workplaces and work colleagues, which means that 'workers cannot sustain supportive relations with one another' (Sennett, 2012: 192).

Sennett traces this also in how we organize work, lamenting the rise of teamwork and management practices which recommend the rotation of employees to avoid group think or workers becoming too attached to one another. This produces an isolatory effect and increases anxiety, as discussed in the introduction to this chapter, accelerating workers' withdrawals either through complacency and detachment, or narcissism. Scharff (2016) observed a similar effect of neoliberalism, which responsibilizes the individual with their own productivity, their health and well-being, despite our best knowledge that these three factors are related and that health in particular is for many of us outside of our control and likely varying across our life cycle. As before, it returns us to Kittay's (1999) and Fineman's (2020) argument that our justice system centring the rational autonomous individual is not fit for purpose because any of us, beyond predictable periods of dependency in infancy and old age, could become dependent at any point in time through illness or accidents—and because derivative dependency is a reality and affecting predominately women.

Instead, as explored in Chapter 1, we are expected to run our lives like a business, 'embracing risks, learning from knock-backs and staying positive', 'constantly active and still lacking time' (Scharff, 2016: 113–114). There is no space for acknowledging the vulnerability fundamental to the human condition (Fineman, 2020; Kittay, 1999). That we require social support from others around us and are interdependent throughout our lives. And this is seen both here and in the previous section.

Throughout this book, we have seen that the focus on relationships, on depending on others, is much stronger in the rhetoric of the German partners than the UK partners. This had a gendered effect for the women's careers. The German respondents talked about relying on the support of family friends and instrumental ties in their careers, but respondents also reported having a difficult time when such relationships were lacking, and, with the vast majority of partners and senior management in accountancy being male, women are less likely to have access to this sort of relationship than men (Hudson, Netto, Noon, Sosenko, de Lima, and Kamenou-Aigbekaen, 2017; Kanter, 1977).

But how are such relations at work shaped by, and shaping, the way we centre work in our lives? There is a significant literature on the work-life balance of accountants. Some of this was discussed in Chapter 2 and revisited where relevant throughout the book. Crompton and Lyonette (2011) argued that work-life balance was a key reason why women failed to rise through the ranks, and indeed, as Chapter 5 showed, making partnership in the UK involved a gender role reversal for many of the women interviewed. This is somewhat in step with the 'felicitous work-life balance' Rottenberg problematizes in her work on US executive women, and the presentation of neoliberal feminism as a hollowed-out project of the self, rather than a meaningful critique of capitalism and the structural constrains and disadvantages women face. There is also an emerging insightful literature on overworking, and Lupu and Rokka (2021) show how employees in professional service firms often overwork as a result of trying to exercise control. The focus in this chapter is on the notion of work centrality and the extent to which the women interviewed were able to meaningfully carve out space for other life domains, demonstrating the ways in which work was for the majority the central activity around which other life domains are organized which must give way when necessary. From a work centrality point of view, there were relatively few differences in their talk across national borders. As mentioned earlier in this chapter, all women worked long hours. But there were some interesting contrasts when talking about the meaningfulness of what accountants do and the toll that working at the top of their profession takes on their health and bodies. This will be explored in the second subsection, which focuses on the accounts of the ten partners who noted that their life almost exclusively focused on work.

Work, other life domains, and work-life balance

Researchers distinguish between five life domains: work, family, leisure, community, and religion (Sharabi, 2017).

As Table 6.4 indicates, ten of the sixty women said that they focused predominantly on work (1) and of these seven worked in Big-4 firms; twenty-two respondents stressed the importance of time for oneself and hobbies in addition to their careers (2); fourteen women said that if they were not working they were predominantly spending time with their children and their husbands (3); and fourteen women felt that it was important to also have time for their own interests aside from work and family (4).

In her seminal article *Inequality Regimes*, Acker (2006: 448) noted that 'work is organized on the image of a white man who is totally dedicated to the work and who has no responsibilities for children or family demand other than earning a living. Eight hours of continuous work away from the living space, arrival on time, total attention to the work, and long hours if requested

Table 6.4 Work centrality and how respondents described the focus of their 'work-life' balance

Firm size	Work			Work/Life			Work/Family			Work/Life/ Family		
Country	GER	UK	Total	GER	UK	Total	GER	UK	Total	GER	UK	Total
Small	0	1	1	4	1	5	2	2	4	3	0	3
Medium	1	1	2	3	7	10	2	5	7	3	5	8
Big-4	4	3	7	5	2	7	2	1	3	1	2	3
Total	5	5	10	12	10	22	6	8	14	7	7	14

are all expectations that incorporate the image of the unencumbered worker. Flexibility to bend these expectations is more available to high-level managers', thus noting that there are gender and class (as well as race and other intersecting) dimensions to how inequality regimes operate. In line with the high work centrality typically observed among high status professionals, work was the key life domain around which other life domains were organized among the respondents in this study. A lot remains unknown about how female partners in professional service firms organize their lives, and this section therefore contributes to a significant gap in knowledge across borders. Among the sixty respondents, twenty-two said having time to pursue personal interests on a regular basis was important to them. There were some variations here. For example, three women in Germany engaged in sports with other partners at their firms, something not reported by any of the UK respondents. Konstanze, a partner of a small firm in Germany runs ultramarathons[3] and trains with one of the other partners during lunch hours or after work. Meanwhile, Elenor, also a partner in a small German firm, plays in the same handball team as one of the other partners in her firm. Among the partners in the larger firms in Germany, hobbies that involved others were relatively rare. Some tried to regularly attend a gym, others walked, but Konstanze and Elenor were markedly the only ones who regularly engaged in sports with others.[4] In the UK, quite a few partners had horses. This can be a time-consuming hobby to fit around work. Sharon, for example, a partner in a Big-4 firm, moved to a location where she was close to a stable in order to be able to fit her hobby around her work. She elaborates:

'So what I did was move my house so it's down the road from where my horse lives. If I get home before 11 o' clock at night, well 10.30 probably, I will go down and see him. If I get home before 8.30 at night, I ride him. And if I can't ride him, there is a groom who can ride to keep him fit'.

(Sharon, Big-4 firm, UK, 41/0)

Martha, who had moved to the Cornish countryside for family reasons, noted that as a couple they decided for her husband to give up his job so that

---

[3] Ultramarathons are any running events longer than a marathon of 42.195 km. This may include 24-hour races.
[4] This corresponds to a discussion by Warren (2003) and Kilkey and Perrons (2010), who note that there are different qualitative dimensions to time. In this case, it appears that the respondents found it difficult to have sufficient 'synchronic' time, which means that they 'have time' at the same time as others. In their UK-based study, Kilkey and Perrons (2010) also relate this to social class, noting the on average more flexible hours and shifts of manual workers, for example (2010: 8).

they could keep horses without her having to step away from her work. She explains:

> 'I'm the main breadwinner but he worked. It was just a nightmare. He would ring me to say there was a storm and we were worried about the horses being out. Now, he does the mucking out and all that. I just find that it makes my life a lot easier'.
>
> **(Martha, medium-sized firm, UK, 54/0)**

This was a notable difference across the narratives in Germany and the UK—the referral to husbands in their talk. This is something that was explored in more depth in Chapter 5, where the UK respondents frequently referred to their husbands as being involved in childcare so that the women could work like normative fathers might. Similarly, here, Martha's husband gave up his work to support their joint lifestyle and her career. Tracy and her partner made a similar decision. Having previously worked in different locations, Tracy had been the one to commute to their permanent home. She recalls this as a difficult situation, noting:

> 'It was difficult and I think after six months we definitely had enough because, when I went home, it was almost like going to someone else's home. Because my husband had kind of changed things to how he wanted them and say, I put something here, he'd say "That doesn't go there". It was quite weird really … It was affecting my marriage. So, we took the decision that our marriage was more important than the money. We took a more than 50 per cent drop in income at the time … But once I got the job here I was earning more than the both of us had ever earned between us so we took the decision that he may as well (stay home). Actually, he really is good. He does all the shopping, the washing, the cleaning, the gardening. I don't have to worry about any of that'.
>
> **(Tracy, medium-sized firm, UK, 46/0)**

In similar ways to the accounts shared in Chapter 5, the unencumbered norm here is left intact and a gender reversal takes place in the household in order to accommodate this.

Among those with children, the respondents described how they fit their family commitments around work during the week. Lauren, a partner in one of the medium-sized UK firms, mostly focused on work or her family and household commitments and stressed that she really enjoyed both seeing her son and doing the household chores.

> 'It's either work or family. I don't know what to do if I do get an hour. I get lost cause I don't know what to do with myself. I have a cleaner. But everything else … It's my

relaxation. I do the cooking, the ironing, help with homework. All the social, all the house bills and finance and that kind of thing'.

(Lauren, medium-sized firm, UK, 36/1)

Dunja, a partner at one of the Big-4 firms in the UK, shared how she would rush home after work to see her children and put in more hours in the evening:

'I work between 8.30 and 5 and then I usually go home, have dinner, put the kids to bed and I usually start work at about 8 o' clock. So, when you say (can I work) flexibly—I am very flexible (laughs)'.

(Dunja, Big-4 firm, UK, 39/2)

In line with Acker's claims, Dunja had some flexibility here, but it is not clear whether her ability to work anywhere at any time was making it easier to successfully integrate multiple roles, or whether it instead functioned 'as a vehicle for enslavement to work', as Valcour and Hunter argue (2005: 62; also see Chung, 2022). In Dunja's case, her laughter may indicate sarcasm or irony, yet she really seemed to enjoy her role as well as her family life. In contrast to Lauren, Dunja employed a nanny who also took care of much of the household chores and noted that her husband was 'very flexible' in the case of emergencies. This then meant that she was able to engage in activities that she personally cared for a little bit more than she used to. She notes:

'Given the hours that I work, I work usually Monday to Friday, I try not to work on the weekends. That's usually the family. I try to see my kids every day. It doesn't always happen, if you have to go out, you know, for a dinner or something like that. But I try to see the kids every day, whether that is in the morning or the evening that will vary. What else? I go to pilates. I do pilates once a week. I do try to carve out time for myself on a Friday afternoon these days. That's my new regime'.

(Dunja, Big-4 firm, UK, 39/2)

Dunja was comfortable employing a nanny, answering my question about this with:

'Of course! How do you think I would manage? (laughs)'.

(Dunja, Big-4 firm, UK, 39/2)

Anita, a partner in one of the larger medium-sized firms in Germany, was very strongly against the idea of having a nanny. As noted in Chapter 5, she had managed to negotiate her role part-time and had family help with childcare. She notes:

> 'The question is where you place your work-life-balance. Of course, in Germany you can also work all day very nicely and have some other person look after your child and then you come home at 8 p.m. A man can do that as well as a woman ... A solution would be to have all day care facilities here. But that does not solve the work-life-balance problem for me and especially in England that is a big problem I think because for many women it actually does not translate into work-life-balance, but they work and then they get the kid on top of that or it's reserved for the weekends. I find that difficult'.
>
> **(Anita, medium-sized firm, Germany, 45/1)**

Anita notes that this is 'one of the most exciting subjects of our time: to find a solution for women who want both' children and a career and simultaneously questions the outsourcing of childcare by mothers on the one hand, and the absence of work-life-balance for those same mothers on the other hand. It reinforces the rhetoric encountered among the German partners that children need their mothers, but that partnership is a full-time commitment and that 'having it all' is a fantasy that can only be sustained by outsourcing; thus 'working all day very nicely and hav(ing) some other person look after your child' as Anita puts it. Importantly, her argument that 'a man can do that as much as a woman' is on point as it is precisely descriptive of how, through a gender role reversal and significant outsourcing of care work, the households of the British firm partners are sustained—with or without the presence of children.

Six of the ten women whose lives revolved mainly around work said they were trying to achieve a better balance for themselves, and among those who were regularly engaging in other activities, several mentioned that this was only a recent development. This is a significantly smaller proportion than reported by Lupu and Ruiz-Castro (2021), for example, in their study of male and female professionals working for an international law firm in London, where 30 per cent of male and 50 per cent of female respondents noted that they tried to avoid working long hours. Besides differences in sector, their respondents were also working across levels, and all were parents to at least one child. Interestingly, five women across both groups in my research pointed to the limitations of their bodies and health as the main reason for seeking to shift away from work.

Work stress, health, and fertility

There is a small literature on the effects of stress on executive health. For example, there is concrete albeit dated evidence of the devastating impact of job insecurity on the mental health of executives (McCormick and Cooper, 1988) something I discussed in the first half of this chapter. More broadly, the literature on occupational health and stress is of interest. A US study of over 800 executives who had been referred to stress management found that work was the main stressor for 64 per cent of these patients, and among those 79 per cent noted a 'demand-resource imbalance' as the key driver (Ganesh, Mahapatra, Fuehrer, Folkert, Jack, Jenkins, Bauer, Wahner-Roedler, and Sood, 2018). Interestingly, sex was not a predictor of high stress in this study. There is some work looking more specifically at women executives, notably an older paper by Nelson and Burke (2002), which argued that, at the time, there were differences between the sexes in how stress at work is experienced and that women were more likely to report illnesses but that those illnesses were less likely to be fatal. The authors noted a trend towards convergence in some of these observations. A study on women's occupational health in Spain by de Celis, de Bobadilla-Guemez, Alonso-Almeida, and Velasco-Balmaseda (2017) lists sexual harassment in the workplace and violence against women as a key risk to women—and indeed as noted in Chapter 4, such incidents were reported among the women interviewed here also. These authors, like Burke and Richardson (2009) before them, note a continued absence of good quality research on women's occupational health.

Four of the five respondents who mentioned health problems worked in Big-4 or large medium-sized firms, and three of those were in positions with national or global responsibilities. For instance, Sabine, a partner at a Big-4 firm in Germany, recalls her past working pattern during the first three years after she was appointed to a global role:

> 'I would arrive here at 7 in the morning and leave at 6 in the evening, have dinner and then hop on my exercise bike and then work until midnight. And that's how it was every day. The neighbours did not believe my husband that I even existed. That was a very exhausting time and I got sick regularly and it just did not work anymore'.
>
> **(Sabine, Big-4 firm, Germany, 46/0)**

Her marriage broke down, which she partly attributed to her responsibilities at work. Sabine also highlighted that she made an effort now to delegate as much as possible and that she would sometimes leave the office earlier to do sports and to focus on things 'that are really important' to her at work instead of 'running around everywhere'. Sabine noted that it was a trade-off between gaining a little bit more time on the one hand, and on the other hand losing with respect to the centrality of her position within the firm, stating 'yes of course it is nice when everyone asks for you' but that the way she was working was not sustainable and that it had serious implications on her relationships and health.

Mary, now a partner at one of the larger medium-sized firms in the UK, also struggled to incorporate time for herself with her role as a firm partner with national responsibilities, and also reported getting ill as a key factor which motivated her to reorientate. She explains:

> 'It (work-life-balance) is more important ... I recognize it now. And I recognize its importance now, because I was ill as a result of overwork and I was off work for months and therefore I am very aware of work-life-balance, which I was not before ... It means I am not as committed to the practice as I was before. I don't do the long hours that I used to and I am not prepared to give up my days off and I try to find time to enjoy myself, which I didn't do before ... The job was absolutely everything, which it isn't anymore'.
>
> **(Mary, medium-sized firm, UK, 52/0)**

In a similar way to Sabine in Germany, Mary had to acknowledge the limitations of, and the effects of stress on, her body. For both, there is a clear connection between over work and becoming ill. The action necessary then is to detach somewhat from work. The relation between long working hours and health concerns is not linear. For example, the ways in which longer working hours could impact on health has been shown to be linked to the individual's sense of control over commitments and responsibilities (Bryson, Warner-Smith, Brown, and Fray, 2007). Mary noted that her GP had pressed her to incorporate regular exercise into her weekly routine, but that she had only managed to do so occasionally—perhaps one sign that she did not feel greatly in control. In addition, there was Summer, a partner in a small UK firm in her early forties. She had worked very long hours since joining the firm as a partner a decade earlier. She did not bring up ill health per se, but she noted that she had hoped to have children and that her move into accountancy had been with a view to combining having a family with a career. She shared:

> 'I try. I joined a gym and I am trying to find a hobby so that I have something. I think, because I got to the point where I can't carry on really. I need to address the balance'.

'Do you have children?'

'No. I think also, you know, by now that I thought, I positively would have. It hasn't happened, so I suppose to an extent that was another good reason to go into accountancy, because then you can work from home you can work very flexibly, and I suppose to an extent now I kind of got to the point where that (having children) is not on the cards. Well, something has gotta give now. I can't carry on like this for another 20. You know I've got to do something'.

(Summer, small firm, UK, 44/0)

Summer's vulnerability too is embodied. It is unclear why Summer has not fallen pregnant. But her account resonates with Rottenberg's (2014; 2017) argument that professional women today are expected to put their careers first and delay maternity. The fact that women's fertility declines with age and the low success rates of artificial fertility treatment are casually left unacknowledged in the rhetoric around employer-funded egg-freezing and IVF treatment (e.g. see Bayefsky, 2020), exploiting what is a critical and sustained lack of knowledge about fertility and assisted human reproduction among the general population (Delbaere, Verbiest, and Tyden, 2020; Meissner, Schippert, and von Versen-Hoynck, 2016; Royal College of Obstetricians and Gynaecologists, 2016). For example, the research by Meissner, Schippert, and von Versen-Hoynck (2016: 1) found that the majority of the over 1,100 students surveyed 'planned to have children at an age when women's fertility is already declining'. It is unclear why Summer did not have children, but what is clear is that she dedicated herself to her work expecting that maternity would happen and then naturally cause a reorientation or interruption to this working pattern. With this now less likely, she found that a focus on work alone was not enough. Her focus on work was therefore expected to be a temporary status on the way to a different lifestyle.

There were some interesting contrasts in how the women felt about the meaningfulness of the profession. Freja, for example, was one of three partners who felt that there was now too much emphasis on work-life balance. As a partner at one of the Big-4 firms in Germany, Freja worked in transaction services, often regarded as one of the toughest specialisms. On the subject of work-life balance, she stated:

'(Laughs) That is a term that I cannot hear anymore. It's the other way round. Of course, it is important to have a balanced private life in which one can develop oneself sufficiently within a social context. Yes. But, at the moment, I am starting to think that work-life balance on the job is always somehow something that people who don't really take their job very seriously hide behind, right? We work in a service industry and so you have to accept that the work-life balance is sometimes not right'.

'How important is it to you?'

'Not at all. My client is important to me'.

(Freja, Big-4 firm, Germany, 44/0)

Asked whether she thought it would be possible to organize work in a way that would allow for a shift towards shorter hours, she replied:

'No. That is the market. We have to operate under its rules or we are out. The competition is simply too great'.

'How about if everyone in the market worked differently?'

'They won't. Theoretically not everyone would do that. The first who wouldn't do it, are men'.

(Freja, Big-4 firm, Germany, 44/0)

My question here was motivated by Acker's (2006) notion of an unencumbered ideal worker mentioned earlier. Freja's response shows that she is well aware that this ideal worker is a man. Freja worked very long hours and noted that she dreaded the times when business was slow. I was curious to learn more about whether she found time to pursue other interests as ninety-hour weeks imply working seven-day weeks and at least twelve-hour days. She replied: 'Yes, you learn to cope with less sleep. One doesn't need to sleep that much'. Interestingly, she rejected the thought that individuals perhaps did not need to work that much, stressing the service industry character and at a later stage in the interview pointing out the urgent nature of the business:

'I think it's like a doctor. I mean if you are a doctor and you need to do an operation and someone breaks his leg at 12 pm and you need to operate then you can't say well let's wait till tomorrow morning. In most cases you can't. The ones that can wait, will wait'.

(Freja, Big-4 firm, Germany, 44/0)

I thought that was a very interesting analogy, echoing Anita's response when she talked about the need of children to be looked after by mothers above and in Chapter 5 where she drew a comparison between auditors and astronauts ('That's just how it is. If you fly to the moon you can't just get out of your cabin in the middle of things and take care of your child either' (Anita, medium-sized firm, Germany, 45/1). While Summer, Mary, and Sabine in the UK conceded that their jobs were not more important than their own health and well-being, Freja in Germany compared her job to life-saving and Anita found an analogy to astronauts fitting. However, while Summer, Mary, and Sabine felt that they had reorientated and claimed some of their time back, their lives were very much orientated around work and Freja's claim that 'it is the other way round' is likely a fair observation for many professionals for whom considering work-life balance, in practice, means to work out how to fit family and leisure commitments around work, not vice versa.

This is evident in Dunja's account, for example, who 'tries to see the kids every day' and continues to work after they have gone to sleep. Freja was not the only one who made the analogy to life-saving, albeit in an opposing way. Martha, a partner at a medium-sized firm, had previously spent most of her time working and was now fiercely protective of her personal time. She says:

'I can understand if you were a doctor, a heart surgeon saving lives, doing transplants you know and you're going to have to do crazy hours and be on call. But at the end of the day, I think we're doing accounts, we're doing tax. Let's not delude ourselves (laughs) it gets busy if you're doing transaction work. A lot of clients selling their companies or buying, then you're usually up against strict deadlines and that will be the time some occasionally might be working till 8 o' clock at night but otherwise …'

(Martha, medium-sized firm, UK, 54/0)

Martha simultaneously reinforces and contradicts Freja's argument by suggesting that it would be 'deluded' to think that working in an accountancy firm was like being a surgeon, saving lives, yet at the same time pointing out that working in transactions was an exception and that it did require long hours—albeit occasionally so. This difference may well be due to working in different firm sizes, with Freja a partner in a Big-4 which meant that her work in transaction services was also more specialized. Freja was also based in Germany, which may also have implications. Within the UK context, Martha argued that the idea of working more hours and being constantly available to the client was old-fashioned. Having worked in the City of London for the better part of her career, she had moved to Cornwall for family reasons. She says:

'Some of them are pushing for us to get there earlier. They're making a fatal mistake here. They are aiming to compete with the big boys, alright, and think that means working 24-hour days and be available all days. The way I see it, the big firms have done that in the 80s and they're now getting a bit more sense, a bit more work-life-balance, whereas we're still behind the times'.

(Martha, medium-sized firm, UK, 54/0)

Martha and Freja are keen to protect their own sense of how accountancy should be centred in their lives, whereas Sabine, Mary, and Summer, who had been in situations that were perhaps experienced as less within their control as they struggled with ill health, were less convicted. For others, it was not their bodies but the economy that caused them to evaluate their priorities.

Conclusion

This chapter explored how the female partners in this study talked about the centrality of their work, and in line with what we know about the working patterns of organizational elites, for many work also structured their engagement in other life domains. They worked long hours in both countries and, especially in the UK, some had started to question their commitment to the profession and their firms. The key differences in their talk across national borders was in relation to how they encountered conflict at work, and the extent to which they felt secure in their position. In Chapter 3, I explored the ways in which relationships matters in the careers of the German respondents and were a crucial part of their career histories. They frequently crossed the private and public divide, with partners sharing common interests in sports for example. They also crossed the public and private divide when it came to the subject of motherhood, where one of the respondents for example asked the other firm partners what their thoughts were on her adopting a child and, beyond her account, everyone had a view on how motherhood ought to be done. And, as this chapter shows, boundaries were less evident here also, and some of the respondents recalled what might be considered quite unprofessional and aggressive exchanges lacking respect, often involving men above them in the hierarchy. The women did not necessarily respond at the time, but usually started looking for opportunities elsewhere soon after. In fact, resignations were common and for a range of reasons. The German respondents felt secure in their jobs and their ability to secure new positions.

In many of these accounts, the firms may have had the same name, but the context differs. In Chapter 1 I introduced the work of Weishaupt (2021), who stresses the importance of recognizing Germany's commitment to the social market economy and its manifestation in times of crises. In his work, he traces the coordination of public employment services and social partner organizations and emphasizes the role of these as firm-level 'watch dogs'. Germany only suffered a small rise in unemployment following the Great Recession set off by the financial crisis of 2008 (Statista, 2022b), partly due to its commitment to Kurzarbeit in manufacturing; for example, rather than allow manufacturers to react to crises by firing staff and then rehiring in better times, here the state, unions, and employers coordinated a response where all worked less to avoid layoffs. Similarly, what can be seen in the accounts of the German respondents is a sense of a collective common good among all firm members, for example, the application of pay freezes for everyone rather than the application of redundancies in times of crises. And there have been common crises affecting two countries in the time span relayed by the interviewees.

Perhaps, in Germany, relationships in the industry here may act as a buffer to a profession that was by itself much less exposed to market forces, with the supply of chartered accountants much more tightly controlled. The discussion of redundancies in the UK was also another example of how performance-based decision-making systems can be subject to bias. And it highlights the fragility of formal structures and the role of informal practices and processes in maintaining inequality regimes.

Sennett's, as well as Scharff's, work helps shed light on the ruthlessness of accelerated capitalism in practice within neoliberal regimes, even at the level of working elites. While the German exchanges were also lacking respect, and were at times aggressive, in the UK, instead, there was a void of emotion where responsibility was pushed instead on a system organized around notions of fair competition and meritocracy, burdening the individual with the idea that they, ultimately, did it to themselves. But the respondents resisted the latter, and across these accounts communicated a sense that these were not meritocratic decisions, but that they were gendered. The chapter contributes to our understanding of the extent to which economic crises are experienced in different ways and how this may be a function of the socio-political as well as the professional/occupational context. The German respondents were secure in their knowledge that they had options and that they could always resign, because in Germany the profession functions as its monopolist status suggests it should. In the UK on the other hand, with around fifteen times more members, accountancy was neither their preferred profession in the first place, nor a secure one in times of crisis.

7
Gendered Hierarchies of Dependency, Feminism, and the Commodification of the Self

This research showed how careers and progression to partnership for the women interviewed was managed somewhat differently in these two quite distinct capitalist contexts, and I drew on the Varieties of Capitalism framework to make sense of these differences in the qualitative data. Dany, Mallon, and Arthur (2003) argued that 'career' as a concept lends itself well to analytically connecting individuals, organizations, and social structures (2003: 705). And that has been a key objective in this book and pursued from a feminist perspective.

There is evidence that how people form relationships at work, and how they instrumentalize these relationships, has demographic as well as geographic and/or cultural properties (see e.g. Batjargal, 2007; Burt, Hogarth, and Michaud, 2000). Chapter 3 illustrated the importance of building networks and having social skills in accountancy (Carter and Spence, 2014). The interviews suggested that relationship quality, tie duration, and the extent to which they are drawn upon in advancement to partnership by the women I interviewed differed across borders. The women interviewed in Germany, who have made it to the very top of their profession, were much more likely to draw on long-standing friendships—often with men and professional father figures—than their UK counterparts. In the UK, the emphasis was much more on understanding standardized career structures and processes and working their way through these (see Chapter 2 and Kokot, 2014).

Hierarchies differ to the extent that they favour networks and relationships with others (Germany) or navigating procedures and standardized career structures (UK), but the outcomes are always gendered, albeit in different ways. And these differences may also relate to how much women (and men) can and must depend on others at work. Dependency here, in this specific workplace context, is conceived as one's entanglement in relationships of trust and the degree to which one can advance without it.

Gendered Hierarchies of Dependency. Patrizia Kokot-Blamey, Oxford University Press.
© Patrizia Sofia Kokot-Blamey (2023). DOI: 10.1093/oso/9780199688456.003.0007

Sex matters in at least three different ways. First, tendencies towards homosociality and men's overrepresentation in positions of power in the industry mean that women will find it more difficult than men to access the kinds of networks needed to advance in Germany. Second, relatedly, being dependent on a manager means that such biases are played out again and again across the hierarchy; even if women do have good relationships at work with their superiors, it makes it difficult to challenge problematic behaviour when it occurs, because doing so may result in irreparable damage to a relationship that one depends on. Third, embeddedness in relationships means that one is more likely to be held to account when one seeks to behave in ways that do not conform to cultural or gendered norms and expectations.

This, I argue in Chapter 4, left the women in Germany much more conflicted when it came to admitting to and making sense of sexism in the profession as a collective experience. In contrast, in the UK, the interviewees felt more able to acknowledge constraints and recount moments where they experienced inappropriate behaviour. The literature on post- and neoliberal feminism allows us to make sense of this focus on individual autonomy and choice, but, theoretically, this ought to be less pronounced in the German accounts situated within a Coordinated Market Economy. In the conclusion to that chapter, I point to variegated feminist legacies as well as the Varieties of Capitalism in thinking about why this could be. First, as Offen (1988) reminds us, Germany and the UK have very different feminist legacies, with the UK feminist movements taking a more rights-based approach. Second, I wondered to what extent the higher degree of interdependence and embeddedness observed in the accounts in Germany made a complaint riskier and potentially costly.

This too is explored in Chapter 5, which focused on the subject of motherhood (also see Kokot-Blamey, 2021). In Germany, the women were more frequently confronted with their own reproductive capacity, and becoming a mother was understood to be a burden to the firm and its clients. At the same time, mothers were seen as indispensable for infants and young children, and motherhood was thus regarded to be incompatible with firm partnership. The respondents reproduced this juxtaposition in their accounts, but were also resistant to it in their lives, with a third of the women having children while making partnership. Interestingly, fathers were almost entirely absent in their talk. This was in stark contrast to the accounts in the UK where more of the women had children, almost two thirds, but half of these relied on their husbands to be the primary carer, unencumbering themselves and working like a normative father might. Here, I was struck by how, in an effort to appear gender neutral, firms would burden women by being oblivious to the embodied realities of pregnancy, birth, and maternity. And how the women were rendered speechless lest they be seen to complain about policies that were sold to them as fair, but were drawn up without women and their bodies in mind. Indeed, in some of the cases, the respondents were the first women to join at partner level and this was reflected in the state of the partnership deeds, which are not subject to the same scrutiny as employment contracts might be, because partners are usually self-employed.

Chapter 6 focused on work centrality and job security. In both countries, predictably, the women worked long hours and there were, at times, interesting parallels drawn, comparing accountancy or auditing to the kinds of work astronauts or surgeons might be doing. In both countries, some of the women had dealt with health issues. They talked about stress and that they would try to delegate more and carve out more time for themselves, but this was not usually successful. The talk by the women in the UK was much more marked by job insecurity. And they witnessed redundancies and fell victim to redundancy themselves. Here, there were glimpses of how career structures and performance systems were indeed 'perverted', as Manuela's superior in Germany had suggested; they were used as mirrored shields to suggest to those being let go, first, that they did it to themselves—had they been more competitive or performed better it would have hit someone else—and second, that the firm had no choice, that the market and economy demanded it be so. In Germany, redundancies were not something the respondents talked about. In times of crisis, women were also able to depend on others and they felt secure in their positions. This reflects a broader political commitment in Germany to approaching crises as a collective, albeit a collective that less likely to account for marginalized communities to the same extent.

In the remainder of this concluding discussion, I return to the question asked at the beginning of the book: what do we gain when we let go of the messy but enduring and often dependable relationship-based hierarchies the women relayed to me in Germany, and what in turn do we give up?

The Cost of Embeddedness and the Cost of the Commodification of the Individual

Chapter 1 introduced the Varieties of Capitalism as a lens to think about how the ways in which institutions coordinate nationally may be replicated at the level of one's career. Throughout, the book sought to show that there were differences in how career advancement was negotiated in Germany and the UK, but that the implications were gendered in both instances, albeit in different ways. Chapter 3 showed how in Germany, at the time, many of the women interviewed felt that partnership meant a life-long commitment, and some even likened it to marriage. They talked about joining firms where they had friendships, where their firm became an extension of their family networks and thus of the home environment. Perhaps in these circumstances, making the firm a centre of one's life can be very meaningful. This is not straightforward for women, because the cost of mutuality and reciprocity is conformity, and that includes conforming to gender norms. Chapter 5, for example, explored how in Germany, motherhood was everyone's business. This too is the cost of social embeddedness in collectivism and of depending on one another at work and at home—interpersonal boundaries mean nothing and one's dependency on others can be stifling, as the accounts in Chapter 3 and Chapter 6 showed. But Chapter 3 in particular also showed how the women interviewed in the UK were much more likely to draw on commodified language in their narratives. They talked about spot rates, negotiating standardized processes, and working with recruitment agents to facilitate career moves when they met a stumbling block in their career paths. They dealt with sexual harassment or discrimination at work at arm's length, and negotiated the division of labour between paid and unpaid work within the household through a process of economic cost-benefit analyses (also see Kokot, 2015). In short, they did run their lives as if they were a business (Scharff, 2016)—and in a market economy, businesses can go under and are vulnerable to the ups and downs of the economy around them.

The subject of the commodification of the individual through work and performance management systems has been explored in a range of disciplines. In the health care sector, for example, authors such as Timmermans and Almeling (2009) emphasized how a focus on objectification, commodification, and standardization in medicine is leading towards the 'loss of humanism in medicine, the depersonalization of care, and the replacement of holistic care with bureaucratic control' (2009: 21). Shields and Grant focus on human resource management (HRM) in their critique and note that 'labour commodification is one of the defining characteristics of the market capitalist mode' (2010: 61). They draw attention to the role of HRM, and note how soft HR practices e.g. those focused on employee engagement, psychological contracts, and organizational justice, also 'seek to objectify the worker in the most intimate way'. They argue that the 'latest turn in management's objectification project has been to seek to render human cognition and affects—the basis of the worker's status as a social and organizational subject—classifiable, measurable and, hence, more manipulable' (Shields and Grants, 2010: 71). For Shields and Grants, HRM and performance management systems are not about accountability, fairness, and equality, but about controlling the human subject and depleting him or her of their skills and knowledge, rendering them manipulable and impotent. Butterick and Charlwood (2021) argue that this intensified during the COVID-19 pandemic, and that those in the most commodified jobs were the most vulnerable to this. Butterick and Charlwood claim that HRM and HRM theory have been complicit in 'legitimising the increasing commodification of labour' (2021: 848) and observe that ideological individualism has led to 'wide spread amorality' (2021: 848).

In short, standardized career structures, and the bureaucracies that support them, are turning more intrusive, aiming to affect workers' intimate and emotional lives (Hochschild, 2003; 2012) and controlling their relationships with others. Butterick and Charlwood also warn that the rise of unemployment as a result of the pandemic will exacerbate this problem, giving more power to employers—and women, as shown in Chapter 6 and repeatedly in the data on unemployment following recessions, are particularly vulnerable (Perrons, 2021).

In this book, such issues came to the fore also. The UK women were adaptive and made it through the standardized career system, often at speed. At times, they adopted a depersonalized and commodified language when talking about performance. This was also selectively noticeable in the accounts of the German respondents, although there was more ambivalence in their talk. But in the UK too there was resistance to these sorts of attempts to responsibilize them with the gendered constraints and realities of career advancement. This came through when Tracy told her story of redundancy through gritted teeth. Or when Claire was quite happy to leave rather than sit through another redundancy round unfolding around her amid fabricated and clearly gendered conceptualizations of performance.

An obsession with independence and with counting women at work has produced a myopic and skewed picture on the basis of which we have rested our enthusiastic export of performance and appraisal systems and of standardized career structures that favour performance over experience, and merit over tenure; that values assertiveness over thoughtfulness and consideration (see e.g. Sennett, 2012; also see Orgad and Gill, 2021). This focus on short-termism is corrosive, as Sennett (1998; 2007; 2012) argues. People are discouraged from making long-term meaningful ties with one another and instead are encouraged to focus on collecting 'the evidence', and competencies that might get them promoted.

In the service economy of the twenty-first century, we create little and our jobs are stripped of meaning, and we are stripped of a sense that we matter. In the UK, specifically, there is a disconnect between education, training, and job security, as discussed in Chapter 6. There are fifteen times more chartered accountants in the UK than there are in Germany, and, not surprisingly, they have a sense that they are disposable and that this disposability has a gendered tinge to it. This difference is in line with the Varieties of Capitalism approach which predicts, or describes, that workers in liberal market economies are more likely to develop general skills that are more easily transferrable, whereas those in coordinated market economies are supported by more generous welfare states which favour investment in more specialized skill sets that are less transferrable. But in both countries becoming a chartered accountant requires a significant investment in terms of time and opportunity cost. What, then, is the purpose of professional closure, of adding years of training to one's CV, if it exposes its members regardless to the market forces of supply and demand? We must always hold onto critiques of occupational closure and the ways in which it is classed, racialized, and gendered (Annisette, 2003; Sian, 2006; 2007; 2011; Walker and Shackleton, 1998; Witz, 1992) amongst others, but perhaps it is fair to wonder whether the training of large numbers of public accountants is in the interest of either its members or the public in light of continuous scandals in the industry in both Germany (e.g. see Meyer, 2021 for ZDF.de) and the UK (e.g. see Moyer, 2019 for AccountancyAge). The key conflict of interest lies in the profession's simultaneous involvement in both audit and consultancy (Meuwissen and Quick, 2019). At these numbers, accounting trainees today certainly become clients tomorrow. There are more women making it to the very top in accountancy in the UK, but they also appear to be more vulnerable to suffering redundancy.

Feminist Visions of Equality

Within the feminist literature, a notable split occurs on what equality ought to look like, with the key complication being women's reproductive capacity and what to do about pregnancy, birth, maternity, and, most importantly, the care of little children. The majority of women become mothers in their lifetime. And the majority of men become fathers. In a nutshell, it comes down to whether mothers ought to be unencumbered by focusing on the provision of free childcare, 'enabling' them to work in ways that fathers already feel able to. Or, whether we all ought to centre care and dependency in our lives, organizing work around our commitments to the care of others. The literature on post-feminism/neoliberal feminism that this book draws on extensively in Chapters 4 to 6 has been enriching in showing women's ambivalence towards feminism, towards structural constraints, and towards naming these.

Spearheaded by scholars in Britain, it is also concerned with a focus on allowing women to work and pursue careers like men do, while also being critical of the ways in which work is centred. McRobbie's latest book (2020) sketches out her views about how women feel able, or not, to claim feminism and how this has changed over time in the UK, by moving from a post-feminist space where feminism is seen as no longer needed, towards a liberal and neoliberal feminism that actively embraces the pre-dominantly white, middle- and upper-class overachieving working mother. This opens us to important insights into how our understanding towards what it means to be 'a good woman' is mediated by our cultural contemporary context and that there is an understanding that we must be good workers as well as caring mothers and that these expectations are gendered, classed, and racialized (also see Littler and McRobbie, 2021; Rottenberg; 2017). At the same time, McRobbie also talks about one's ability to pursue a career as an opportunity to fulfil oneself, initially in relation to the division of labour in the household in the 1950s, but later also emphasizing the potential of 'full-time nursery provision for babies and toddlers', which, she stresses, is the 'single most effective route out of poverty for disadvantaged and single-parent households' (2013: 128; 2020). She reminds the reader that free childcare was a socialist aim for some. McRobbie claims there being a 'professionalization of domestic life (which) forcefully reverses the older feminist denunciation of housework as drudgery, and childcare as monotonous and never-ending, by elevating domestic skills and the bringing up of children as worthwhile and enjoyable' (2013: 130; 2020). On the one hand, McRobbie exposes the ways in which women today must achieve both a fulfilling successful career as well as a stable family life, importantly prioritizing the former over the latter. Yet, on the other hand, it bears a hint of a maternal anxiety of its own, and a denial of the possibility that perhaps many working mothers may find domestic work a 'drudgery', may find childcare 'monotonous', and may find the fact that their husbands might be less involved unfair and infuriating, but yet feel that it can be worthwhile, and frequently enjoyable, precisely because it is not 'never-ending'—because children grow up.

What is interesting here is that heteronormative femininity and family life are framed as contradictions to women's ability to achieve in the workplace, but within a broader cultural narrative that has so enthusiastically accepted the idea that it is free childcare, not time, that matters to women, children, and families more broadly. During the 2019 British elections, for example, Labour, the Liberal Democrats, and the Conservatives were falling over themselves to entice voters with promises of free childcare. Albert (2019) in a summary aimed at nursery workers, referred to this fittingly as the 'free childcare arms race'. In 2021, Scottish Labour offered fifty hours of free childcare a week should they have been elected in Scotland (as reported by e.g. Eden for the Evening Standard, 2021). This is the equivalent to saying that two-year olds, taking into account sleep and weekends, should spend 85–100 per cent of their waking hours at a nursery or some other childcare provision, away from their parents. It is close to childcare provision in the *Wochenkrippen* in the former German Democratic Republic, where very young children were kept away from their parents during the working week and only returned at weekends. The detrimental effects of this parental alienation for both parents and children have been documented over the years (see e.g. Stary, 2018, and the footnoted short film for the ZDF, 2019). The problem here is not that some people may very well need fifty hours of childcare, but that many dual earner families where this is the case may wish for more time *with* and not *from* their children and that one might expect to see a range of policies from different and usually opposing parties.

Stephens (2012) reminds us that women (and men) being able to look after their own children, if they so wish, with respect and dignity and supported appropriately by the state, was also always an aim of the women's movement, but one that has been erased as part of a wider pattern of cultural forgetting as a result of creeping neoliberalism and globalization, which glorifies market work over caring for others. A call for free childcare is thus in line with a neoliberal push towards unencumbering both men and women to dedicate themselves fully to paid work and employment under ever more precarious and corrosive conditions, where we are not just encouraged to compete with one another, but also with ourselves (Scharff, 2016; Sennett, 2012).

The idea that we cannot centre children and dependency in our lives for some years without fatally ruining our careers for ever is fraught. Rhetorically, it contributes to the disconnect between job security on the one hand and education, training, and experience on the other hand. Skill depreciation is taken for granted as a given in many economic analyses of the gender pay gap as the 'cost' of leave to women—but I think we ought to take a critical look at these terms and how they are employed to tell predominately women, but also men, that our skills, our experience, all this additional training, depreciates into a puff of smoke if we step outside the labour market for what is a relatively short moment in the bigger scheme of things—the short time that children are truly dependent compared to the forty to fifty years of work we are now expected to accrue before retirement. Who benefits from having us think so? Mostly employers.

The notion that mothers matter to children came through especially in the German accounts explored across Chapters 3 to 5, and culminated problematically in the conclusion that one cannot be a mother and a firm partner. But Germany took a new direction in 2015 with the introduction of much more generous allowances for parental leave of up to three years for mothers and fathers, two of which can be taken at any time between the child's third and his or her eighth birthdays (BMFSJ, 2021a). The employer does not need to agree, and parents are protected from lay-off during that time. In addition, there is Basis-Elterngeld (Parental Allowance, between 300 and 1,800 Euros per month at the time of writing (2022), or around 65 per cent of one's net income before birth, but this rises up to 100 per cent for low earners), which parents can receive for up to fourteen months, and Elterngeld Plus (between 100 and 900 Euros per month, twice as long as Basis-Elterngeld and taken in lieu), which is conceived as a bonus for parents who work part-time during their parental leave and allows parents to extend their allowance, and the Partnerschaftsbonus, which is an additional bonus if both parents are working part-time between twenty-five and thirty-two hours, for four additional months. The latter is also available for single parents (BMFSJ, 2021b). This should over time encourage employers, at point of recruitment, to conceive of men too as potential fathers who may be taking time to care for their children. Importantly, the child and his or her development has been kept in mind here, and parents are able to split their allowance for leave into three parts—for example, after birth, to help settle the child in nursery, and to support the child's transition to school at age 6. This has resulted in a slow but steady increase of fathers claiming entitlements, with 25 per cent of new fathers claiming Elterngeld in 2021 (BMFSJ, 2021a). Elterngeld Plus claims by fathers rose from just under 5 per cent in the third quarter of 2015 to just under 14 per cent two years later (BMFSJ, 2018). There was a significant increase in the number of fathers claiming three or more months of allowances, which was rare before 2015 when the vast majority or 80 per cent of fathers making claims would take two months or less. In addition, a fifth of those making claims in 2017 were planning to take further leave after the child's third birthday.

It is more in line with a feminist vision that centres dependency and care rather than autonomy, independence, and employers. The writings by Eva Feder Kittay (1999) and Julie Stephens (2012) have been inspiring because one can see not just a critique of what is, but also a vision of how we could organize our lives, and that centring care in all our lives and communities *is*, and in fact has always been, at the heart of a feminist vision of the future. Male accountancy partners too are parents and grandparents and have the potential to meaningfully involve themselves in care. Organizing communities, entitlements, and everyday life around work instead is a capitulation to a fabricated panic that, under globalization, capitalists will leave our shores in droves, and that as highly educated Western societies we have nothing to offer but the availability of disenfranchised, pliable workers, whose independence is propped up by the unpaid or underpaid efforts of women.

Kittay and Stephens are honest about the work that women do for others, and about the fact that children, the elderly, and all of us at different points in our life, need care, and that there is a suspicion brewing underneath that the care we give and receive out of love is different than that provided by often underpaid agency workers; that paying changes the relationship between the carer and the cared for. *We can't have it all* is an admission that time matters and that who cares matters. The problem is not that women care, but that many men do not.

Domesticity, Marriage, and the Family under Neoliberalism

Orgad (2019) shows how the women she interviewed felt that they were to blame for the structural constraints that made dual careers and caring for children impossible. It exposed their anger and disappointment and how this is part of a broader responsibilization of the individual, and women in particular under neoliberalism (also see McRobbie (2020); Banet-Weiser, Gill, and Rottenberg (2020)). A focus on women's rage, and disappointment, however, is obscuring that all of these feelings are part of living an ordinary life and neglects to consider also the extent to which domesticity can be a critique of capitalism and a refusal to participate in mass consumption (Stephens, 2012) and the 'Wegwerfgesellschaft'[1]. In the popular imagination, the family is presented to us a key site of women's oppression and exploitation—also from our own children—but this narrative is not likely to resonate with mothers at large who, we know, try hard to look after their young children for a significant proportion of daytime hours themselves in the early years, whether childcare is comparatively cheap but in practice in short supply, such as in Germany, or very costly and available, as in the UK. In Germany and the

---

[1] Literal translation: throw-away-society.

UK, and indeed around the world, women spend more time than men each week caring for little children.

Of course, for a great many, mostly women and children, the family regrettably is also a place of violence and aggression. There are contributory factors, but, as a consistent pattern, we must consider it in any social policies that seek to reallocate the division of labour in private and public life, to keep women, children, and the most vulnerable safe. And it must thus feature as a concern in the implementation of any scheme such as the Elterngeld, Elternzeit, and Partnerschaftsbonus initiatives introduced in Germany.

But it is in the home that we often find the support needed to deal with the disappointments we experience at work, but have been trained never to articulate there, lest it be taken as a moment of great debasement. As Sennett (2012: 136) observes, 'shame has become deeply associated in Western culture with self-control; losing control over your body or your words has become a source of shame. Modern family life, and even modern business practice, has extended the idea of self-containment: dependency on others is taken to be a sign of weakness, a failure of character; in raising children or at work, our institutions seek to promote autonomy and self-sufficiency; the autonomous individual appears free'. Importantly, he argues that this preoccupation with autonomy and independence is context-specific and not universal, albeit leaking across cultural and geographical divides and chipping away at our sense of togetherness both at home and at work.

Resisting the Upside-down World in Feminist Visions of a Future under Capitalism

The standardization of career structures results in more women at top levels at work. But we must consider the wider implications of this sort of strategy for our conceptualizations of equality—beyond accountancy and beyond the workplace. Capitalism through its division of the public from the private is a disaster for women, and in this book I argued that there are no gender-neutral hierarchies at work; both relationship- and structure-based hierarchies have gendered effects. Yet, if capitalism is not going anywhere fast, like Power (2022) recently noted, then we must still hold onto a feminist vision of what is right and resist the narratives 'of a world indeed turned upside down, where solutions have become problems, and problems solutions' (Stephens, 2012: 23). Caring well for our most vulnerable, the elderly and young children—rather than self-care. Developing and maintaining relationships of trust in our homes, at work, and within our communities. Allowing for differences of being and disagreements in thinking. Valuing experience and a history of servitude to others. Employers cannot be trusted to prioritize morally; it is not in their interest. But the state could.

As I write this in Spring 2022, there is a war at the doors to Europe, prices are increasing, and fear of escalation, fear of job losses, and rising interest rates are all reasonable concerns. An apprehension towards the idea of a strong state is not unfounded, particularly for women and marginalized communities. Since the onset of the COVID-19 pandemic, we have learnt that even the most hands-off and liberal of states can trap us in our homes for months on end, mask us, and demand we work while simultaneously looking after and overseeing the education of our children. That a liberal state can require the most underpaid, casualized, and racialized workers leave their children in care, despite the, at the time, unknown risks exposure to the virus could bring, and work on the frontline, propping up historically underfunded social care and health services as well as the education sector. At this moment in time, or perhaps as always, the political parties in both Britain and in Germany are writing manifestos not with a vision of what they conceive to be right, but on the basis of what polls well with voters—and voters are exhausted.

As Stephens (2012: 15) observes, the 'new, unencumbered (motherless) self is celebrated and defined by its separateness, autonomy, and purported freedom of choice'. Power (2022: 41) makes a similar point with regards to paternalism, arguing that 'today paternalism is not only absent, but extensively vilified when it is understood to be merely another expression of patriarchy'. This claim is interesting because when we look back at the history of accounting, we hear of figures like Isobel Guthrie in Scotland (Shackleton, 1998), or Mary Harris Smith and H.M. Claridge, who were able to fight for entrance in the accountancy profession because of the standing of their fathers (ICAEW, 2015[2]). And in Germany women told me about the friendships with often older men who supported them in a fatherly way and for many years. Both Anita and Elenor laughed, perhaps uncomfortably or self-consciously, when they recounted making partnership and how much they drew on these friends in their ascent. I wonder to what extent this laughter was also a foreboding that they knew that admission and advancement by the grace of father was on the way out and that women today must fight alongside men in the disingenuous slog that is performance management in

---

[2] Smith' father was a banker and Claridge's father the president of the ICAEW when she was admitted in 1920.

organizational meritocracies, where women enter the race, first, with a ticking clock over their heads, and then frequently with childcare strapped to their legs—unless they find, in time, the right sort of partner. Like Rottenberg (2017) notes, professional women are to delay maternity and to focus on career success first. Artificial reproductive technologies are embraced by large employers, to keep in check women's anxieties about the realities of fertility and of what is lost when the clock stops ticking. Like the free buffets of the early 2000s, the resulting policies are designed to keep us working, worrying only about the next step on the ladder, rather than the things we could be doing instead.

Appendix

Appendix Table 1: Respondents' characteristics, Germany

Pseudonym	Firm Size	Age	Marital Status	Children	Socio-Economic	Migrant Background
Andrea	S	50	Married	2	Middle Class	No
Angela	M	55	Married	2	Middle Class	No
Anita	M	45	Married	1	Middle Class	No
Barbara	S	38	Married	0	Middle Class	No
Beate	L	44	Married	1	Middle Class	No
Bettina	M	43	Partner	1	Middle Class	No
Birte	M	47	Married	0	Upper Class	No
Brigitte	L	41	Married	0	Middle Class	No
Chloe	L	52	Single	1	Middle Class	No
Elenor	M	51	Married	0	Middle Class	No
Elisabeth	M	55	Single	0	Working Class	No
Freja	L	44	Single	0	Upper Class	Other EU
Hannah	M	48	Divorced	1	Middle Class	No
Jana	M	42	Partner	0	Working Class	No
Johanna	S	53	Married	1	Middle Class	No
Julia	L	41	Partner	0	Middle Class	No
Katja	L	40	Partner	0	Middle Class	No
Katrin	L	44	Partner	1	Middle Class	No
Konstanze	S	42	Married	0	Middle Class	No
Manuela	L	47	Single	0	Middle Class	No
Melanie	S	58	Married	2	Upper Class	No
Nadine	S	46	Divorced	0	Middle Class	No
Nadja	L	46	Partner	0	Middle Class	No
Nina	L	39	Married	0	Middle Class	No
Pauline	S	41	Married	2	Middle Class	No
Sabine	L	46	Divorced	0	Middle Class	No
Sabrina	L	42	Married	0	Middle Class	Other EU
Stephanie	S	39	Married	1	Middle Class	No
Susanne	M	53	Married	2	Working Class	No
Vanessa	S	44	Partner	0	Middle Class	No

Appendix Table 2: Respondents' characteristics, United Kingdom

Pseudonym	Firm Size	Age	Marital Status	Children	Socio-Economic	Ethnicity
Abbie	M	46	Married	2	Middle Class	White British
Alice	M	47	Married	2	Middle Class	White British
Anastasia	L	36	Married	1	Middle Class	White British
Apoorva	S	37	Married	2	Working Class	Asian- or Black Caribbean-British
Carolyn	S	39	Married	0	Upper Class	White British
Chelsea	M	48	Divorced	0	Working Class	White British
Christiane	L	43	Married	2	Middle Class	White British
Claire	M	43	Married	2	Middle Class	White British
Daisy	L	37	Married	1	Middle Class	White British
Denise	S	39	Married	2	Middle Class	White British
Dunja	L	39	Married	2	Working Class	Asian- or Black Caribbean-British
Emily	M	46	Married	2	Middle Class	White British
Frances	L	39	Married	2	Middle Class	White British
Henrietta	M	49	Married	2	Middle Class	White British
Kelly	M	49	Married	0	Working Class	White British
Kerry	M	38	Married	2	Middle Class	White British
Lauren	M	36	Married	1	Middle Class	White British
Leslie	L	52	Single	0	Working Class	White British
Madie	M	38	Married	0	Middle Class	White British
Marina	L	59	Married	2	Middle Class	EU, White Other
Martha	M	54	Married	0	Working Class	White British
Martine	M	53	Married	2	Upper Class	White British
Mary	M	52	Married	0	Middle Class	White British
Meredith	M	44	Married	2	Working Class	White British
Natasha	M	47	Married	2	Middle Class	White British
Paris	M	49	Single	0	Middle Class	White British
Sarah	M	45	Single	0	Middle Class	Asian- or Black Caribbean-British
Sharon	L	41	Single	0	Middle Class	White British
Summer	S	44	Married	0	Middle Class	White British
Tracy	M	46	Married	0	Middle Class	White British

Methodological Note

This book is based on sixty interviews with women partners in Germany and the UK which were recorded and transcribed and mainly took place at the respondents' offices during 2009 and 2010, lasting between forty-five and ninety minutes. The interviews were in-depth, semi-structured, thereafter transcribed and then analysed in NVivo. I focused on recruiting women in partnership positions in small, medium-sized, and large accounting firms. Both equity and salaried partners were included. The respondents were aged between 31–59 years with a median and mean age of 44. Most of the participants identified as white, middle-class, and heterosexual, reflecting, besides their minority status as women, the broader lack of diversity at the top of organizational hierarchies in both Germany (Coester, 2018) and the UK (Cox, 2018).

The analysis of the interview is limited to women who did make partnership and therefore does not include any insights into the experiences of those who left the profession. This is of particular relevance in the context of this book, since, arguably, those who did successfully negotiate their way towards partnership positions may feel very differently about their careers in accountancy and the extent to which their status as women may be relevant to it, compared to those who left the profession (see Anderson, Vinnicombe and Singh, 2010 for a discussion of women partners leaving the profession).

There are various reasons why I focused on female partners only. The main purpose of the wider research context was to examine career advancement, and it is partners who can ultimately reflect upon the full range of experiences, including changing firms and going to smaller firms if partnership was denied in large firms. This is one of the reasons why respondents were recruited across firm sizes, which allowed me to think about the organizational context and the ways in which it may shape the women's experiences of day-to-day practices. I use the term sex throughout to denote biological sex, and gender to refer to socially constructed stereotypes of what is understood as appropriate feminine or masculine behaviours, roles, and attributes, which limit women and men in daily life. I also use the term gendered as an adjective to refer to bias—e.g. 'the effects of this policy are gendered' (to mean the policy affects men and women differently)—as well as in established terms such as the gender pay gap which represents the pay gap between men and women.

Class was a contested term, and the respondents had very different views on what it means to have a middle-class upbringing, pointing for example to location and time as mediating factors. I asked the respondents about their parents' education and employment with an understanding that class has significant generational properties, especially in the UK (Chan and Boliver, 2013; Clark and Cummins, 2015), but also in Germany (see e.g. Dodin, Findeise, Henkel, et al., 2021 or Hertel and Groh-Samberg, 2014). I then offered an assessment, which they could accept, reject, or discuss further.

With regards to 'ethnic origin', I was concerned about using the most appropriate terminology within the local context and settled on two different approaches. The term 'race' is used and constructed differently in different countries. Miles and Torres (1999), in their study, for example examine how the term is frequently used in conjunction with 'relations' in the UK and US context, whereas this construction was largely absent in academic discourses in France and Germany, thus reminding us of the historic and cultural dimensions of the term Knapp (2005). In Germany, I enquired whether a 'migration background' existed and asked for further details where appropriate. Equality and diversity questionnaires at the time were relatively unusual in Germany, which also reflects how analytical categories such as class and race are often culturally specific and understood differently across borders (Gutierrez Rodriguez, 1999). In the UK, I adopted the terminology frequently used by employers, which presents the respondents with a questionnaire that incorporates sixteen different categories.

Data collection and analysis took place simultaneously and informed one another following Corbin and Strauss' (2008) procedural guide to grounded theory techniques. This is referred to as theoretical sampling and, in conjunction with the concept of constant comparison (Glaser and Strauss, 1968; Suddaby, 2006), lies at the heart of the approach. Theoretical sampling is a 'cumulative' and 'concept-driven' process, and insights gained from early data collection impact on later data collection stages, which in return influence the analysis (Corbin and Straus, 2008: 144). This is repeated until 'conceptual saturation' is reached. There is, therefore, some flexibility in the data collection process to follow up conceptual leads arising from the data already gathered and analysed (Harry, Sturges, and Klingner, 2005). This may alter inclusion criteria as the study progresses, for example. Grounded theory has been subjected to feminist critiques of positivist understandings of objectivity (Hall and Callery, 2001; Olesen, 2007). Hall and Callery (2001), for example, note that some users of grounded theory 'treat interview and participant observation data as though they mirror informants' realities' (2001: 257), rather than treating it as subjective and context-dependent accounts and acknowledging that the researcher herself is an active producer of knowledge (Charmaz, 2006).

Given the qualitative nature of the project, the aim is not to generalize from the analysis of the women's experiences, but to 'produce' knowledge that can make a difference to women's lives and that is grounded in their daily experiences (Letherby, 2003). This is particularly relevant in workplace-related research where we too frequently treat men's experiences as if they were neutral and the default.

References

Abraham, M. (2016). 'Pay formalization revisited: considering the effects of manager gender and discretion on closing the gender wage gap'. *Academy of Management Journal 60*(1), 26–54.
Accountancy Daily. (2020). 'Ex Big Four staff chair majority of audit committees'.
Accounting Today. (2018). 'Firms need to protect themselves against potential harassment lawsuits'.
Acker, J. (1990). 'Hierarchies, jobs, bodies: a theory of gendered organizations'. *Gender & Society 4*(2), 139–158.
Acker, J. (1993). 'The gender regime of Swedish banks'. *Scandinavian Journal of Management 10*, 117–130.
Acker, J. (2006). 'Inequality regimes. Gender, class, and race in organizations'. Paper presented at the Sociologists for Women in Society Feminist Lecture.
Adamson, M. (2017). 'Postfeminism, neoliberalism and a "successfully" balanced femininity in celebrity CEO autobiographies'. *Gender, Work & Organization, 24*(3), 314–327.
Adamson, M., & Kelan, E. (2019). '"Female Heroes": celebrity executives as postfeminist role models'. *British Journal of Management, 30*(4), 981–996.
Adapa, S., Rindfleish, J., & Sheridan, A. (2016). '"Doing gender" in a regional context: explaining women's absence from senior roles in regional accounting firms in Australia'. *Critical Perspectives on Accounting, 35*, 100–110.
Adapa, S., & Sheridan, A. (2021). 'A case of multiple oppressions: women's career opportunities in Malaysian SME accounting firms'. *The International Journal of Human Resource Management, 32*(11), 2416–2442.
Albert, A. (2019). '2019 Election: Conservatives, Labour and Lib Dems locked in "free" childcare "arms race"'. https://www.daynurseries.co.uk/news/article.cfm/id/1618098/election-conservatives-labour-lib-dems-locked-in-free-childcare-arms-race.
Alvesson, M., & Billing, Y. D. (2009). *Understanding Gender and Organizations*. Second Edition. London: Sage.
Ames, D. R., & Flynn, F. J. (2007). 'What breaks a leader: the curvilinear relation between assertiveness and leadership'. *Journal of Personality and Social Psychology, 92*(2), 307.
Amis, J. M., Mair, J., & Munir, K. A. (2020). 'The organizational reproduction of inequality'. *Academy of Management Annals, 14*(1), 195–230.
Anand, R., & Winters, M.-F. (2008). 'A retrospective view of corporate diversity training from 1964 to the present'. *Academy of Management Learning & Education, 7*(3), 356–372.
Anderson, J. C., Johnson, E. N., & Reckers, P. M. (1994). 'Perceived effects of gender, family structure, and hysical appearance on career progression in public accounting: a research note'. *Accounting, Organizations and Society, 19*(6), 483–491.
Anderson, D., Vinnicombe, S., & Singh, V. (2010). 'Women partners leaving the firm: choice, what choice?' *Gender in Management: An International Journal, 25*(3), 170–183.
Anderson-Gough, F., Grey, C., & Robson, K. (2000). 'In the name of the client: the service ethic in two professional services firms'. *Human Relations, 53*(9), 1151–1174.
Anderson-Gough, F., Grey, C., & Robson, K. (2005). '"Helping them to forget.": the organizational embedding of gender relations in public audit firms'. *Accounting, Organizations and Society, 30*(5), 469–490.

References

Annisette, M. (2003). 'The colour of accountancy: examining the salience of race in a professionalisation project'. *Accounting, Organizations and Society, 28*(7-8), 639–674.

Annisette, M., & Neu, D. (2004). 'Accounting and empire: an introduction'. *Critical Perspectives on Accounting,* 15, 1–4.

Armitage, T. (2007). 'Merkel helps German mums shed "raven mother" tag'. *Reuters.* https://www.reuters.com/article/uk-germany-childcare-idUKL2758192720070307.

Arthur, M. B., & Rousseau, D. M. (Eds.). (1996). *The boundaryless career: A new employment principle for a new organizational era.* New York: Oxford University Press.

Babcock, L., Laschever, S., Gelfand, M., & Small, D. (2003). 'Nice girls don't ask'. *Harvard Business Review, 81*(10), 14–14.

Baker, D. T., & Brewis, D. N. (2020). 'The melancholic subject: a study of self-blame as a gendered and neoliberal psychic response to loss of the 'perfect worker'. *Accounting, Organizations and Society,* 82, 101093.

Banet-Weiser, S. (2018). *Empowered: popular feminism and popular misogyny.* Durham: Duke University Press.

Banet-Weiser, S., Gill, R., & Rottenberg, C. (2020). 'Postfeminism, popular feminism and neoliberal feminism? Sarah Banet-Weiser, Rosalind Gill and Catherine Rottenberg in conversation'. *Feminist theory, 21*(1), 3–24.

Bariola, N., & Collins, C. (2021). 'The gendered politics of pandemic relief: labor and family policies in Denmark, Germany, and the United States during COVID-19'. *American Behavioral Scientist, 65*(12), 1671–1697.

Barker, P. C., & Monks, K. (1998). 'Irish women accountants and career progression: a research note'. *Accounting, Organizations and Society, 23*(8), 813–823.

Barthold, J. A., Myrskylä, M., & Jones, O. R. (2012). 'Childlessness drives the sex difference in the association between income and reproductive success of modern Europeans'. *Evolution and Human Behavior, 33*(6), 628–638.

Batjargal, B. (2007). 'Comparative social capital: networks of entrepreneurs and venture capitalists in China and Russia'. *Management and Organization Review, 3*(3), 397–419.

Bauman, Z. (2000). *Liquid modernity* Cambridge: Polity.

Bauman, Z. (2002). 'Foreword', in U. Beck & E. Beck-Gernsheim (Eds.), *Individualization: institutionalized individualism and its social and political consequences,* p. x. London: Sage.

Bayefsky, M. J. (2020). 'Legal and ethical analysis of advertising for elective egg freezing'. *Journal of Law, Medicine & Ethics, 48*(4), 748–764.

Beattie, V. (2014). 'Accounting narratives and the narrative turn in accounting research: issues, theory, methodology, methods and a research framework'. *The British Accounting Review, 46*(2), 111–134.

Beck, T., & Kotz, H.-H. (2017). *Ordoliberalism: a German oddity?.* London: CEPR Press.

Beck, U., & Beck-Gernsheim, E. (Eds.) (2002). *Individualization: institutionalized individualism and its social and political consequences.* Vol. 13. London: Sage.

Bedard, J. (1989). 'Expertise in auditing: myth or reality'. *Accounting Organizations and Society, 14*(1/2), 113–131.

Béland, D., Cantillon, B., Hick, R., & Moreira, A. (2021). 'Social policy in the face of a global pandemic: policy responses to the COVID-19 crisis'. *Social Policy & Administration, 55*(2), 249–260.

Benschop, Y., & Meihuizen, H. E. (2002). 'Keeping up gendered appearances: representations of gender in financial annual reports'. *Accounting, Organizations and Society, 27*(7), 611–636.

Bertrand, M., & Hallock, K. F. (2001). 'The gender gap in top corporate jobs'. *ILR Review, 55*(1), 3–21.

Beynon, J. (1985). 'Institutional change and career histories in a comprehensive school', in S. J. Ball & I. F. Goodson (Eds.), *Teachers' Lives and Careers*, pp. 159–181. London: Taylor and Francis.

Bisiada, M. (2021). 'Movement or debate? How #MeToo is framed differently in English, Spanish and German Twitter discourse', in M. Bisiada (Ed.), *Empirical studies in translation and discourse*. Berlin: Language Science Press. https://library.oapen.org/bitstream/handle/20.500.12657/48441/external_content.pdf?sequence=1#page=125.

BMFSJ. (2018). 'Bericht über die Auswirkungen der Regelungen zum Elterngeld Plus und zum Partnerschaftsbonus sowie zur Elternzeit'. *Deutscher Bundestag*. https://www.bmfsfj.de/resource/blob/121264/6bfce747d8a948b19ddbeb73e4bfdaef/bericht-elterngeldplus-data.pdf.

BMFSJ. (2021a). 'Familienleistungen: Elternzeit'. https://www.bmfsfj.de/bmfsfj/themen/familie/familienleistungen/elternzeit/elternzeit-73832#:~:text=W%C3%A4hrend%20der%20Elternzeit%20d%C3%BCrfen%20Eltern,sondern%20auf%20den%20monatlichen%20Durchschnitt.

BMFSJ. (2021b). 'Familienleistungen: Elterngeld'. https://www.bmfsfj.de/bmfsfj/themen/familie/familienleistungen/elterngeld/elterngeld-73752?view=).

Bone, J. (2012). 'The deregulation ethic and the conscience of capitalism: how the neoliberal "free market" model undermines rationality and moral conduct'. *Globalizations, 9*(5), 651–665.

Bourdieu, P. (1990). *The logic of practice*. Redwood City: Stanford University Press.

Bowles, H. R., Babcock, L., & Lai, L. (2007). 'Social incentives for gender differences in the propensity to initiate negotiations: sometimes it does hurt to ask'. *Organizational Behavior and Human Decision Processes, 103*(1), 84–103.

Bradley, H., & Healy, G. (2008). *Ethnicity and gender at work: inequalities, careers and employment relations*. Basingstoke: Palgrave.

BRAK. (2019). 'Mitglieder 2019'. https://www.brak.de/fileadmin/04_fuer_journalisten/statistiken/2019/grosse-mitgliederstatistik_2019.pdf.

Broadbridge, A. (2010). 'Social capital, gender and careers: evidence from retail senior managers'. *Equality, Diversity and Inclusion: An International Journal 29*(8), 815–834.

Brown, J., & Dillard, J. (2015). 'Opening accounting to critical scrutiny: towards dialogic accounting for policy analysis and democracy'. *Journal of Comparative Policy Analysis: Research and Practice, 17*(3), 247–268.

Bryson, A., Joshi, H., Wielgoszewska, B., & Wilkinson, D. (2021). 'A short history of the gender wage gap in Britain'. *Oxford Review of Economic Policy, 36*(4), 836–854.

Bryson, L., Warner-Smith, P., Brown, P., & Fray, L. (2007). 'Managing the work–life rollercoaster: private stress or public health issue?' *Social Science & Medicine, 65*(6), 1142–1153.

Buchheit, S., Dalton, D. W., Harp, N. L., & Hollingsworth, C. W. (2016). 'A contemporary analysis of accounting professionals' work-life balance'. *Accounting Horizons, 30*(1), 41–62.

Bueskens, P. (2016). 'Matricentric feminism is a gift to the world'. *Matricentric Feminism: Theory, Activism, Practice*.

Bujaki, M. L., Durocher, S., Brouard, F., & Neilson, L. C. (2021). 'Conflicting accounts of inclusiveness in accounting firm recruitment website photographs'. *European Accounting Review, 30*(3), 473–501.

Bunting, M. (2020). *Labours of love: the crisis of care*. London: Granta Books.

Burke, R. J., & Richardsen, A. M. (2009). 'Work experiences, stress and health among managerial women: research and practice', in C. L. Cooper, J. C. Quick, & M. J. Schabracq (Eds.), *International Handbook of Work and Health Psychology*, pp. 147–170. Chichester: John Wiley.

References

Burt, R. S., Hogarth, R. M., & Michaud, C. (2000). 'The social capital of French and American managers'. *Organization Science, 11*(2), 123–261.

Burt, R. S. (1992). *Structural holes: the social structure of competition*. Cambridge: Harvard University Press.

Busch, A. (2005). 'Globalisation and national varieties of capitalism: the contested viability of the "German Model"'. *German Politics, 14*(2), 125–139.

Butler, J. (1990). 'Gender trouble, feminist theory, and psychoanalytic discourse'. *Feminism/postmodernism, 327*, 324–340.

Butler, J. (2004). *Undoing gender*. New York: Routledge.

Butterick, M., & Charlwood, A. (2021). 'HRM and the COVID-19 pandemic: how can we stop making a bad situation worse?' *Human Resource Management Journal, 31*(4), 847–856.

Canada, J., Kuhn, J. R., & Sutton, S. G. (2008). 'Accidentally in the public interest: the perfect storm that yielded the Sarbanes-Oxley act'. *Critical Perspectives on Accounting, 19*(7), 987–1003.

Care Collective (2020). *The care manifesto*. London: Verso.

Carli, L. L., & Eagly, A. H. (2007). 'Overcoming resistance to women leaders: the importance of leadership style', in Kellerman, B. and Rhode, D. L. (eds). *Women and leadership: the state of play and strategies for change* (127–148). Hoboken: Jossey-Bass.

Carmona, S., & Ezzamel, M. (2016). 'Accounting and lived experience in the gendered workplace'. *Accounting, Organizations and Society, 49*, 1–8.

Carter, C. A. S. H., 2014 (2004). 'Being a successful professional: an exploration of who makes partner in the Big 4'. *Contemporary Accounting Research, 31*(4), 949–981.

Castilla, E. J. (2008). 'Gender, race, and meritocracy in organizational careers'. *American Journal of Sociology, 113*(6), 1479–1526.

Castro, M. R., & Holvino, E. (2016). 'Applying intersectionality in organizations: inequality markers, cultural scripts and advancement practices in a professional service firm'. *Gender, Work & Organization, 23*(3), 328–347.

Chan, T. W., & Boliver, V. (2013). 'The grandparents' effect in social mobility: evidence from British birth cohort studies'. *American Sociological Review, 78*(4), 662–678.

Chapman, E., & Gubi, P. M. (2019). 'An exploration of the ways in which feelings of "maternal ambivalence" affect some women'. *Journal of Illness, Crisis & Loss 30*(2), 92–106.

Chapman, J. (2009). 'Not another bloody cop show: *Life on Mars* and British television drama'. *Film International, 7*(2), 6–19.

Charmaz, K. (2006). *Constructing grounded theory: a practical guide through qualitative analysis*. Thousand Oaks: Sage Publications.

Chen, W.-H., & Hou, F. (2019). 'The effect of unemployment on life satisfaction: a cross-national comparison between Canada, Germany, the United Kingdom and the United States'. *Applied Research in Quality of Life, 14*(4), 1035–1058.

Cheng, G. H.-L., & Chan, D. K.-S. (2008). 'Who suffers more from job insecurity? A meta-analytic review'. *Applied Psychology, 57*(2), 272–303.

Chung, H. (2022). *The flexibility paradox: why flexbiel working leads to (self-)exploitation*. Bristol: Bristol University Press.

Chia, Y. M. (2003). 'Career drivers of junior auditors: an exploratory study'. *Managerial Auditing Journal, 18*(2), 100–111.

Childs, M. (2018). 'Ernst & Young partner alleges sexual harassment at firm'. *Barrons*. https://www.barrons.com/articles/ernst-young-partner-alleges-sexual-harassment-at-firm-1524083557

Choi, J. H., Kim, J. B., Liu, X., & Simunic, D. A. (2008). 'Audit pricing, legal liability regimes, and Big 4 premiums: theory and cross-country evidence'. *Contemporary Accounting Research, 25*(1), 55–99.

Chua, W. F., & Poullaos, C. (1998). 'The dynamics of "closure" amidst the construction of market, profession, empire and nationhood: an historical analysis of an Australian accounting association, 1886–1903'. *Accounting, Organizations and Society, 23*(2), 155–187.

Chua, W. F., & Poullaos, C. (2002). 'The Empire Strikes Back? An exploration of centre–periphery interaction between the ICAEW and accounting associations in the self-governing colonies of Australia, Canada and South Africa, 1880–1907'. *Accounting, Organizations and Society, 27*(4-5), 409–445.

Chung, H., & Thewissen, S. (2011). 'Falling back on old habits? A comparison of the social and unemployment crisis reactive policy strategies in Germany, the UK and Sweden'. *Social Policy & Administration, 45*(4), 354–370.

Clark, G., & Cummins, N. (2015). 'Intergenerational wealth mobility in England, 1858–2012: surnames and social mobility'. *The Economic Journal, 125*(582), 61–86.

Coester, C. (2018). 'When German companies talk about "diversity", they only mean women. Adding women to executive boards does not a diversity-management strategy make. Handelsblatt. https://www.handelsblatt.com/today/opinion/vielfalt-when-german-companies-talk-about-diversity-they-only-mean-women/23582984.html

Collective, T. C. (2020). *The care manifesto*. London: Verso.

Collins, C., Landivar, L. C., Ruppanner, L., & Scarborough, W. J. (2020). 'COVID-19 and the gender gap in work hours'. *Gender, Work & Organization, 28*, 101–112.

Collinson, D., & Hearn, J. (1994). 'Naming men as men: implications for work, organization and management'. *Gender, Work & Organization, 1*(1), 2–22.

Collinson, M., & Collinson, D. (1996). '"It's only Dick": the sexual harassment of women managers in insurance sales'. *Work, Employment and Society, 10*(1), 29–56.

Corbin, J., & Strauss, A. (2008). *Basics of qualitative research: techniques and procedures for developing grounded theory*. Thousand Oaks: Sage Publications.

Cox, J. (2018). 'Black, Asian and minority ethnic groups still grossly underrepresented in UK management, study finds'. *The Independent*. https://www.independent.co.uk/news/business/news/black-asian-minority-ethnic-groups-bme-uk-management-diversity-study-a7846671.html

Crompton, R., & Lyonette, C. (2008a). 'Who does the housework? The division of labour within the home'. *British Social Attitudes, 24*, 53.

Crompton, R., & Lyonette, C. (2008b). 'Mothers' employment, work-life conflict, careers and class'. In Scott, J., Dex, S. and Joshi, H. (eds.). *Women and Employment: Changing Lives and New Challenges*, 213–233, Cheltenham: Edward Elgar.

Crompton, R., & Lyonette, C. (2011). 'Women's career success and work–life adaptations in the accountancy and medical professions in Britain'. *Gender, Work & Organization, 18*(2), 231–254.

Crompton, R., & Sanderson, K. (1990). *Gendered jobs and social change*. London: Routledge.

Dahl, R. A. (2005). *Who governs? Democracy and power in an American city*. New Haven: Yale University Press.

Dahlander, L., & McFarland, D. A. (2013). 'Ties that last: tie formation and persistence in research collaborations over time'. *Administrative Science Quarterly, 58*(1), 69–110.

Dalal, R. S., 2005. (2005). 'A meta-analysis of the relationship between organizational citizenship behavior and counterproductive work behavior'. *Journal of Applied Psychology, 90*(6), 12–41.

Dalton, D. W., Cohen, J. R., Harp, N. L., & McMillan, J. J. (2014). 'Antecedents and consequences of perceived gender discrimination in the audit profession'. *Auditing: A Journal of Practice & Theory, 33*(3), 1–32.

Dambrin, C., & Lambert, C. (2008). 'Mothering or auditing? The case of two Big Four in France'. *Accounting, Auditing and Accountability Journal, 21*(4), 474–506.

Dambrin, C., & Lambert, C. (2012). 'Who is she and who are we? A reflexive journey in research into the rarity of women in the highest ranks of accountancy'. *Critical Perspectives on Accounting, 23*(1), 1–16.

Dany, F., Mallon, M., & Arthur, M. (2003). 'The odyssey of career and the opportunity for international comparison'. *International Journal of Human Resource Management, 14*(5), 705–712.

de Celis, I. L.-R., de Bobadilla-Güémez, S. F., del Mar Alonso-Almeida, M., & Velasco-Balmaseda, E. (2017). 'Women's occupational health and safety management: an issue for corporate social responsibility'. *Safety Science, 91*, 61–70.

de Vries, M., Blomme, R., & De Loo, I. (2021). 'Part of the herd or black sheep? An exploration of trainee accountants' suffering and modes of adaptation'. *Critical Perspectives on Accounting 83*, 102353.

DeAngelo, L. E. (1981). 'Auditor size and audit quality'. *Journal of Accounting and Economics 3*, 183–199.

Debus, M. E., Probst, T. M., Koenig, C. J., & Kleinmann, M. (2012). 'Catch me if I fall! Enacted uncertainty avoidance and the social safety net as country-level moderators in the job insecurity–job attitudes link'. *Journal of Applied Psychology, 97*(3), 690–698.

Delbaere, I., Verbiest, S., & Tydén, T. (2020). 'Knowledge about the impact of age on fertility: a brief review'. *Upsala Journal of Medical Sciences, 125*(2), 167–174.

Deloitte. (2000). Women's Initiative Annual Report 2000. http://www.public.deloitte.com/wiar/2000/main.swf

Deloitte. (2008). Women's Initiative Annual Report 2007. http://www.deloitte.com/assets/Dcom-UnitedStates/Local%20Assets/Documents/us_win_2007annualreport082908opt.pdf

Deloitte (2015). Deloitte Impact Report. http://www.deloitte.co.uk/impact/uploads/downloads/Deloitte-Impact-Report-2015.pdf.

Dempsey, K. (2002). 'Who gets the best deal from marriage: women or men?' *Journal of Sociology 38*(2), 91–110.

Dienel, C. (2003). 'Die Mutter und ihr erstes Kind: individuelle und staatliche Arrangements im europäischen Vergleich'. *Zeitschrift für Familienforschung, 15*(2), 120–144.

Dietz, G., Gillespie, N., & Chao, G. T. (2010). 'Unravelling the complexities of trust and culture'. In Saunders, M., Skinner, D., Dietz, G., Gillespie, N. and Lewicki, R. (Eds.). *Organizational Trust: A Cultural Perspective*, 3–41, Cambridge: Cambridge University Press.

Dobbin, F., Schrage, D., & Kalev, A. (2015). 'Rage against the iron cage: the varied effects of bureaucratic personnel reforms on diversity'. *American Sociological Review, 80*(5), 1014–1044.

Dobbin, F, & Kalev, A. (2022). *Getting to diversity: what works and what doesn't*. Cambridge: Harvard University Press.

Dodin, M., Findeisen, S., Henkel, L., Sachs, D., & Schuele, P. (2021). Social Mobility in Germany. *CESifo Working Paper, 9200*.

Doralt, W. D., Hellgardt, W., A., et al. (2008). 'Auditors' liability and its impact on the European financial markets'. *Cambridge Law Journal, 67*(1), 62–88.

Doucet, A. (2006). '"Estrogen-filled worlds": fathers as primary caregivers and embodiment'. *The Sociological Review, 54*(4), 696–716.

Douglas, M. (1966). *Purity and danger: an analysis of the concepts of pollution and taboo*. London: Routledge.

Downar, B., Ernstberger, J., & Koch, C. (2021). 'Who makes partner in Big 4 audit firms?—Evidence from Germany. *Accounting, Organizations and Society, 91*, 101176.

Doyle, E., Frecknall-Hughes, J., & Summer, B. (2014). 'Ethics in tax practice: a study of the effect of practitioner firm size'. *Journal of Business Ethics, 122*, 623–641.

Duncan, C., & Loretto, W. (2004). 'Never the right age? Gender and age-based discrimination in employment'. *Gender, Work & Organization, 11*(1), 95–115.

Durocher, S., Bujaki, M., & Brouard, F. (2016). 'Attracting millennials: legitimacy management and bottom-up socialization processes within accounting firms'. *Critical Perspectives on Accounting, 39*, 1–24.

Dwyer, P. D., & Roberts, R. W. (2004). 'The contemporary gender agenda of the US public accounting profession: embracing feminism or maintaining empire?' *Critical Perspectives on Accounting, 15*(1), 159–177.

Eagly, A. H., & Carli, L. L. (2007). 'Women and the labyrinth of leadership'. *Harvard Business Review 85*(9), 62.

Eby, L. T., Butts, M., & Lockwood, A. (2003). 'Predictors of success in the era of the boundaryless career'. *Journal of Organizational Behavior, 24*(6), 689–708.

Edeh, N. A., Riley, S., & Kokot-Blamey, P. (2021). 'The production of difference and "becoming Black": the experiences of female Nigerian doctors and nurses working in the National Health Service'. *Gender, Work & Organization, 29*(2), 520–535.

Eden, T. (2021). 'Scottish Labour to launch manifesto with pledge to expand free childcare'. https://www.standard.co.uk/news/uk/scotland-holyrood-childcare-scottish-nhs-b931046.html

Edlund, J., & Öun, I. (2016). 'Who should work and who should care? Attitudes towards the desirable division of labour between mothers and fathers in five European countries'. *Acta Sociologica, 59*(2), 151–169.

Elvin-Nowak, Y. (1999). 'The meaning of guilt: a phenomenological description of employed mothers' experiences of guilt'. *Scandinavian Journal of Psychology, 40*(1), 73–83.

Ely, K. M. (1995). 'Operating lease accounting and the market's assessment of equity risk'. *Journal of Accounting Research, 33*(2), 397–415.

England, P. (1989). 'A feminist critique of rational-choice theories: implications for sociology'. *The American Sociologist, 20*(1), 14–28.

Esping-Andersen, G. (1990). *The three worlds of welfare capitalism*. Oxford: Polity Press.

Esping-Andersen, G. (2000). 'Multi-dimensional decommodification: a reply to Graham Room'. *Policy & Politics, 28*, 353–359.

Estevez-Abe, M. (2002). *Gendering the Varieties of Capitalism*. Paper presented at the Female Employment and Fertility Conference, Yale University.

Estevez-Abe, M. (2005). 'Gender bias in skills and social policies: the varieties of capitalism perspective on sex segregation'. *Social Politics 12*(2), 180–215.

Estevez-Abe, M., Iversen, T., & Soskice, D. W. (2001). 'Social protection and the formation of skills: a reinterpretation of the welfare state', in P. A. Hall & D. W. Soskice (Eds.), *Varieties of capitalism: the institutional foundations of comparative advantage*, pp. 145–183. Oxford: Oxford University Press.

Evans, C., & Rumens, N. (2020). 'Gender inequality and the professionalisation of accountancy in the UK from 1870 to the interwar years'. *Business History, 64*(7), 1–16.

EY. (2021). 'EY strengthens UK partnership with 103 new equity partners'. https://www.ey.com/en_uk/news/2021/07/ey-strengthens-uk-partnership-with-new-equity-partners#:~:text=In%202019%2C%20EY%20set%20ambitious,progress%20on%20diversity%20and%20inclusiveness.

Families, W. (2019). 'Modern families index 2019'. https://www.workingfamilies.org.uk/wp-content/uploads/2019/02/BH_MFI_Report_2019_Full-Report_Final.pdf.

Fernando, D. & Prasad, A. (2018). 'Sex-based harassment and silencing in academia: how people are led to reluctant acquiescence'. *Human Relations, 72*(10), 1565–1594.

Fineman, M. A. (2000). 'Contract and care'. *Chi.-Kent L. Rev., 76*, 1403.

Fineman, M. A. (2008). 'The vulnerable subject: anchoring equality in the human condition'. *Yale JL & Feminism, 20*, 1.
Fineman, M. A. (2017). 'Vulnerability and inevitable inequality'. *Oslo L. Rev., 4*, 133.
Fineman, M. A. (2020). 'Beyond equality and discrimination'. *SMU L. Rev. F., 73*, 51.
Fleetwood, S. (2007). 'Why work–life balance now?' *The International Journal of Human Resource Management, 18*(3), 387–400.
Foster, D. J., & Wass, V. J. (2011). 'The ideal worker and capitalist forms of production: Can employees with impairments ever achieve organisational fit?'
Foucault, M. (2010 [1979]). *The birth of biopolitics: lectures at the College de France*. Basingstoke: Palgrave Macmillan.
Fraser, N. (2009). 'Social justice in the age of identity politics'. *Geographic Thought: A Praxis Perspective, 72*, 91.
Fraser, N. (2013). *Fortunes of feminism: from state-managed capitalism to neoliberal crisis*. London: Verso Books.
Fraser, N. (2017). 'Progressive neoliberalism versus reactionary populism: a Hobson's choice', in H. Geiselberger (Ed.), *The great recession* (29–42). St Ives: Clays.
Fraser, N., & Gordon, L. (1994). 'A genealogy of dependency: tracing a keyword of the U.S. welfare state'. *Signs: Journal of Women in Culture and Society, 19*(2), 309.
FRC. (2005). 'Professional oversight board. Key facts and trends in the accountancy profession'. https://www.frc.org.uk/getattachment/62052bf3-6ede-4e59-8efc-a90c13349fd8/ACF18F5.pdf
FRC. (2014). 'Key facts and trends in the accountancy profession'. https://www.frc.org.uk/Our-Work/Publications/FRC-Board/Key-Facts-and-Trends-in-the-Accountancy-Profession.pdf.
FRC. (2021). 'Key facts and trends in the accountancy profession'. https://www.frc.org.uk/getattachment/669f6196-5a08-4a0b-aad3-b1915d4a6e4e/FRC-Key-Facts-Trends-2021.pdf.
FRC. (2022). 'Key facts and trends in the accountancy profession'. https://www.frc.org.uk/getattachment/e9fb0109-5f0f-4f7f-9dd9-4e9135e51e93/FRC-Key-Facts-and-Trends-in-the-Accountancy-Profession_August-2022.pdf.
Gallie, D., & Russell, H. (2009). 'Work-family conflict and working conditions in Western Europe'. *Social Indicators Research, 93*(3), 445–467.
Gammie, E., & Gammie, B. (2007). *Women of ICAS reaching the top: the demise of the glass ceiling*. Edinburgh: The Institute of Chartered Accountants of Scotland.
Ganesh, R., Mahapatra, S., Fuehrer, D. L., Folkert, L. J., Jack, W. A., Jenkins, S. M., & Sood, A. (2018). 'The stressed executive: sources and predictors of stress among participants in an executive health program'. *Global Advances in Health and Medicine, 7*: 1–9.
Gatrell, C., Cooper, C. L., & Kossek, E. E. (2017). 'Maternal bodies as taboo at work: new perspectives on the marginalizing of senior-level women in organizations'. *Academy of Management Perspectives, 31*(3), 239–252.
Gebreiter, F. (2021). 'A profession in peril? University corporatization, performance measurement and the sustainability of accounting academia'. *Critical Perspectives on Accounting, 87*: 1022921.
Geist, C. (2005). 'The welfare state and the home: regime difference in the domestic division of labour'. *European Sociological Review, 21*(1), 23–41.
Ghouri, F. (2021). 'Deloitte faces lawsuit by former employee over harassment claims. *City Am*. https://www.cityam.com/deloitte-faces-lawsuit-by-former-employee-over-harassment-claims/.
Gill, M. (2009). *Accountants' truth*. Oxford: Oxford University Press.

References

Gill, R. (2007). 'Postfeminist media culture: elements of a sensibility'. *European Journal of Cultural Studies, 10*(2), 147–166.

Gill, R., K. Kelan, E., & M. Scharff, C. (2017). 'A postfeminist sensibility at work'. *Gender, Work & Organization, 24*(3), 226–244.

Gill, R., & Orgad, S. (2017). 'Confidence culture and the remaking of feminism'. *New Formations, 91*(91), 16–34.

Gill, R., & Scharff, C. (eds) (2011). *New femininities: postfeminism, neoliberalism, and subjectivity*. London: Palgrave Macmillan.

Gilman, C. P. (1903). *The home: its work and influence*. Walnut Creek: Rowman Altamira.

Gilman, C. P. (2020). *Women and economics*. Oakland: University of California Press.

Glaser, B., & Strauss, A. (1968). *The discovery of grounded theory: strategies for qualitative research*. London: Weidenfeld and Nicolson.

Glick, P., & Fiske, S. T. (1996). 'The ambivalent sexism inventory: differentiating hostile and benevolent sexism'. *Journal of Personality and Social Psychology, 70*(3), 491–512.

Goetz Jr, J. F., Morrow, P. C., & McElroy, J. C. (1991). 'The effect of accounting firm size and member rank on professionalism'. *Accounting, Organizations and Society, 16*(2), 159–165.

Goldin, C., & Rouse, C. (2000). 'Orchestrating impartiality: the impact of "blind" auditions on female musicians'. *American Economic Review, 90*(4), 715–741.

Gould, A., Barry, M. & Wilkinson, A., (2015). 'Varieties of capitalism revisited: current debates and possible directions/Les varietes du capitalisme revisitees: debats actuels et avenues possibles'. *Relations Industrielles/Industrial Relations, 70*(4), 587–620.

Government Equalities Office (2021). '2020 Sexual Harassment Survey'. https://assets.publishing.service.gov.uk/government/uploads/system/uploads/attachment_data/file/1002873/2021-07-12_Sexual_Harassment_Report_FINAL.pdf.

Granleese, J., & Sayer, G. (2006). 'Gendered ageism and "lookism": a triple jeopardy for female academics. *Women in Management Review, 21*(6), 500–517.

Granovetter, M. (1973). 'The strength of weak ties'. *American Journal of Sociology, 78*, 1360–1380.

Granovetter, M. (1974). *Getting a job: a study of contacts and careers*. Chicago: University of Chicago Press.

Grosser, K., & Tyler, M. (2021). 'Sexual harassment, sexual violence and CSR: radical feminist theory and a human rights perspective'. *Journal of Business Ethics, 177*(2), 217-232.

Gruner, S. (2010). 'The others don't want …' small-scale segregation: hegemonic public discourses and racial boundaries in German neighbourhoods'. Journal of Ethnic and Migration Studies. 36(2), 275–292.

Gutierrez Rodriguez, E. (1999). *Intellektuelle Migrantinnen—Subjektivitaeten im Zeitalter von Globalisierung*. Opladen, Leske und Budrich

Hall, P. A., & Soskice, D. W. (2001). *Varieties of capitalism: the institutional foundations of comparative advantage*. Oxford: Oxford University Press.

Hall, W. A., & Callery, P. (2001). 'Enhancing the rigor of grounded theory: incorporating reflexivity and relationality'. *Qualitative Health Research, 11*(2), 257–272.

Hancké, B., Rhodes, M., & Thatcher, M. (2007). *Beyond varieties of capitalism: conflict, contradictions, and complementarities in the EuropeaneEconomy*. Oxford: Oxford University Press.

Hantrais, L. (1995). 'A comparative perspective on gender and accountancy'. *European Accounting Review, 4*(2), 197–215.

Harper, J., Boivin, J., O'Neill, H., Brian, K., Dhingra, J., Dugdale, G., Balen, A. (2017). 'The need to improve fertility awareness'. *Reproductive Biomedicine & Society Online, 4*, 18–20.

Harry, B., Sturges, K., & Klingner, J. (2005). 'Mapping the process: an exemplar of process and challenge in grounded theory analysis'. *Educational Researcher, 34*(2), 3–13.

References

Harvey, D. (2007). *A brief history of neoliberalism*. Oxford: Oxford University Press.

Hattrup, K., Ghorpade, J., & Lackritz, J. R. (2007). 'Work group collectivism and the centrality of work a multinational investigation'. *Cross-Cultural Research, 41*(3), 236–260.

Hayes, N., Introna, L. D., & Kelly, P. (2018). 'Institutionalizing inequality: calculative practices and regimes of inequality in international development'. *Organization Studies, 39*(9), 1203–1226.

Haynes, K. (2008a). 'Moving the gender agenda or stirring chicken's entrails?' *Accounting, Auditing and Accountability Journal, 21*(4), 539–555.

Haynes, K. (2008b). '(Re) figuring accounting and maternal bodies: the gendered embodiment of accounting professionals'. *Accounting, Organizations and Society, 33*(4–5), 328–348.

Haynes, K. (2008c). 'Transforming identities: accounting professionals and the transition to motherhood'. *Critical Perspectives on Accounting, 19*(5), 620–642.

Haynes, K. (2017). 'Accounting as gendering and gendered: a review of 25 years of critical accounting research on gender'. *Critical Perspectives on Accounting, 43*, 110–124.

Hays, S. (1998). *The cultural contradictions of motherhood*. New Haven: Yale University Press.

Healy, G. (1999). 'Structuring commitments in interrupted careers: career breaks, commitment and the life cycle in teaching'. *Gender, Work & Organization, 6*(4), 185–201.

Healy, G., & Ahamed, M. M. (2019). 'Gender pay gap, voluntary interventions and recession: the case of the British financial services sector'. *British Journal of Industrial Relations, 57*(2), 302–327.

Heilman, M. E. (2012). 'Gender stereotypes and workplace bias'. *Research in Organizational Behavior, 32*, 113–135.

Heilman, M. E., Wallen, A. S., Fuchs, D., & Tamkins, M. M. (2004). 'Penalties for success: reactions to women who succeed at male gender-typed tasks'. *Journal of Applied Psychology, 89*(3), 416.

Henry, M. G. (2003). '"Where are you really from?": representation, identity and power in the fieldwork experiences of a South Asian diasporic'. *Qualitative Research, 3*(2), 229–242.

Hertel, F. R., & Groh-Samberg, O. (2014). 'Class mobility across three generations in the US and Germany'. *Research in Social Stratification and Mobility, 35*, 35–52.

Highhouse, S., Zickar, M. J., & Yankelevich, M. (2010). 'Would you work if you won the lottery? Tracking changes in the American work ethic'. *Journal of Applied Psychology, 95*(2), 349.

Hines, R. D. (1988). 'Financial accounting: in communicating reality, we construct reality'. *Accounting, Organizations and Society, 13*(3), 251–261.

Hochschild, A., & Machung, A. (1989). *Working parents and the revolution at home*. New York: Viking.

Hochschild, A. R. (2003). *The commercialization of intimate life: notes from home and work*. San Francisco and Los Angeles: University of California Press.

Hochschild, A. R. (2012). *The outsourced self: intimate life in market times*. New York: Metropolitan Press.

Hofstede, G. (2001). *Culture's consequences: comparing values, behaviors, institutions and organizations across nations*. Thousand Oaks: Sage Publications.

Holck, L., 2018. 'Unequal by structure: exploring the structural embeddedness of organizational diversity'. *Organization, 25*(2), 242–259.

Holgersson, C. (2013). 'Recruiting managing directors: doing homosociality'. *Gender, Work & Organization, 20*(4), 454–466.

Holt, D. T., Markova, G., Dhaenens, A. J., Marler, L. E., & Heilmann, S. G. (2016). 'Formal or informal mentoring: what drives employees to seek informal mentors?' *Journal of Managerial Issues, 28*(1–2), 67–82.

Hopkins, A. (2005). 'Pricewaterhouse v. Hopkins: a personal account of a sexual discrimination plaintiff'. *Hofstra Labor & Employment Law Journal, 22*, 357–416.

Hudson, M., Netto, G., Noon, M., Sosenko, F., De Lima, P., & Kamenou-Aigbekaen, N. (2017). 'Ethnicity and low wage traps: favouritism, homosocial reproduction and economic marginalization'. *Work, Employment and Society*, 31(6), 992–1009.

Ibarra, H. (1992). 'Homophily and differential returns: sex differences in network structure and access in an advertising firm'. *Administrative Science Quarterly*, 37(3), 422–447.

ICAEW. (2015). 'Timeline 1914–1938'. https://www.icaew.com/library/historical-resources/timeline/1914-1938

ICAEW. (2021). 'Fifth of FTSE 100 CEOs are accountants'. https://www.icaew.com/insights/features/archive/fifth-of-ftse-100-ceos-are-accountants

IAEW. (2023). *Credit Suisse: unpacking the fallout.* https://www.icaew.com/insights/viewpoints-on-the-news/2023/mar-2023/credit-suisse-unpacking-the-fallout.

IFRS. (2022). 'About the International Accounting Standards Board (Board)'. https://www.ifrs.org/groups/international-accounting-standards-board/

Jacobs, K. (2003). 'Class reproduction in professional recruitment: examining the accounting profession'. *Critical Perspectives on Accounting*, 14(5), 569–596.

Jeacle, I. (2008). 'Beyond the boring grey: the construction of the colourful accountant'. *Critical Perspectives on Accounting*, 19(8), 1296–1320.

Jensen, T. (2014). 'Mothers and the academy'. *Feminist Theory*, 15(3), 345–351.

Jeny, A., & Santacreu-Vasut, E. (2017). 'New avenues of research to explain the rarity of females at the top of the accountancy profession'. *Palgrave Communications*, 3(1), 1–10.

Jeremiah, E. (2006). 'Motherhood to mothering and beyond: maternity in recent feminist thought'. *Journal of the Motherhood Initiative for Research and Community Involvement*, 8(1), 21–33.

Jiang, L., & Johnson, M. J. (2017). 'Meaningful work and affective commitment: a moderated mediation model of positive work reflection and work centrality'. *Journal of Business and Psychology*, 33, 545–558.

Jiang, L., & Lavaysse, L. M. (2018). 'Cognitive and affective job insecurity: a meta-analysis and a primary study'. *Journal of Management*, 44(6), 2307–2342.

Johnson, E. N., Lowe, D. J., & Reckers, P. M. (2008). 'Alternative work arrangements and perceived career success: current evidence from the big four firms in the US'. *Accounting, Organizations and Society*, 33(1), 48–72.

Johnston, D. D., & Swanson, D. H. (2006). 'Constructing the "good mother": the experience of mothering ideologies by work status'. *Sex Roles*, 54(7), 509–519.

Joshi, A., Son, J., & Roh, H. (2015). 'When can women close the gap? A meta-analytic test of sex differences in performance and rewards'. *Academy of Management Journal*, 58(5), 1516–1545.

Kalleberg, A. L. (2018). *Precarious lives: job insecurity and well-being in rich democracies.* Hoboken: John Wiley & Sons.

Kamla, R. (2012). 'Syrian women accountants' attitudes and experiences at work in the context of globalization'. *Accounting, Organizations and Society*, 37(3), 188–205.

Kanter, R. M. (1977). *Men and women of the corporation.* New York: Basic Books.

Kattenbach, R., Schneidhofer, T. M., Lücke, L. M., Loacker, B., Schramm, F., & Mayrhofer, W. (2014). 'A quarter of a century of job transitions in Germany'. *Journal of Vocational Behavior*, 84(1), 49–58.

Kelan, E. (2009a). *Performing gender at work.* Basingstoke: Palgrave Macmillan.

Kelan, E. K. (2009b). 'Gender fatigue: the ideological dilemma of gender neutrality and discrimination in organizations'. *Canadian Journal of Administrative Sciences/Revue Canadienne des Sciences de l'Administration*, 26(3), 197–210.

Kellermann, K. L. (2021). *Trust we lost: The Treuhand experience and political behavior in the former German Democratic Republic.* Paper presented at the CIW Discussion Paper,

No. 3/2021, Westfälische Wilhelms-Universität Münster, Centrum für Interdisziplinäre Wirtschaftsforschung (CIW), Münster.

Khalifa, R. (2013). 'Intra-professional hierarchies: the gendering of accounting specialisms in UK accountancy'. *Accounting, Auditing & Accountability Journal, 26*(8), 1212– 1245.

Kidder, D. L. (2002). 'The influence of gender on the performance of organizational citizenship behaviors'. *Journal of Management, 28*(5), 629–648.

Kilkey, M., & Perrons, D. (2010). 'Gendered divisions in domestic work time: the rise of the (migrant) handyman phenomenon'. *Time & Society, 19*(2), 239–264.

Kim, N., You, J., & Lee, E. (2022). 'Varying importance of the work-life balance dimension of career success for Korean accountants: the effects of gender and generation'. *SHS Web of Conferences. Part of a study conducted on request of the Korean Institute of Certified Public Accountants.* https://www.shs-conferences.org/articles/shsconf/pdf/2022/02/shsconf_ies2021_01002.pdf.

Kim, S. N. (2004). 'Imperialism without empire: silence in contemporary accounting research on race/ethnicity'. *Critical Perspectives on Accounting, 15*(1), 95–133.

Kirkham, L. M. (1992). 'Integrating herstory and history in accountancy'. *Accounting, Organizations and Society, 17*(3-4), 287–297.

Kirkham, L. M., & Loft, A. (1993). 'Gender and the construction of the professional accountant'. *Accounting, Organizations and Society, 18*(6), 507–558.

Kirton, G., & Green, A.-M. (2005). 'Gender, equality and industrial relations in the "New Europe": an introduction'. *European Journal of Industrial Relations, 11*(2), 141–149.

Kirton, G., & Robertson, M. (2018). 'Sustaining and advancing IT careers: women's experiences in a UK-based IT company'. *The Journal of Strategic Information Systems, 27*(2), 157–169.

Kittay, E. F. (1999). *Love's labor: essays on women, equality and dependency.* New York: Routledge.

Kittay, E. F. (2011). 'The ethics of care, dependence, and disability'. *Ratio Juris, 24*(1), 49–58.

Klasen, O. (2014). 'Wo kommst du her? "Nachbohren geht in Richtung Rassismus"', Sueddeutsche Zeitung. https://www.sueddeutsche.de/leben/wo-kommst-du-her-nachbohren-geht-in-richtung-rassismus-1.2217486

Knapp, G.-A. (2005). 'Intersectionality–ein neues Paradigma feministischer Theorie? Zur transatlantischen Reise von Race, Class, Gender'. *Feministische Studien, 23*(1), 68–81.

Kokot, P. (2014). 'Structures and relationships: women partners' careers in Germany and the UK'. *Accounting, Auditing & Accountability Journal, 27*(1), 48–72.

Kokot, P. (2015). 'Let's talk about sex(ism): cross-national perspectives on women partners' narratives on equality and sexism at work in Germany and the UK'. *Critical Perspectives on Accounting, 27,* 73–85.

Kokot-Blamey, P. (2021). 'Mothering in Accounting: feminism, motherhood, and making partnership in accountancy in Germany and the UK. *Accounting, Organizations and Society, 93,* 101255.

Konrad, A. M., Kramer, V., & Erkut, S. (2008). 'Critical mass: the impact of three or more women on corporate boards'. *Organizational Dynamics, 37*(2), 145–164.

Kornberger, M., Carter, C., & Ross-Smith, A. (2010). 'Changing gender domination in a Big Four accounting firm: flexibility, performance and client service in practice'. *Accounting, Organizations and Society, 35*(8), 775–791.

Kornberger, M., Justesen, L., & Mouritsen, J. (2011). '"When you make manager, we put a big mountain in front of you": an ethnography of managers in a Big 4 accounting firm. *Accounting, Organizations and Society, 36*(8), 514–533.

Kulich, C., Trojanowski, G., Ryan, M. K., Alexander Haslam, S., & Renneboog, L. D. (2011). 'Who gets the carrot and who gets the stick? Evidence of gender disparities in executive remuneration'. *Strategic Management Journal*, *32*(3), 301–321.

Kumra, S., & Vinnicombe, S. (2008). 'A study of the promotion to partner process in a professional services firm: how women are disadvantaged'. *British Journal of Management*, *19*, S65–S74.

Kyriakidou, O., Kyriacou, O., Özbilgin, M., & Dedoulis, E. (2016). 'Equality, diversity and inclusion in accounting'. *Critical Perspectives on Accounting*, *35*, 1–12.

Lamont, M., & Lareau, A. (1988). 'Cultural capital: allusions, gaps and glissandos in recent theoretical developments'. *Sociological Theory*, *6*(2), 153–168.

Leahy, M., & Doughney, J. (2006). 'Women, work and preference formation: a critique of Catherine Hakim's preference theory'. *Journal of Business Systems, Governance and Ethics*, *1*(1), 37–48.

Leddy-Owen, C. (2014). 'Reimagining Englishness: "Race", class, progressive English identities and disrupted English communities'. *Sociology*, *48*(6), 1123–1138.

Lee, T. (1995). 'The professionalization of accountancy: a history of protecting the public interest in a self-interested way'. *Accounting, Auditing & Accountability Journal*, *8*(4), 48–69.

Lehman, C. R. (1992). '"Herstory" in accounting: the first eighty years'. *Accounting, Organizations and Society*, *17*(3–4), 261–285.

Letherby, G. (2003). *Feminist research in theory and practice*. Buckingham: Open University Press.

Lewis, P., Benschop, Y., & Simpson, R. (2017a). 'Postfeminism, gender and organization'. *Gender, Work and Organization*, *24*(3), 213–225.

Lewis, P., Benschop, Y., & Simpson, R. (2017b). 'Postfeminism: negotiating equality with tradition in contemporary organisations', in Lewis, Patricia and Benschop, Yvonne and Simpson, Ruth, eds., *Postfeminism and organization* (3–18). Abingdon: Routledge.

Lewis, S. (2001). 'Restructuring workplace cultures: the ultimate work-family challenge?' *Women in Management Review* *16*(1), 21– 29.

Lief Cabaser. (2021). KPMG Agrees to $10M Deal to End 10-Year Gender Discrimination Suit

Lightbody, M. G. (2009). 'Turnover decisions of women accountants: using personal histories to understand the relative influence of domestic obligations'. *Accounting History*, *14*(1–2), 55–78.

Lincoln, J. R., & Miller, J. (1979). 'Work and friendship ties in organizations: a comparative analysis of relation networks'. *Administrative Science Quarterly*, *24*(2), 181–199.

Lipman-Blumen, J. (1976). 'Toward a homosocial theory of sex roles: an explanation of the sex segregation of social institutions'. *Signs: Journal of Women in Culture and Society*, *1*(3, Part 2), 15–31.

Little, B., & Tang, W.-Y. (2008). 'Age differences in graduate employment across Europe'. http://oro.open.ac.uk/10753/1/reflex_report_5.pdf: Higher Education Funding Coucil for England.

Littler, J., & McRobbie, A. (2021). 'Beyond anti-welfarism and feminist social media mudslinging: Jo Littler interviews Angela McRobbie'. *European Journal of Cultural Studies*, *25*(1), 327–334.

Loeb, S. E. (1971). 'A survey of ethical behavior in the accounting profession'. *Journal of Accounting Research*, *9*(2), 287–306.

Loft, A. (1992). 'Accountancy and the gendered division of labour: a review essay'. *Accounting, Organizations and Society*, *17*(3–4), 367–378.

Low, M., Davey, H., & Hooper, K. (2008). 'Accounting scandals, ethical dilemmas and educational challenges'. *Critical Perspectives on Accounting, 19*(2), 222–254.

Lowinsky, N. R. (1992). *Stories from the motherline: reclaiming the mother-daughter bond, finding our feminine souls*. Los Angeles: Tarcher.

Lowy, M. (2021). *The maternal experience: encounters with ambivalence and love*. Abingdon: Routledge.

Lupu, I. (2012). 'Approved routes and alternative paths: the construction of women's careers in large accounting firms. Evidence from the French Big Four'. *Critical Perspectives on Accounting, 23*(4–5), 351–369.

Lupu, I. (2013). *Contradictory Discourses and the Identity Work of Mother Managers in the Accounting Profession*. Unpublished working paper

Lupu, I., & Castro, M. R. (2021). 'Work-life balance is a cycle, not an achievement'. *Harvard Business Review*. https://hbr.org/2021/01/work-life-balance-is-a-cycle-not-an-achievement.

Lupu, I., Spence, C., & Empson, L. (2018). 'When the past comes back to haunt you: the enduring influence of upbringing on the work–family decisions of professional parents'. *Human Relations, 71*(2), 155–181.

Lutter, M. (2015). 'Do women suffer from network closure? The moderating effect of social capital on gender inequality in a project-based labor market, 1929 to 2010'. *American Sociological Review, 80*(2), 329–358.

Lyness, K. S., & Heilman, M. E. (2006). 'When fit is fundamental: performance evaluations and promotions of upper-level female and male managers'. *Journal of Applied Psychology, 91*(4), 777.

Macdonald, K. M. (1984). 'Professional formation: the case of scottish accountants'. *The British Journal of Sociology, 35*(2), 174–189.

Mandel, H., & Shalev, M. (2009). 'Gender, class and varieties of capitalism'. *Social Politics, 16*(2), 161–181.

Manning, A., & Mazeine, G. (2020). *Subjective job insecurity and the rise of the precariat: evidence from the UK*. Germany and the United States: CEP Discussion Papers dp1712, Centre for Economic Performance, LSE.

Markus, H. B. (1996). *Der Wirtschaftsprüfer: Entstehung und Entwicklung des Berufes im nationalen und internationalen Bereich*. Munich: Verlag C.H. Beck.

Markus, H. B. (2021). *The history of the German public accounting profession*. London: Routledge.

Marriage, M. (2019). 'Betrayed by the Big Four: whistleblowers speak out'. *Financial Times*. https://www.ft.com/content/78f46a4e-0a5c-11ea-bb52-34c8d9dc6d84

Martin, P. Y. (2006). 'Practicing gender at work: further thoughts on reflexivity'. *Gender, Work and Organization, 13*(3), 254–276.

Marx, K. (1844). 'Estranged Labour', in J. Gingell, A. Little, & C. Winch (Eds.), *Modern political thought: a reader*, 248– 289. London: Routledge.

McCall, L., & Orloff, A. S. (2005). 'Introduction to special issue of social politics: "gender, class, and capitalism"'. *Social Politics: International Studies in Gender, State and Society, 12*(2), 159–169.

McCormick, I. A., & Cooper, C. L. (1988). 'Executive stress: extending the international comparison'. *Human Relations, 41*(1), 65–72.

McDowell, L. (1997). *Capital culture: gender at work in the city*. Vol. 21. Oxford: Blackwell.

McDowell, L. (2010). 'Capital culture revisited: sex, testosterone and the city'. *International Journal of Urban and Regional Research, 34*(3), 652–658.

McDowell, L., Ray, K., Perrons, D., Fagan, C., & Ward, K. (2005). 'Women's paid work and moral economies of care'. *Social & Cultural Geography, 6*(2), 2019–2235.

McKinley, S., Pany, K., & Reckers, P. M. (1985). 'An examination of the influence of CPA firm type, size, and MAS provision on loan officer decisions and perceptions'. *Journal of Accounting Research, 23*(2), 887–896.

McManus, L., & Subramaniam, N. (2009). 'Ethical evaluations and behavioural intentions of early career accountants: the impact of mentors, peers and individual attributes'. *Accounting & Finance, 49*(3), 619–643.

McNicholas, P., Humphries, M., & Gallhofer, S. (2004). 'Maintaining the empire: Maori women's experiences in the accountancy profession'. *Critical Perspectives on Accounting, 15*(1), 57–93.

McPherson, M., Smith-Lovin, L. and Cook, J.M. (2001). 'Birds of a feather: homophily in social networks'. *Annual Review of Sociology, 27*(1), 415–444.

McRobbie, A. (2004). 'Post-feminism and popular culture'. *Feminist Media Studies, 4*(3), 255–264.

McRobbie, A. (2005). *The uses of cultural studies: a textbook*: Thousand Oaks: Sage.

McRobbie, A. (2007). 'Top girls? young women and the post-feminist sexual contract'. *Cultural Studies, 21*(4–5).

McRobbie, A. (2020). *Feminism and the politics of resilience: essays on gender, media and the end of welfare*. Cambridge: Polity Press.

Mehreen, A., Hui, Y., & Ali, Z. (2019). 'A social network theory perspective on how social ties influence perceived employability and job insecurity: evidence from school teachers'. *Social Network Analysis and Mining, 9*(25): 17.

Meisenbach, R. J. (2010). 'The female breadwinner: phenomenological experience and gendered identity in work/family spaces'. *Sex Roles, 62*(1), 2–19.

Meissner, C., Schippert, C., & von Versen-Höynck, F. (2016). 'Awareness, knowledge, and perceptions of infertility, fertility assessment, and assisted reproductive technologies in the era of oocyte freezing among female and male university students'. *Journal of Assisted Reproduction and Genetics, 33*(6), 719–729.

Merriam-Webster. (2022). https://www.merriam-webster.com/dictionary/perverse.

Meuwissen, R., & Quick, R. (2019). 'The effects of non-audit services on auditor independence: an experimental investigation of supervisory board members' perceptions'. *Journal of International Accounting, Auditing and Taxation, 36.* 100264.

Meyer, C. (2021). 'Skandale und Interessenkonflikte: Die Krux mit den Wirtschaftsprüfern'. https://www.zdf.de/nachrichten/wirtschaft/wirecard-wirtschaftspruefung-big-four-100.html

Miles, R., & Torres, R. (1999). 'Does "race" matter? Transatlantic perspectives on racism and "race relations"', in L. Torres, F. Miron & J. Inda (Eds.), *Race, identity, and citizenship: a reader,* 19–38. Malden: Blackwell.

Molina, O., & Rhodes, M. (2007). 'The political economy of adjustment in mixed market economies: a study of Spain and Italy', in B. Hancké, M. Rhodes & M. Thatcher (Eds.), *Beyond varieties of capitalism: conflict, contradictions, and complementarities in the European economy,* 223–252. Oxford: Oxford University Press.

Moore, S. (2009). '"No matter what I did I would still end up in the same position": age as a factor defining older women's experience of labour market participation'. *Work, Employment and Society, 23*(4), 655–671.

Morgan, L. A., & Martin, K. A. (2006). 'Taking women professionals out of the office: the case of women in sales'. *Gender & Society, 20*(1), 108–128.

Morse, N. C., & Weiss, R. S. (1955). 'The function and meaning of work and the job'. *American Sociological Review, 20*(2), 191–198.

Moyer, S. (2019). 'The top UK accounting scandals of 2019'. https://www.accountancyage.com/2019/12/09/the-top-uk-accounting-scandals-of-2019/

Nelson, D. L., & Burke, R. J. (2002). 'Women executives: health, stress, and success'. *Academy of Management Perspectives, 14*(2), 107–121.

Netto, G., Noon, M., Hudson, M., Kamenou-Aigbekaen, N., & Sosenko, F. (2020). 'Intersectionality, identity work and migrant progression from low-paid work: a critical realist approach'. *Gender, Work & Organization, 27*(6), 1020–1039.

Neu, D. (1999). '"Discovering" indigenous peoples: accounting and the machinery of empire'. *Accounting Historians Journal, 26*(1), 53–82.

Neumann, C., & von Hammerstein, K. (2008). 'Ich will einen starken Staat'. *Der Spiegel,* 42.

Nichols, D., Robinson, R. K., Reithel, B. J., & Franklin, G. M. (1997). 'An exploratory study of sexual behavior in accounting firms: do male and female CPAs interpret sexual harrassment differently?' *Critical Perspectives on Accounting, 8*(3), 249–264.

Noon, M. (2018). 'Pointless diversity training: unconscious bias, new racism and agency'. *Work, Employment and Society, 32*(1), 198–209.

Nussbaum, M., & Sen, A. (1993). *The quality of life.* Oxford: Oxford University Press.

OECD (2014. 'At what age do university students earn their first degree?' Education Indicators in Focus. https://www.oecd.org/education/skills-beyond-school/EDIF_23%20eng%20(2014)EN.pdf.

O'Reilly, A. (2016). *Matricentric feminism: theory, activism, and practice.* York, Canada: Demeter Press.

O'Reilly, A. (2016b). 'We need to talk about patriarchal motherhood: essentialization, naturalization and idealization in Lionel Shriver's *We Need to Talk about Kevin*'. *Journal of the Motherhood Initiative for Research and Community Involvement, 7*(1), 64–81.

Oakley, A. (1981). *From here to maternity: becoming a mother.* Harmondsworth: Penguin.

Offen, K. (1988). 'Defining feminism: a comparative historical approach'. *Signs: Journal of Women in Culture and Society, 14*(1), 119–157.

Ogharanduku, B. E., Jackson, W. J., & Paterson, A. S. (2021). 'Beautiful SWAN, or ugly duckling? The attempt to reduce gender inequality by the Society of Women Accountants of Nigeria'. *Critical Perspectives on Accounting, 79*, 102245.

Oksala, J. (2013). 'Feminism and neoliberal governmentality'. *Foucault Studies,* 16, 32–53.

Olesen, V. L. (2007). 'Feminist qualitative research and grounded theory: complexities, criticisms, and opportunities', in A. Bryant & K. Charmaz (Eds.), *The Sage Handbook of Grounded Theory,* 417. Thousand Oaks: Sage Publications.

ONS. (2016). 'Women shoulder the responsibility of "unpaid work"'. https://www.ons.gov.uk/employmentandlabourmarket/peopleinwork/earningsandworkinghours/articles/womenshouldertheresponsibilityofunpaidwork/2016-11-10.

ONS. (2019). 'Domestic abuse victim characteristics, England and Wales, year ending March 2019'. https://www.ons.gov.uk/peoplepopulationandcommunity/crimeandjustice/articles/domesticabusevictimcharacteristicsenglandandwales/yearendingmarch2019.

ONS. (2020). 'Parenting in lockdown: Coronavirus and the effects on work-life balance'. https://www.ons.gov.uk/peoplepopulationandcommunity/healthandsocialcare/conditionsanddiseases/articles/parentinginlockdowncoronavirusandtheeffectsonworklifebalance/2020-07-22.

Orgad, S. (2019). *Heading home: motherhood, word, and the failed promise of equality.* New York: Columbia.

Orgad, S., & De Benedictis, S. (2015). 'The "stay-at-home" mother, postfeminism and neoliberalism: content analysis of UK news coverage'. *European Journal of Communication, 30*(4), 418–436.

Orgad, S., & Gill, R. (2021). *Confidence culture.* Durham: Duke University Press.

Orloff, A. (1996). 'Gender in the welfare state'. *Annual Review of Sociology, 22*, 51–78.

Orloff, A. S. (1993). 'Gender and the social rights of citizenship: the comparative analysis of gender relations and welfare states'. *American Sociological Review*, 58(3), 303–328.
Orloff, A. S. (2006). 'From maternalism to "employment for all": state policies to promote women's employment across the affluent democracies', in Jonah, L. (Ed.) (2006) *The state after statism: new state activities in the era of globalization and liberalization*, pp. 230–268. Cambridge: Harvard University Press.
Orloff, A. S. (2009). 'Gendering the comparative analysis of welfare states: an unfinished agenda'. *Sociological Theory*, 27(3), 317–343.
Orloff, A. S. (2011). 'Policy, politics, gender. Bringing gender to the analysis of welfare states'. *Sociologica, January-April*(1), 1–20.
Osman, M. (2021). 'UK public understanding of unconscious bias and unconscious bias training'. *Psychology*, 12(7), 1058–1069.
Patten, D. M. (1995). 'Supervisory actions and job satisfaction: an analysis of differences between large and small public accounting firms'. *Accounting Horizons*, 9(2), 17–28.
Perrons, D. (2021). *Is austerity gendered?* Cambridge: Polity Press.
Peterson, H. (2015). *Fifty shades of freedom. Voluntary childlessness as women's ultimate liberation*. Paper presented at the Women's studies international forum.
Pfau-Effinger, B. (2002). 'Changing welfare states and labour markets in the context of European gender arrangements'. In Jørgen Goul Andersen, and Per H. Jensen (eds), *Changing Labour Markets, Welfare Policies and Citizenship*, pp. 235–256. Bristol: Policy Press.
Pfau-Effinger, B., & Smidt, M. (2011). 'Differences in women's employment patterns and family policies: Eastern and Western Germany'. *Community, Work & Family*, 14(2), 217–232.
Podsakoff, P. M., MacKenzie, S. B., Paine, J. B., & Bachrach, D. G. (2000). 'Organizational citizenship behaviors: a critical review of the theoretical and empirical literature and suggestions for future research'. *Journal of Management*, 26(3), 513–563.
Power, N. (2022). *What do men want? Masculinity and its discontents*. London: Penguin.
PwC. (2021). 'Women in business'. https://www.pwc.co.uk/careers/student-careers/undergraduate-graduate-careers/our-programmes/women-in-business.html.
Rhoten, D., & Pfirman, S. (2007). 'Women in interdisciplinary science: exploring preferences and consequences'. *Research Policy*, 36(1), 56–75.
Rich, A. (1986). *Of woman born: motherhood as experience and institution. 1976*. New York.
Rivera, L. A., & Tilcsik, A. (2019). 'Scaling down inequality: rating scales, gender bias, and the architecture of evaluation'. *American Sociological Review*, 84(2), 248–274.
Robertson, L. G., Anderson, T. L., Hall, M. E. L., & Kim, C. L. (2019). 'Mothers and mental labor: a phenomenological focus group study of family-related thinking work'. *Psychology of Women Quarterly*, 43(2), 184–200.
Roth, W. D. & Sonnert, G. (2010). 'The costs and benefits of "red tape": anti-bureaucratic structure and gender inequity in a science research organization'. *Social Studies of Science* 41(3), 385–409.
Rothschild, K. W. (1993). 'Like a Lehrstueck by Brecht: notes on the German reunification drama'. *Cambridge Journal of Economics*, 17(3), 259–266.
Rottenberg, C. (2014). 'The rise of neoliberal feminism'. *Cultural Studies*, 28(3), 418–437.
Rottenberg, C. (2017). 'Neoliberal feminism and the future of human capital'. *Signs: Journal of Women in Culture and Society*, 42(2), 329–348.
Royal College of Obstetricians and Gynaecologists (2016). 'Young people "missing out" on parenthood due to a lack of knowledge about their fertility'. https://www.rcog.org.uk/en/news/young-people-missing-out-on-parenthood-due-to-a-lack-of-knowledge-about-their-fertility/.
Rubery, J. (2009). 'How gendering the varieties of capitalism requires a wider lens'. *Social Politics*, 16(2), 192–203.

Ruckdeschel, K. (2009). 'Rabenmutter contra mère poule: Kinderwunsch und Mutterbild im deutsch-französischen Vergleich'. *Zeitschrift für Bevölkerungswissenschaft, 34*(1), 105–134.

Ruddick, S. (1995). *Maternal thinking: towards a politics of peace*. Boston: Beacon Press.

Rundschau, F. (2008). IG Metall bleibt unbeirrbar auf Acht-Prozent-Kurs. 9 October.

Sadler, E., & Wessels, J. S. (2019). 'Transformation of the accounting profession: an autoethnographical reflection of identity and intersectionality'. *Meditari Accountancy Research, 27*(3), 448–471.

Sanford Heisler. (2015). 'KPMG Gender Discrimination Case'. https://www.sanfordheisler.com/case/discrimination-harassment/kpmg-gender-discrimination-case/.

Santora, J. C. (2007). 'Assertiveness and effective leadership: is there a tipping point?' *Academy of Management Perspectives, 21*(3), 84–86.

Schaefer, J., & Zimmer, M. (1995). 'Gender and earnings of certain accountants and auditors: a comparative study of industries and regions'. *Journal of Accounting and Public Policy, 14*(4), 265–291.

Scharff, C. (2011). 'Disarticulating feminism: individualization, neoliberalism, and the othering of "Muslim women"'. *European Journal of Women's Studies 18*(2), 119–134.

Scharff, C. (2012). *Repudiating feminism: young women in a neoliberal world*. Farnham: Ashgate.

Scharff, C. (2016). 'The psychic life of neoliberalism: mapping the contours of entrepreneurial subjectivity'. *Theory, Culture & Society, 33*(6), 107–122.

Scharff, C. (2017). *Gender, subjectivity, and cultural work: the classical music profession*: Abingdon: Routledge.

Scharff, C. (2018). 'Inequalities in the classical music industry: the role of subjectivity in constructions of the "ideal" classical musician', in Dromey, C and Haferkorn, J. (eds.) (2018) *The classical music industry*, pp. 96–111. New York: Routledge.

Scholtes, B. (2021). After the Wirecardscandal: New rules for auditors are not convincing. https://www.deutschlandfunk.de/nach-dem-wirecard-skandal-neue-regeln-fuer.724.de.html?dram:article_id=490968.

Sellers, R. D., & Fogarty, T. J. (2010). 'The making of accountants: the continuing influence of early career experiences'. *Managerial Auditing Journal, 25*(7), 701–719.

Sennett, R. (1998). *The corrosion of character: the personal consequences of work in the new capitalism*. New York: W.W. Norton & Co.

Sennett, R. (2007). *The culture of the new capitalism*. New Haven: Yale University Press.

Sennett, R. (2012). *Together: the rituals, pleasures and politics of cooperation*. New Haven: Yale University Press.

Shackleton, K. (1998). *Female entry to public accounting in Scotland, 1900–1930: the impact of the Sex Disqualification (Removal) Act 1919*. Paper presented at the Second Asian Pacific Interdisciplinary Research in Accounting Conference, Osaka, Japan.

Shackleton, K. (1999). 'Gender segregation in Scottish chartered accountancy: the deployment of male concerns about the admission of women, 1900–1925'. *Accounting, Business & Financial History 9*(1), 135–156.

Sharabi, M. (2017). 'The meaning of work dimensions according to organizational status: does gender matter?' *Employee Relations 39*(5), 643– 659.

Sharabi, M. (2017). 'Work, family and other life domains centrality among managers and workers according to gender'. *International Journal of Social Economics 44*(10), 1307– 1321.

Sharabi, M., & Harpaz, I. (2010). 'Improving employees' work centrality improves organizational performance: work events and work centrality relationships'. *Human Resource Development International, 13*(4), 379–392.

Shields, J., & Grant, D. (2010). 'Psychologising the subject: HRM, commodification, and the objectification of labour'. *The Economic and Labour Relations Review, 20*(2), 61–76.

Sian, S. (2006). 'Inclusion, exclusion and control: the case of the Kenyan accounting professionalisation project'. *Accounting, Organizations and Society, 31*(3), 295–322.

Sian, S. (2007). 'Reversing exclusion: the Africanisation of accountancy in Kenya, 1963–1970'. *Critical Perspectives on Accounting, 18*(7), 831–872.

Sian, S. (2011). 'Operationalising closure in a colonial context: the Association of Accountants in East Africa, 1949–1963'. *Accounting, Organizations and Society, 36*(6), 363–381.

Sian, S. (2021). 'Off-ramps and on-ramps: career continuity and discontinuity in professional accountancy'. *Critical Perspectives on Accounting, 91*, 102410.

Sikka, P., Willmott, H., & Lowe, T. (1989). 'Guardians of knowledge and public interest: evidence and issues of accountability in the UK accountancy profession'. *Accounting, Auditing & Accountability Journal, 2*(2), 0–0.

Slotkin, J. (2007). 'Rabenmutter and the glass ceiling: an analysis of role conflict experienced by women lawyers in Germany compared with women lawyers in the United States'. *California Western International Law Journal, 38*(2), 287–329.

Smith-Lovin, L. &. McPherson, J.M. (1993). 'You are who you know: a network approach to gender'. In England, P. (ed.), *Theory on Gender/Feminism on Theory.* 223–251. New York: Aldine.

Smithson, J., & Stokoe, E. H. (2005). 'Discourses of work–life balance: negotiating "genderblind" terms in organizations'. *Gender, Work & Organization, 12*(2), 147–168.

Spence, C., Carter, C., Belal, A., Husillos, J., Dambrin, C., & Archel, P. (2016). 'Tracking habitus across a transnational professional field'. *Work, Employment and Society, 30*(1), 3–20.

Spence, C., Dambrin, C., Carter, C., Husillos, J., & Archel, P. (2016). 'Global ends, local means: cross-national homogeneity in professional service firms'. *Human Relations, 68*(5), 765–788.

Stary, U. (2018). 'Wochenkrippen und Kinderwochenheime in der DDR'. B. f. p. Bildung. https://www.bpb.de/themen/deutschlandarchiv/262920/wochenkrippen-und-kinderwochenheime-in-der-ddr/.

Statista. (2022a). 'Average age of first degree university graduates in Germany from 2003 to 2020 (in years)*'. https://www.statista.com/statistics/584325/first-degree-university-graduates-age-germany/

Statista. (2022b). 'Unemployment rate of the largest economies in Europe from 1980 to 2021'. https://www.statista.com/statistics/1173907/unemployment-in-largest-european-countries

Statista. (2022c). 'Number of Deloitte employees worldwide from 2010 to 2021, by region'. https://www.statista.com/statistics/189032/people-of-deloitte-member-firms-since-2010-by-region/#:~:text=Deloitte%20employed%20around%20345%2C000%20people,revenue%20growth%20across%20all%20regions.

Statista. (2022d). 'Number of PwC employees worldwide from 2010 to 2021'. https://www.statista.com/statistics/484581/number-of-employees-of-pwc/

Statista. (2022e). 'KPMG—statistics & facts'. https://www.statista.com/topics/2612/kpmg/#:~:text=Currently%20headquartered%20in%20Amstelveen%2C%20in,with%20Deloitte%2C%20EY%20and%20PwC.

Statista. (2022f). 'Number of employees of EY worldwide from 2009 to 2021, by region'. https://www.statista.com/statistics/189247/number-of-employees-of-ernst-young-by-area/

Statistisches Bundesamt (2019). 'Drei von vier Müttern in Deutschland waren 2019 erwerbstätig'. Pressemitteilung Nr. N 017 vom 5. März 2021. https://www.destatis.de/DE/Presse/Pressemitteilungen/2021/03/PD21_N017_13.html

Stehr, C. (2013). 'Grosse Zahlen, grosse Qualen'. *Der Spiegel.* https://www.spiegel.de/karriere/wirtschaftspruefer-krisensicherer-job-mit-haken-a-899201.html

References

Stephens, J. (2012). *Confronting postmaternal thinking: feminism, memory, and care*. New York: Columbia University Press.

Suddaby, R. (2006). 'From the editors: what grounded theory is not'. *Academy of Management Journal, 49*(4), 633–642.

Suhr, F. (2020)., Corona: Vor allem Mütter stecken beim Job zurück. https://de.statista.com/infografik/21727/umfrage-zu-eltern-im-home-office-waehrend-der-corona-pandemie/.

Sullivan, A. (2022). 'It is mothers, not fathers, who pay the price of parenthood'. *The Guardian*. https://www.theguardian.com/world/2022/mar/09/it-is-mothers-not-fathers-who-pay-the-price-of-parenthood

Sullivan, S. E., & Arthur, M. B. (2006). 'The evolution of the boundaryless career concept. Examining physical and psychological mobility'. *Journal of Vocational Behavior, 69*, 19–29.

Sutherland, J.-A. (2010). 'Mothering, guilt and shame'. *Sociology Compass, 4*(5), 310–321.

Szostak, R. (2007). 'How and why to teach interdisciplinary research practice'. *Journal of Research Practice, 3*(2), 1–16.

Tax Notes (2021). 'Settlement reached in discrimination suit against KPMG'. Tax Notes. https://www.taxnotes.com/research/federal/other-documents/other-court-documents/settlement-reached-in-discrimination-suit-against-kpmg/4c60y.

Thelen, K. (2012). 'Varieties of capitalism: trajectories of liberalization and the new politics of social solidarity'. *Annual Review of Political Science, 15*, 137–159.

Thompson, P. S., Bergeron, D. M., & Bolino, M. C. (2020). 'No obligation? How gender influences the relationship between perceived organizational support and organizational citizenship behavior'. *Journal of Applied Psychology, 105*(11), 1338.

Timmermans, S., & Almeling, R. (2009). 'Objectification, standardization, and commodification in health care: a conceptual readjustment'. *Social Science & Medicine, 69*(1), 21–27.

Tinker, T. (1985). *Paper prophets: a social critique of accounting*. New York: Praeger

Topping, A. (2020). 'UK working mothers are "sacrificial lambs" in coronavirus childcare crisis'. *The Guardian*. https://www.theguardian.com/money/2020/jul/24/uk-working-mothers-are-sacrificial-lambs-in-coronavirus-childcare-crisis

Trilling, L. (1972). *Sincerity and authenticity*. Cambridge: Harvard University Press.

Underhill, C. M. (2006). 'The effectiveness of mentoring programs in corporate settings: a meta-analytical review of the literature'. *Journal of Vocational Behavior, 68*(2), 292–307.

U.S. Court (1989). 'Price Waterhouse v. Hopkins', 490 U.S. 228. http://supreme.justia.com/us/490/228/case.html.

Valcour, P. M., & Hunter, L. W. (2005). 'Technology, organizations, and work-life integration', in E. E. Kossek & S. J. Lambert (Eds.), *Work and life integration: organizational, cultural, and individual perspectives*, 61–84. New Jersey: Lawrence, Erlbaum Associates Publishers.

Vidwans, M., & Du Plessis, R. A. (2020). 'Crafting careers in accounting: redefining gendered selves'. *Pacific Accounting Review, 32*(1), 32– 53.

Vieten, H. R. (1995). 'Auditing in Britain and Germany compared: professions, knowledge and the state'. *European Accounting Review, 4*(3), 485–514.

Wager, M. (2000). 'I. Childless by choice? Ambivalence and the female identity'. *Feminism & Psychology, 10*(3), 389–395.

Wajcman, J. (1998). *Managing like a man: women and men in corporate management*: Cambridge: Polity Press.

Walby, S. (2007). 'Complexity theory, systems theory, and multiple intersecting social inequalities'. *Philosophy of the Social Sciences, 37*(4), 449–470.

Walker, D. (2014). 'Public audit fights back: insisting on government transparency worldwide'. *The Guardian*. https://www.theguardian.com/public-leaders-network/2014/apr/07/public-audit-fights-back-transparency-governments.

Walker, S., & Shackleton, K. (1998). 'A ring fence for the profession: advancing the closure of British accountancy 1957–1970'. *Accounting, Auditing & Accountability Journal, 11*(1), 34–71.

Walton, P. (1993). 'Introduction: the true and fair view in British accounting'. *European Accounting Review, 2*(1), 49–58.

Warren, S., & Brewis, J. (2004). 'Matter over mind? Examining the experience of pregnancy'. *Sociology, 38*(2), 219–236.

Warren, T. (2003). 'Class and gender-based working time? Time poverty and the division of domestic labour'. *Sociology, 37*(4), 733–752.

Webber, A. (2021). 'EY partner fined after sexually harassing employee on skiing trip'. *Personnel Today*. https://www.personneltoday.com/hr/ey-partner-fined-after-sexually-harassing-employee-on-skiing-trip/.

Weeden, K. A. (2002). 'Why do some occupations pay more than others? Social closure and earnings inequality in the United States'. *American Journal of Sociology, 108*(1), 55–101.

Weishaupt, J. T. (2021). 'German labour market resilience in times of crisis: revealing coordination mechanisms in the social market economy'. *German Politics, 30*(3), 360– 379.

Welsh, M. J. (1992). 'The construction of gender: some insights from feminist psychology'. *Accounting, Auditing & Accountability Journal, 5*(3), 0–0.

West, C., & Zimmerman, D. H. (2002). 'Doing gender', in S. Fenstermaker & C. West (Eds.), *Doing gender, doing difference. Inequality, power, and institutional change*. New York: Routledge

Whiting, R. H., Gammie, E., & Herbohn, K. (2015). 'Women and the prospects for partnership in professional accountancy firms'. *Accounting & Finance, 55*(2), 575–605.

Whiting, R. H., & Wright, C. (2001). 'Explaining gender inequity in the New Zealand accounting profession'. *The British Accounting Review, 33*(2), 191–222.

Wiese, A. (2006). 'Transformation in the South African chartered accountancy profession since 2001: a study of the progress and the obstacles black trainee accountants still encounter'. *Meditari Accountancy Research, 14*(2), 151– 167.

Wigdor Law (2018). 'Wigdor LLP represents female partner at Ernst & Young in claims of sexual harassment, gender discrimination and retaliation'. https://www.wigdorlaw.com/ernst-young-partner-sexual-harassment-retaliation/.

Wilkinson, M. A. (2019). 'Authoritarian liberalism in Europe: a common critique of neoliberalism and ordoliberalism'. *Critical Sociology, 45*(7-8), 1023–1034.

Williamson, S., & Foley, M. (2018). 'Unconscious bias training: the "silver bullet" for gender equality?' *Australian Journal of Public Administration, 77*(3), 355–359.

Willmott, H. (1986). 'Organising the profession: a theoretical and historical examination of the development of the major accountancy bodies in the UK'. *Accounting, Organizations and Society, 11*(6), 555–580.

Windsor, C., & Auyeung, P. (2006). 'The effect of gender and dependent children on professional accountants' career progression'. *Critical Perspectives on Accounting, 17*(6), 828–844.

Witz, A. (1992). *Professions and patriarchy*. London: Routledge.

Woolcock, M., (2010). 'The rise and routinization of social capital, 1988–2008'. *Annual Review of Political Science, 13*. 469–487.

WPK. (2005). 'Statistische Informationen zu unseren Mitgliedern Stand 1.7.2005'. http://www.wpk.de/pdf/wpk-statistiken_juli_2005.pdf
WPK. (2015). Mitgliederstatistik der WPK—Stand 1. Juli 2015: Wirtschaftsprüferkammer.
WPK. (2022). Mitgliederstatistik der WPK—Stand 1. January.
Young, B. (2017). 'Is Germany's and Europe's crisis politics ordoliberal and/or neoliberal?', in Biebrichter, T. and Vogelmann, F. (eds.). *The birth of austerity*, 221–238, London: Rowman and Littlefield International.
ZDF. (2019). '*Wenn die Eltern Fremde sind—Kinder in DDR-Wochenheimen—Frontal 21*'. https://www.youtube.com/watch?v=2DTaJCy8Qm8.

Index

For the benefit of digital users, indexed terms that span two pages (e.g., 52–53) may, on occasion, appear on only one of those pages.

Tables and figures are indicated by an italic *t* and *f*, following the paragraph number.

A

ACCA (Association of Chartered Certified Accountants, UK), 23–24
  female membership, 25, 26*t*, 123–124
  membership, 24–25
  training, 25–26
accountancy, 17, 19
  activities and services of, 19–21
  chartered/'public accountants', 19–21
  demand for accountancy services, 21–22
  as elite profession, 1, 21, 22–23, 107–108, 112
  Germany, 3, 19–21, 23
  history of, 19–23, 29–30
  importance of, 19–22
  monopolist status of, 3, 19–23, 149
  professional closure, 3, 19, 22–23, 29–30, 154
  professionalization of, 19–21, 132, 151–152
  as protected occupation, 19
  Royal Charter, 151–152
  scandals, 19–21, 154
  Scotland, 22–23
  standard-setting procedures, 21–22
  UK, 19–23, 132
  Vereidigte Buchführer, 23–24
  wealth distribution and, 21
  Wirtschaftsprüfer, 19–21, 23–25
  women's advancement at Big-4 Firms, 27, 31–32
  women's entrance and rise in, 22, 29–30
  women's representation and advancement in accounting research, 29
accountancy: Germany/UK comparison, 37–38, 53
  accountancy industry as larger in the UK, 1, 23–26, 50, 53, 154
  accountancy institutes, 23–24
  accountancy qualification: transferability of skills, 5, 24–25, 154
  audit industry, 23–26
  British focus on standardization, competition, and performance, 3
  British market-type structures, 2
  education system and training routes, 25–26, 81, 116, 123–124, 154
  employee turnover, 117–118, 134–135
  gender equality, 26–27, 37–38
  gender pay gap, 28–29
  German coordination and cooperation, 3, 86–87
  German monopolist status, 3, 149
  German relationship-based careers, 2
  professional organization and women's representation, 23
  proportion of women in accounting profession, 25*t*, 25–26, 37–38, 123–124
  SMEs, 50, 53
  unpleasant experiences at work, 3
  Wirtschaftsprüfer/British accountants comparison, 24–26
  see also women at partnership level in Germany; women at partnership level in the UK
accountancy: women at partnership level, 12–13
  Big-4 Firms, 27–28
  childlessness, 92–93, 112–113, 136, 145–146
  motherhood and, 36–37
  organizational structures, 39
  part-time vs full-time commitment, 2–3, 33–34
  promotion to partnership as partly negotiated through gender, 28
  underrepresentation, 1, 23–24, 26–28, 112
  webs of relationships, 39

accountancy: women at partnership level, (*Continued*)
  see also women at partnership level in Germany; women at partnership level in the UK
accountancy: women's underrepresentation in, 1, 32
  Canada, 32
  Germany, 1, 25–26, 31–32, 66, 102–103, 123–124
  Malaysia, 32–33
  UK, 25–27, 72–73, 128, 129
  underrepresentation at top levels, 1, 23–24, 26–28, 31–33, 66, 72–73, 112, 128–129, 151
  women's representation and advancement in accounting research, 29
Accounting Today, 28–29
Acker, J., 6, 57, 141–142
  informal practices, 49
  unencumbered worker, 30–31, 108–109 n.2, 140, 147
Adapa, S., 32–34
age
  'double jeopardy of gendered ageism', 81
  reproduction and, 69–70, 81, 97–98, 110–111, 146, 161–162
  sexism and, 78, 97–98, 110–111
Ali, Z., 116
Almeling, R., 153–154
Anderson-Gough, F., 36–37, 89–90, 96–97
Anglo-Saxon context, 8–11, 117–118, 135–136
Arthur, M., 150
Arthur, M. B., 11
Australia, 33–34

B
Bakhtin, Mikhail, 136
Banet-Weiser, S., 159–160
Bauman, Z., 117
Beck, T., 8
Bédard, J., 19–21
Big-4 Firms, 21–22
  flexibility, 141–142
  gender equality, diversity, and inclusion, 27–28
  graduate recruitment practices, 30–31
  influence in politics and business, 19–21
  institutionalized aspects of 'behaving, acting, talking, looking', 33–34
  mentorship, 58–59
  sex discrimination, 28–29
  sexual harassment, 28–29
  training and networking, 116
  UK, 116, 123–124
  women at partnership level, 27–28
  women at partnership level in Germany, 41–42, 44, 54–55, 57, 68–69, 75, 82, 130–131, 144, 146
  women at partnership level in the UK, 47, 50, 57–59, 71, 73, 83, 103–106, 108, 128, 141
  women's advancement at, 27, 31–32
  work centrality, 148
  work-life balance, 34
  see also Deloitte; EY; KPMG; PwC
Bisiada, M., 86–87
body (female body)
  fertility, 146, 161–162
  maternal body as social pollutant, 88, 92–93, 95, 102–105, 112–113
  maternal body as taboo, 92, 110, 151–152
  menopause, 69–70, 92–93
  menstruation, 92–93
  physical aspects of pregnancy, 35–37, 92–93, 151–152
  reproductive capacity, 12–15, 93, 97–98, 104–105, 109–111, 151–152, 155–156
Bone, J., 117
Bourdieu, P., 31–32
Brewis, J., 92–93
Brouard, F., 32
Brown, J., 117
Buchheit, S., 34
Bueskens, P., 36–37, 90–91, 98, 109
Bujaki, M. L., 32
Burke, R. J., 61, 143–144
Butterick, M., 153–154

C
Canada, 32
capitalism
  accelerated capitalism, 9–10, 117–118, 127–128, 137, 149
  androcentrism of, 11–12
  artificial divide of public/private life, and valorization of paid over unpaid care work, 69–70

Index

dependency, capitalism, and the state, 4
domesticity and, 159–160
effects of advanced capitalism on women, 1
elite: detachment from responsibilities to others, 127–129
feminism, women's careers, and, 11
neoliberalism and, 9–10
resisting the capitalist upside-down world in feminist visions of a future, 160
self-worth as linked to one's work, 135–136
welfare states and, 6–7
women and, 160–161
women's advancement under, 18
see also VoC
career advancement
access to networks and, 39
accounting research on, 29
firm size and female representation, 33–34
Germany/UK comparison: career structures and career advancement, 2, 40t, 59, 60f, 152–153
importance of titles in Germany, 31–32
language and, 31–32
'macho' culture and gendered career advancement process, 31–32
motherhood and, 35–37
social capital and, 31–32
women at partnership level in Germany, 41–44
women at partnership level in the UK, 46–50
women's advancement at Big-4 Firms, 27, 31–32
women's career advancement and dependency, 17–18
see also promotion
Carli, L. L., 102
Carter, C., 34
Carter, C. A., 31–32
Castilla, E. J., 39
Chao, G. T., 8–9
Charlwood, A., 153–154
Chia, Y., 29–30
children and childcare, 35–36, 155–157
free childcare, 156–157
gender equality and, 155–158

German Parental Allowances (Elterngeld), 158
Germany: childcare as mother's care, 98, 142–143, 147, 151–152, 158
Germany/UK comparison: women at partnership level and childcare arrangements, 94t, 94–95
institutionalization of, 13–14, 112, 141
men as carers, 158–159
motherhood and *mental load*, 89–90, 99
mothers' guilt, 99, 110–111
outsourcing care responsibilities, 11–12, 69, 98–99, 112, 141–143
'Tagesmutter' (childminder), 98
UK, 103, 105–106, 141–142, 156–157
UK: reversing of gender roles, 2–3, 70, 94–95, 106, 109–111, 120, 138, 140–141, 143, 151–152
'Wochenkrippen'/Wochenheime, 13–14, 156–157
see also motherhood; reproduction and care work
CIMA (Chartered Institute of Management Accountants, UK), 25
CIPFA (Chartered Institute of Public Finance and Accountancy, UK), 25
Claridge, H.M., 161–162
class, 64, 165
class/gender/race intersections, 5–6, 8–9, 21, 156
occupational closure and, 154
relationship-based careers and, 57, 60–61
sexism and, 81, 85
social capital and, 39
standardization of career structures and, 57
women at partnership level in Germany, 82
women at partnership level in the UK, 82–85
work centrality and, 140
Collins, C., 113–114
Collinson, D., 76
Collinson, M., 76
commodification of the self, 18, 152, 153–154
women at partnership level in the UK, 2, 49, 61–62, 152–154
'confidence culture', 64–66

Cooper, C. L., 88, 92–93, 95, 96–98, 102–105, 109–110, 112–113
COVID-19 pandemic, 113–114, 153–154, 161
  Germany, 8
  inequitable division of household and economic labour, 113–114
  liberal state and, 161
  US, 113–114
Crompton, R., 5–6, 138

D
Dahl, R. A., 21–22
Dahlander, L., 61–62
Dalal, R. S., 54
Dalton, D. W., 34
Dambrin, C., 36–37
Dany, F., Mallon, M., 150
de Bobadilla-Güemez, S. F., 143–144
Debus, M. E., 115–116
de Celis, I. L.-R., 143–144
de-commodification, 6–7
del Mar Alonso-Almeida, M., 143–144
Deloitte
  2015 Deloitte Impact Report, 27–28
  women at partnership level, 27–28
  see also Big-4 Firms
dependency, 15, 17–18, 57
  dependency, capitalism, and the state, 4
  feminist ethics of care, 13–14
  gendered gatekeeping relationships of dependency, 8–9, 138
  Germany and relationships of dependency, 138
  women's career advancement and, 17–18
  see also gendered hierarchies of dependency: Germany/UK comparison
derivative dependency, 13–14, 117, 137–138
Dhaenens, A. J., 58–59
Dietz, G., 8–9
Dillard, J., 117
discretionary behaviour, 9–10, 54
discrimination, 2, 18
  CME and statistical discrimination, 5
  labour market, 6
  see also gender in/equality; gender pay gap; sexism
Dobbin, F., 57–59
domesticity
  anger and disappointment with, 156–157, 159–160
  capitalism and, 159–160
  domesticity, marriage, and family under neoliberalism, 159
domestic work
  motherhood and *the second shift*, 89–90
  outsourcing domestic work, 98, 141–142
  UK: household chores delegated to husbands, 107
  women's centrality in, 6, 89–90
Douglas, Mary, 88, 92–93, 95, 96, 104–105, 112–113
Downar, B., 31–32
Duncan, C., 81
Durocher, S., 32

E
Eagly, A. H., 102
economy, 148–149
  entering the profession and, 119
  Germany: pay freezes, 125, 130–131, 149
  Germany: reunification and internet boom as factor in female partners accountants' career advancement, 118, 119t, 121–122, 130
  recessions and reunification, 118–124
  redundancies and, 124
  UK: contracts and household economics, 103, 109–110
  UK: recession/economic downturn as factor in female partners accountants' career advancement, 118, 119t, 124, 128
  women at partnership level in Germany, 118, 119t, 121–124, 130, 149
  women at partnership level in the UK, 118–121, 123–124
  see also job in/security; redundancy
embeddedness in relationships, 12–13, 61, 150
  complaints and confrontations as risky, 86–87, 151
  cost of, 86–87, 151, 152
  homosociality and men's over-representation in positions of power, 151
  job insecurity and, 116
  motherhood and, 151–154

private/public life blurred lines, 110
  sexism and, 151
  vulnerability due to, 151
  women at partnership level in Germany and relationship-based careers, 2, 39–40, 57, 59, 61–62, 71, 110, 121, 131, 134–135, 138, 149–152
  women at partnership level in Germany and relationship-based hierarchies, 2, 4–5, 61–62, 110, 150
  see also gendered hierarchies of dependency: Germany/UK comparison; relationships at work
employment
  accountancy: Germany/UK comparison on employee turnover, 117–118, 134–135
  employability and job performance, 116
  LME, 39
  market-driven employment strategies, 39–40
  traditional model of, 39–40
  see also labour force; short-terminism
Empson, L., 89–90
Enron, 21
equality, *see* gender in/equality
Erkut, S., 102
Ernstberger, J., 31–32
Esping-Andersen, G., 4, 6–7
Estévez-Abe, M., 5–6, 61, 123–124
EU (European Union)
  austerity measures, 8–9
  education system, 25–26
Evans, C., 22–23
EY (Ernst & Young)
  women at partnership level, 27–28
  see also Big-4 Firms

F
feminism
  European contexts, 13–14, 36–37
  feminist research, 13–14
  feminist visions of equality, 155
  Germany, 68, 86–87, 151
  liberal feminism, 36–37, 105–106, 109, 156
  popular feminism, 64–66
  repudiation of, 64–65, 85–86
  resisting the capitalist upside-down world in feminist visions of a future, 160
  restoring motherhood to central place within feminism, 113–114
  rights-based approach, 13–14, 86–87, 151
  sameness/difference dogma, 13–14, 36–37, 93, 105–106
  'second-wave feminism', 64–65, 113–114
  UK, 13–14, 36–37, 86–87, 105–106, 151
  US, 13–14, 86–87
  victimization associated with, 68
  women's careers, capitalism, and, 11
  see also matricentric feminism; neoliberal feminism; post-feminism
feminist ethics of care, 1, 12–14, 16–17, 69–70, 88
financial crisis (2008/2009), 64
  Germany, 8–9, 149
financial services, 9–10, 120
  as gendered and masculinized arena, 63–64
Financial Times, 28–29, 117–118
Fineman, M. A., 14–15, 137–138
firm size
  female representation and, 33–34
  structure and bureaucracy, 33–34
  see also SME
Fiske, S. T., 63–64, 86
flexibility
  accounting partnerships, 120, 141
  Big-4 firms, 141–142
  literature on, 34
  public accountancy, 120
  SMEs, 33–34
  UK, 37–38, 120, 141
  see also part-time working
Fogarty, T. J., 116
Foucault, M., 11–12, 65–66
France, 36–37, 61, 92–93
Fraser, N., 11–12, 57
FRC (Financial Reporting Council, UK), 23–24, 26–27
Fuchs, D., 54

G
Gatrell, C., 88, 92–93, 95, 96–98, 102–105, 109–110, 112–113
Gebreiter, F., 30–31
Gendered Hierarchies of Dependency, 17
  feminist ethics of care, 1, 12–13, 16–17
  interdisciplinary analysis, 1, 16–17
  interviews, 15–16

Gendered Hierarchies of Dependency (*Continued*)
  political economy, 1, 4, 16–17
  research methodology, 15–17
  respondents, 15–165, 16*t*
  scope and limitations, 15
  terminology, 17, 165
gendered hierarchies of dependency:
  Germany/UK comparison, 1, 39, 61–62, 150
  dependency, definition of, 150
  gendered outcomes, 150–151, 160–161
  Germany: relationship-based careers, 2, 39–40, 57, 59, 61–62, 71, 110, 121, 131, 134–135, 138, 149–152
  Germany: relationship-based hierarchies, 2, 4–5, 61–62, 110, 150
  homosociality and, 8–9, 151
  UK: standardized career structures, 2, 39–40, 44–47, 59, 60–62, 132, 150, 152–154
  vulnerability, 151
  see also embeddedness in relationships
gendered power relations, 8–9
gender in/equality, 16–18, 26–27
  access to accountancy profession and, 93
  accountancy: Germany/UK comparison, 26–27, 37–38
  Big-4 Firms, 27–28
  children and childcare, 155–158
  feminist visions of equality, 155
  Germany, 93
  private-public sphere and, 69–70
  promotion to partnership as partly negotiated through gender, 28
  redundancy and gender, 60–61, 127, 128, 149, 154
  standardization of career structures and, 160–161
  UK, 37–38, 93
  women's ability to pursue a career, 155–156
  see also sexism
gender pay gap, 28–30
  maternal pay gap, 35
  pay discrimination, 28–29
  skill depreciation and, 157–158

Germany
  2008/2009 financial crisis, 8–9, 149
  accountancy, 3, 19–21, 23
  accountancy institutes, 23–24
  audit industry, 23–26
  childcare as mother's care, 98, 142–143, 147, 151–152, 158
  Christian Democrats, 8–9
  as CME, 3–6, 151
  coordination and cooperation, 2–5, 8–9, 86–87, 149
  COVID-19 pandemic, 8
  EU, austerity measures, 8–9
  feminism, 68, 86–87, 151
  fiscal discipline, 8–9
  GDR (German Democratic Republic), 13–14, 118, 121–122, 156–157
  gender equality, 93
  job in/security, 115–116, 118, 124, 136–137
  motherhood career paradox, 90–91
  "ordoliberalism", 2, 8–9, 130, 136–137
  parental leave, 158
  Parental Allowances (Elterngeld), 158, 160
  promotion in accounting, 52–57
  relationships of dependency, 138
  relationships and strong networks, 4–5, 8–9
  social market economy, 8–9, 149
  work centrality, 136–137
  see also accountancy: Germany/UK comparison; gendered hierarchies of dependency: Germany/UK comparison; Wirtschaftsprüfer; women at partnership level in Germany
Gill, Rosalind, 11–12, 64–66, 85–86, 123–124, 159–160
  postfeminism, 68–69, 85
Gillespie, N., 8–9
Gilman, C. P., 13–14
Glick, P., 63–64, 86
globalization, 9–10, 89–90, 157, 158–159
Goetz Jr, J. F., 33–34
Gordon, L., 57
governmentality, 11–12, 65–66
Granleese, J., 81
Grant, D., 153–154
Grey, C., 36–37, 89–90, 96–97

Gruner, S., 82
Guardian, The, 24–25
Guthrie, David, 23
Guthrie, Isobel Clyne, 23, 161–162

H
Hall, P. A.: *Varieties of capitalism*, 4, 61, 123–124
 see also VoC
Harp, N. L., 34
Haynes, K., 29–30, 36–37, 89–90, 92–93, 96–97
Hays, S., 90–91
Heilman, M. E., 54
Heilmann, S. G., 58–59
Henry, M. G., 82
Hines, Ruth, 19–21
Hochschild, A. R., 137
Hogarth, R. M., 61
Hollingsworth, C. W., 34
Holt, D. T., 58–59
homophily, 1, 60, 61–62
 disadvantages for women working within male-dominated professions, 8–9
 gender, race, and class implications, 8–9
 homosociality, 8–9, 151
 primary ties as homophilous, 41–42
 relationships at work and, 8–9, 61, 151
 US, 61–62
Hong Kong, 29–30
Hopkins, Ann, 28
Hudson, M., 83
Hui, Y., 116
human capital
 gender-bias in CMEs, 5
 neoliberalism and, 11–12, 117
Hunter, L. W., 141–142
husbands, 77, 156
 Germany: absence of husbands in partner accountants' talks, 94–95, 98, 99–100, 106, 109–110, 140, 151–152
 as part-time workers, 70, 106, 107
 supporting women's careers, 32–33, 129, 140
 UK: reversing of gender roles, 2–3, 70, 94–95, 106, 109–111, 120, 138, 140–141, 143, 151–152

I
IASB (International Accounting Standards Board), 21–22
Ibarra, H., 61
ICAEW (Institute of Chartered Accountants in England and Wales), 21–24, 36–37, 161–162 n.11
 female membership, 25, 26t, 123–124
 membership, 24–25
 training, 25–26
ICAS (Institute of Chartered Accountants in Scotland), 23–24, 36–37
 female membership, 25, 26t
 membership, 24–25
'ideal worker', 14–15, 30–31, 108–109 n.2, 147
 see also unencumbered norm
IdW (Institut der Wirtschaftsprüfer—association of chartered accountants, Germany), 23–24
 voluntary membership, 23–24

J
Jeacle, I., 24–25
Jensen, T., 35
Jeny, A., 31–32
job in/security, 2, 18, 115–116, 148, 161
 accountancy as 'safe' career, 117–118, 120, 122
 disconnection between job security, education and training, 154, 157–158
 embeddedness in relationships and, 116
 Germany, 115–116, 118, 136–137
 Germany: education/job insecurity negative relationship, 124
 health and, 115–116, 143–144
 as key stressor, 115–116, 143–144
 networks and, 116
 sociological perspectives on, 117
 UK, 3, 115–116, 118
 uncertainty avoidance, 115–116
 unemployment, 123–124, 127–128, 149, 154
 women at partnership level in Germany, 134–135, 149, 152
 women at partnership level in the UK, 3, 120–121, 134–135, 149, 152, 154
 work centrality and, 3, 130, 135–137
 see also economy; redundancy

K
Kalev, A., 57–59
Kamenou-Aigbekaen, N., 83
Kanter, R. M., 9–10, 63–64, 76, 102
Kassman, Donna, 28–29
Kellermann, K. L., 121
Kilkey, M., 140 n.4
Kim, N., You, J., 34–35
Kirkham, L. M., 22–23
Kittay, Eva Feder, 14–15, 17, 91, 137–138, 158–159
Klasen, O., 82
Kleinmann, M., 115–116
Knapp, G.-A., 165
Koch, C., 31–32
Koenig, C. J., 115–116
Konrad, A. M., 102
Kornberger, M., 34
Kossek, E. E., 88, 92–93, 95, 96–98, 102–105, 109–110, 112–113
Kotz, H.-H., 8
KPMG
  sex discrimination, 28–29
  women underrepresentation at the top level, 27–28
  see also Big-4 Firms
Kramer, V., 102
Kumra, S., 31–32

L
labour force
  dual-earner couples, 30–31
  female breadwinners, 107, 115–116, 129, 134–135, 140
  male breadwinner model, 13–14, 115–116
  VoC: CME/LME comparison, 4–7
  women as part of, 13–14
  see also employment
labour market
  de-commodification and, 6–7
  domestic labour market, 6
  gender segregation, 6
  labour market insecurity, 115–116
  VoC: CME/LME comparison, 4–7, 123–124
  women's more frequent interruptions in, 123–124
Lambert, C., 36–37
Landivar, L. C., 113–114

Lee, E., 34–35
Lehman Brothers, 21
Letherby, G., 13–14
Lightbody, M. G., 35–36, 92–93, 96–97
Lincoln, J. R., 41–42
Loeb, S., 33–34
Loft, A., 22–23
Loretto, W., 81
Lowinsky, N., 36–37, 89–90
Lupu, I., 89–90, 92–93, 138, 143
Lutter, M., 61–62
Lyness, K. S., 54
Lyonette, C., 138

M
M&A (Mergers and Acquisitions), 19–21
'macho' culture, 31–32
McDowell, Linda, 64
McElroy, J. C., 33–34
McFarland, D. A., 61–62
McRobbie, Angela, 11–12, 64–65, 68, 156, 159–160
Malaysia, 32–34
Mallon, M., 150
management studies, 'female deficit' in, 9–10
Mandel, H., 5–7
Manning, A., 115–118
Markova, G., 58–59
Markus, H. B., 19–21, 23, 121
Marler, L. E., 58–59
Marx, Karl, 137
masculinity, 8–9, 64, 160
maternity leave, 32–33
  "macho maternity", 36–37
  returning to work after maternity leave, 88, 103, 128
  returning to work part-time after maternity leave, 93
  women at partnership level in Germany, 98, 102–103
  women at partnership level in the UK, 94, 103–105, 109–113
  see also motherhood; pregnancy and birth
matricentric feminism, 89–91, 93, 96, 102–103, 105–107, 109, 113–114
Mazeine, G., 115–118
Mehreen, A., 116
Meisenbach, R. J., 107
menopause, 69–70, 92–93

menstruation, 92–93
mentorship
  formal/informal mentoring, 58–59
  women at partnership level in Germany, informal mentorship, 2, 39–40, 44–45, 58–59
  women at partnership level in the UK, 46–47, 49, 57–59
meritocracy, 55–56, 64–67, 69–70, 85, 149, 154, 161–162
Merkel, Angela, 8–9
#MeToo, 86–87
Michaud, C., 61
Miller, J., 41–42
misogyny, 33–34
Moore, S., 80
Morrow, P. C., 33–34
Morse, N. C., 135–136
motherhood, 2, 18, 88
  accountancy: women at partnership level, 36–37
  career advancement and, 35–37
  centring mothers in accountancy, 112
  childlessness, 92–93, 112–113, 136, 145–146
  as choice, 69, 85–86, 100–103, 112–113
  CME and, 5–6
  delaying maternity, 146, 161–162
  embeddedness in relationships and, 151–154
  empowered mothering, 88–90, 98, 100
  "high flying working mother", 36–37
  intensive mothering, 88, 90–91, 103
  literature on, 35–37
  "macho maternity", 36–37
  maternal body as social pollutant, 88, 92–93, 95, 102–105, 112–113
  maternal body as taboo, 92, 110, 151–152
  maternal pay gap, 35
  motherhood as institution, 88–90, 98, 103, 110, 112–113
  motherhood as institution/mothering as experience and practice, distinction between, 89–90
  mother identity, 36–37
  mothering and motherhood in accounting, 93–106, 109–110
  mothers as part-time workers, 2–3, 88, 93, 95, 96–98, 100, 101–102, 108, 109–111, 142

normalization of parenting as synonymous with mothering, 69
private-public sphere and, 2, 99, 102–103, 105–107, 109, 110, 112–114, 149, 152–153
technology, women's bodies and, 12
UK: contracts and household economics, 103, 109–110
UK: reversing of gender roles, 2–3, 70, 94–95, 106, 109–111, 120, 138, 140–141, 143, 151–152
unencumbered norm and, 89–90, 107, 110, 112–114, 151–152, 155–156
women at partnership level in Germany, 2–3, 69, 70, 88, 93, 95–98, 109–111, 142, 149, 151–153
women at partnership level in the UK, 2–3, 88, 94, 103–106, 110–111
see also children and childcare; maternity leave; matricentric feminism; motherhood career paradox; postmaternal thinking; pregnancy and birth; reproduction and care work
motherhood career paradox, 159–160
  Germany, 90–91
  motherhood vs professionalism, 92–93, 96–97
  'Mutterbild', 90–91, 99
  'Rabenmutter', 99 n.1
  UK, 88, 92–93
  women at partnership level in Germany, 2–3, 52–53, 68–69, 85–86, 88, 93, 95, 100–102, 108, 109–110, 112–113, 143, 151–152, 158
  see also motherhood
Motherline, 36–37, 89–90

N
Neilson, L. C., 32
Nelson, D. L., 143–144
neoliberal feminism, 17–18, 65–66, 151, 155–156
  work-life balance and, 65–66, 136, 138
neoliberalism, 117–118
  accelerated capitalism and, 9–10, 117–118, 127–128, 137, 149
  accountants and accounting 'as a primary enabler of neoliberal logic', 117

neoliberalism, (Continued)
  capitalism and, 9–10
  domesticity, marriage, and family under, 159
  free childcare, 157
  human capital and, 11–12, 117
  individual responsibility and, 11, 85, 117, 137–138, 151
  isolatory effect of, 117–118
  postmaternal thinking and, 109
  short-terminism, 11, 137–138
  UK, 108–109, 117–118
  unencumbered norm, 157
  women and, 11–12
  work centrality and neoliberal capitalism, 135–136
nepotism, 41–42
Netto, G., 83
Noon, M., 83
Nussbaum, M., 14–15

O
Oakley, A., 89–90
Offen, K., 13–14, 86–87, 151
"ordoliberalism", 8
  Germany, 2, 8–9, 130, 136–137
O'Reilly, A., 36–37, 89–91, 100, 101, 109, 110–111
  maternal studies, 88
  matricentric feminism, 113–114
Orgad, S., 64–66, 159–160
organizational structures
  Anglo-Saxon model, 9–11, 117–118
  firm-size element and, 33–34
  male dominate of organizational hierarchies, 9–10
  see also standardization of career structures
Orloff, Ann, 6–7, 17, 35, 109

P
part-time working, 2–3, 33–34
  husbands/partners as part-time workers, 70, 106, 107
  mothers as part-time workers, 2–3, 88, 93, 95, 96–98, 100, 101–102, 108, 109–111, 142
  returning to work part-time after maternity leave, 93
  UK, 70, 106, 107
paternalism, 161–162

patriarchy, 65–66, 89–91, 98, 161–162
Patten, D., 33–34
performance, 154, 161–162
  counterproductive work behaviour, 54
  employability and job performance, 116
  gender and, 54, 154
  'ideal worker', 30–31
  OCB (organizational citizenship behaviour), 54
  task performance, 54
  women at partnership level in Germany, 54
  women at partnership level in the UK, 46–47
Perrons, D., 140 n.4
PIE audit firms (public interest entity), 26–27
political economy, 1, 4, 16–17
post-feminism, 18, 65–66, 136, 151, 155–156
  as 'backlash against feminism', 68
postmaternal thinking, 88–90, 109, 112–113
  see also motherhood
Power, N., 160–162
pregnancy and birth, 15, 28–29, 35, 103–105, 155–156
  physical aspects of, 35–37, 92–93, 151–152
  see also maternity leave; motherhood
private-public sphere
  capitalism and, 69–70
  gender inequalities in, 69–70
  Germany: private/public life blurred lines, 2–3, 96, 110, 149, 152–153
  motherhood and, 2, 99, 102–103, 105–107, 109, 110, 112–114, 149, 152–153
  relationships in, 8–9, 44–45, 59
Probst, T. M., 115–116
promotion
  Germany: making partnership process, 46–48, 54
  Germany: promotion in accounting, 52–57
  job posting systems, formal job ladders and diversity, 57
  promotion to partnership as partly negotiated through gender, 28
  standardized career structures, 57
  UK: making partnership process, 47–48

Index

UK: promotion in accounting, 57–59
women losing out on promotions/salary hikes as they don't ask for them, 55–56
see also career advancement
PwC (PricewaterhouseCoopers)
Price Waterhouse v. Hopkins, 28
sex discrimination, 28
women at entrance level, 27–28
women at partnership level, 27–28
see also Big-4 Firms

R

race and ethnicity, 81, 85
racism, 82, 84
xenophobia, 82
see also class/gender/race intersections
redundancy
economy and, 124
gender and, 60–61, 127, 128, 149, 154
'merit-based' protocol, 128
restrictive non-disclosure agreements, 28–29
self-employment and, 127
women at partnership level in Germany, 58–59, 124, 125, 130, 134, 152
women at partnership level in the UK, 3, 51–52, 58–62, 124, 125t, 125–129, 132, 149, 152, 154
see also job in/security; resignation
relationships at work, 150
absence of, 11
gender, race, and class, 60–61
Germany, instrumental/primary ties, 41–42, 44, 59
Germany, relationships of trust, 3, 43
homophily and, 8–9, 61, 151
instrumental/primary ties, 41–42, 61
narcissism and complacency, 136 n.2, 137–138
personal relationships as disadvantageous, 60–61
'repair work' and, 127–128
short-terminism and, 9–11, 127–128, 137–138
standardized career structures and, 154
trust, absence of, 127–128
UK, instrumental ties, 47–48
withdrawal and isolation of individuals, 9–10, 127–128, 136, 137–138

women at partnership level in Germany, 2, 4–5, 39–40, 44, 55–57, 59, 61–62, 71, 86–87, 110, 121, 131, 134–135, 138, 140, 149, 150–152
women at partnership level in the UK, 46–47, 49, 51–52, 57, 61–62
see also embeddedness in relationships
reproduction and care work
age and, 69–70, 81, 97–98, 110–111, 146, 161–162
artificial reproductive technologies, 161–162
caring well for our most vulnerable, 160–161
challenges posed to working women by, 15, 30–31, 35–36, 69
females executives and, 30–31
fertility, 146, 161–162
gender equality and, 155–156
outsourcing care responsibilities, 11–12, 69, 98–99, 112, 141–143
women's centrality in care, 12–15, 35, 69–70, 89–90, 98, 109, 117, 159–162
women's reproductive capacity, 12–15, 93, 97–98, 104–105, 109–111, 151–152, 155–156
women's unpaid care work, 69–70, 113–114
see also children and childcare; domestic work; motherhood
Republic of Ireland, 24–25
resignation
restrictive non-disclosure agreements and, 28–29
women at partnership level in Germany, 124, 130–134, 149
see also redundancy
Rich, Adrienne, 89–90
Richardsen, A. M., 143–144
rights-based approaches
feminism, 13–14, 86–87, 151
women at partnership level in the UK, 2, 71, 103, 132
Robson, K., 36–37, 89–90, 96–97
Ross-Smith, A., 34
Rottenberg, Catherine, 117, 159–162
neoliberal feminism, 11–12, 49, 65–66, 138

Rottenberg, Catherine, (*Continued*)
  outsourcing care responsibilities, 11–12, 69
  technology, women's bodies and motherhood, 12
  work-life balance, 136, 138, 146
Rousseau, D. M., 11
Rubery, J., 5–6
Ruckdeschel, K., 90–91, 100, 101
Ruiz-Castro, M., 143
Rumens, N., 22–23
Ruppanner, L., 113–114

S
Sanderson, K., 5–6
Santacreu-Vasut, E., 31–32
Sayer, G., 81
Scarborough, W. J., 113–114
Schaefer, J., 29–30
Scharff, Christina, 9–10, 64–65, 68, 138
  neoliberalism and individual responsibility, 11, 137–138
  neoliberalism and women, 11–12, 149
  repudiation of feminism, 85–86
Schrage, D., 57–59
Scotland, 22–23
Seehofer, Horst, 8–9
self-employment, 105–106, 127, 151–152
self-worth as linked to one's work, 9–10, 135–136
Sellers, R. D., 116
Sen, A., 14–15
Sennett, Richard, 17, 60–61, 89–90
  accelerated capitalism and neoliberalism, 9–10, 117–118, 127–128, 149
  cooperation, 9–10, 136
  elites, 127–130
  'fetish of assertiveness', 9–10
  linking sense of one's worth to one's work, 9–10, 135–136
  narcissism and complacency, 136 n.2, 137–138
  'repair work', 127–128
  rotation of employees, 137–138
  shame and self-control, 160
  short-terminism, 9–11, 39, 127–128, 137–138, 154
  'subjunctive mood', 9–10

Sex Disqualification (Removal) Act, 23
sexism, 18, 63–66, 85
  Big-4 Firms, 28–29
  class/gender/race intersections, 81, 85
  dismissing or problematizing sexism, 74, 85–86
  embeddedness in relationships and, 151
  hostile/benevolent sexism, 63–64
  motherhood and discrimination, 97
  'new sexual contract', 64–65
  positive discrimination, 63–64, 71, 72
  sex discrimination, 28–29, 32–33, 51–52, 63, 66, 69–70
  sex discrimination: lawsuits and employment tribunals, 23–24, 28–29, 63, 77–78
  time and age, 78, 97–98, 110–111
  UK, 64, 76
  US, 76
  VoC and, 78, 151
  women at partnership level in Germany, 2, 66, 74–78, 80–82, 85–87, 151
  women at partnership level in the UK, 2, 71, 74, 76, 77–86, 132, 151
  see also gender in/equality
sexual harassment, 74, 76, 77, 143–144
  Big-4 Firms, 28–29
  UK, 76, 152–153
Shalev, M., 5–7
Sheridan, A., 32–34
Shields, J., 153–154
short-terminism, 9–11, 39, 127–128, 154
  neoliberalism and, 11, 137–138
SMEs (Small and Medium-sized Enterprises)
  accountancy: Germany/UK comparison, 50, 53
  female representation in, 33–34
  flexibility, 33–34
  women at partnership level in Germany, 39–41, 52–53, 66, 72–73, 96–97, 99, 101–102, 142
  women at partnership level in the UK, 50, 58–59, 61–62, 77, 78, 80, 84, 104–105, 119–121, 125–128, 141, 145, 148
Smith, Mary Harris, 23, 161–162
Smithson, J., 34–37
social capital, 1
  economic outcomes and, 39

education and training, and
  networks, 116
 importance of, 39
 importance in making partnership, 31–32
Society of Incorporated Accountants and Auditors, 23
Sosenko, F., 83
Soskice, D. W.: *Varieties of capitalism*, 4, 61, 123–124
 see also VoC
Spence, C., 89–90
Spence, H., 31–32
Spiegel, 24–25
standardization of career structures, 132
 gender equality and, 160–161
 promotion and, 57
 relationships at work and, 154
 women at partnership level in Germany, 52, 55–57
 women at partnership level in the UK, 2, 39–40, 44–47, 59, 60–62, 132, 150, 152–154
state
 dependency, capitalism, and the state, 4
 liberal state, 161
 responsibility towards a 'vulnerable subject', 14–15
 strong state, 161
 welfare state regimes, 4, 6–7, 117–118
 welfare states and capitalism, 6–7
Stephens, Julie, 35, 57, 113–114, 158–161
 parenthood, 90–91, 157
 postmaternal thinking, 88–90, 109, 112–113
 unencumbered self, 161–162
Stokoe, E. H., 34–37

T
Tamkins, M. M., 54
Timmermans, S., 153–154
Tinker, T., 21–22, 117
Treuhandanstalt (*Trust Agency*), 121
Trilling, L., 136 n.2

U
UK (United Kingdom)
 accountancy, 19–23, 132
 accountancy industry, 1, 23–26, 50, 53, 154
 accountancy institutes, 23–24
 audit industry, 23–25
 Big-4 Firms, 116, 123–124
 children and childcare, 103, 105–106, 141–142, 156–157
 City of London, 64, 148
 feminism, 13–14, 36–37, 86–87, 105–106, 151
 flexibility, 37–38, 120, 141
 gender equality, 37–38, 93
 job in/security, 3, 115–116, 118
 as LME, 2, 4, 5, 24–25
 motherhood career paradox, 88, 92–93
 neoliberalism, 108–109, 117–118
 part-time working, 70, 106, 107
 promotion in accounting, 57–59
 sexism, 64, 76
 sexual harassment, 76, 152–153
 work centrality, 3, 136–137
 see also accountancy: Germany/UK comparison; gendered hierarchies of dependency: Germany/UK comparison; women at partnership level in the UK
unemployment, 123–124, 127–128, 149, 154
 see also job in/security
unencumbered norm, 141
 motherhood and, 89–90, 107, 110, 112–114, 151–152, 155–156
 neoliberalism and, 157
 unencumbered self, 161–162
 unencumbered worker, 18, 30–31, 89–90, 108–109, 140, 147
US (United Sates), 33–34, 39
 COVID-19 pandemic, 113–114
 feminism, 13–14, 86–87
 financial elite at New York City, 127–128
 gender pay gap, 29–30
 homophily, 61–62
 outsourcing care responsibilities, 11–12, 69
 relationships and networks, 61–62
 sex discrimination: lawsuits and employment tribunals, 28
 sexism, 76
 work centrality, 136–137
 work-life balance, 138

V
Valcour, P. M., 141–142
Velasco-Balmaseda, E., 143–144

Index

Vieten, H., 24–25
Vinnicombe, S., 31–32
VoC (Varieties of Capitalism), 4–8, 59, 88, 117–118, 150, 152–153
　CME (Coordinated Market Economy), 4
　CME/LME comparison, 4–7, 123–124, 136–137, 154
　CMEs/LMEs merging, 8
　corporate governance, 4
　critiques of, 4–7
　France, 61
　gender blindness of, 5, 61
　Germany as CME, 3–6, 151
　Germany/UK comparison: career structures and career advancement, 59, 60f
　human capital, 5
　institutional complementarities, 6–7
　industrial relations, 4
　inter-firm relations, 4
　labour force, 4–7
　labour market, 4–7, 123–124
　LME (Liberal Market Economy), 4, 39
　motherhood, 5–6
　relationship between firms and their employees, 4
　sexism and, 78, 151
　social protections, 6–7, 154
　UK as LME, 2, 4, 5, 24–25
　vocational training and education, 4–7, 24–25, 123–124
　work centrality, 136–137
　see also Hall, P. A.: *Varieties of capitalism*; Soskice, D. W.: *Varieties of capitalism*
'vulnerability theory', 14–15

W

Walker, D., 24–25
Wallen, A. S., 54
Warren, S., 92–93
Warren, T., 140 n.4
Weber, Max, 127–128, 135–136
Weeden, K., 33–34
Weishaupt, J. T., 8–9, 117–118, 149
Weiss, R. S., 135–136
Wirecard, 19–21
Wirtschaftsprüfer, 19–21, 23–24, 121
　stereotypes of, 24–25
　WP exam, 24–25, 55–56, 122, 132
women at partnership level in Germany (accountancy), 1, 150
　age, 81
　appraisal systems, 57
　Big-4 Firms, 41–42, 44, 54–55, 57, 68–69, 75, 82, 130–131, 144, 146
　career progression, 41–44
　career structures and career advancement, 2, 40t, 59, 60f, 152–153
　closure mechanism, 3
　dependencies of loyalty and discretion, 2, 86–87
　entering the profession, 121–124
　friendships in career-making, 2–3, 39–40t, 41, 57, 138, 150, 161–162
　headhunters, 50
　instrumental/primary ties, 41–42, 44, 59
　interdependence with the other partners, 44
　larger firms, 39–40
　managing others and developing talent, 52
　marital status and childcare arrangements, 94t, 94–95
　mentorship, 2, 39–40, 44–45, 58–59
　partnership as full-time commitment, 2–3, 93, 95–96, 100, 108–111
　partnership as long-term commitment, 3, 43, 51–52, 57, 152–153
　performance, 54
　private/public life blurred lines, 2–3, 96, 110, 149, 152–153
　promotion/making partnership process, 46–48, 54
　qualifications, role of, 3
　relationship-based careers, 2, 39–40, 57, 59, 61–62, 71, 110, 121, 131, 134–135, 138, 149–152
　relationship-based hierarchies, 2, 4–5, 61–62, 110, 150
　relationships of trust, 3, 43
　relationships with managers and career advancement, 2, 39–40, 44, 55–56, 59, 86–87, 151
　relationships with other partners at their firms, 140
　shared profits, 43

SMEs, 39–41, 52–53, 66, 72–73, 96–97, 99, 101–102, 142
standardized career structures, 52, 55–57
underrepresentation, 31–32, 66
vulnerability, 110, 151
women proportion at partnership level, 154
see also accountancy: women at partnership level; economy; job in/security; husbands; motherhood; motherhood career paradox; redundancy, resignation; sexism; work centrality; work-life balance
women at partnership level in the UK (accountancy)
advertisements, 51–52, 61–62, 121
age, 81
appraisal systems, 47–48, 59
Big-4 Firms, 47, 50, 57–59, 71, 73, 83, 103–106, 108, 128, 141
career progression, 46–50
career structures and career advancement, 2, 40*t*, 59, 60*f*, 152–153
commodification of the self, 2, 49, 61–62, 152–154
entering the profession, 119–121, 123–124
headhunters and recruitment agents, 40*t*, 50, 59, 61–62, 121, 131, 152–153
instrumental ties, 47–48
internal hierarchies/structures, 41, 49, 59
managing others and developing talent, 57
marital status and childcare arrangements, 94*t*, 94–95
market-type structures, 2–3, 51–52, 59, 60–62, 103, 108–109, 121, 131, 150
mentors and counsellors, 46–47, 49, 57–59
performance, 46–47
promotion/making partnership process, 47–48
relationships at work, 46–47, 49, 51–52, 57, 61–62
rights-based approach, 2, 71, 103, 132
self-employment, 105–106, 127, 151–152
senior executives, interaction with, 49

SMEs, 50, 58–59, 61–62, 77, 78, 80, 84, 104–105, 119–121, 125–128, 141, 145, 148
standardization of human resource management, 3
standardized career structures, 2, 39–40, 44–47, 59, 60–62, 132, 150, 152–154
underrepresentation, 26–27, 72–73, 128, 129
vulnerability, 3, 59, 61–62, 105–106, 154
women proportion at partnership level, 154
see also accountancy: women at partnership level; economy; job in/security; motherhood; redundancy; sexism; work centrality; work-life balance
work centrality, 2, 18, 115–116, 149, 152, 161–162
Big-4 firms, 148
fertility and, 146
Germany, 136–137
health and, 115–116, 135–136, 143, 152
high work centrality, 135–136, 140
job in/security and, 3, 130, 135–137
long working hours, 6, 34, 135, 138, 141, 143, 144–149, 152
meaningfulness of the profession, 146, 149, 152–153
neoliberal capitalism and, 135–136
overworking, 135, 138, 144
stress and, 135–136, 143, 152
UK, 3, 136–137
US, 136–137
VoC perspective on, 136–137
women at partnership level in Germany, 138*t*, 139–140, 144, 146–149, 152–153
women at partnership level in the UK, 138*t*, 139–140, 145–149, 152
work-life balance and, 134–138, 144–145
work culture
long hours culture, 6, 34, 135, 138, 141, 143, 144–149, 152
male work culture, 6
unpaid overtime, 6
work-life balance, 3, 115–116, 149, 152
Big-4 firms, 34
executive women's work-family balance, 136

work-life balance, (*Continued*)
  'felicitous work-life balance', 136, 138, 156
  'gender blind' policies, 34-35
  literature on, 34-35, 138
  neoliberal feminism and, 65-66, 136, 138
  US, 138
  women at partnership level in Germany, 138*t*, 139-140, 142-144, 146, 147
  women at partnership level in the UK, 138*t*, 139-142, 145, 147-148

  work-centrality and, 134-138, 144-145

WPK (Wirtschaftsprüferkammer—professional institute of chartered accountants, Germany), 23-24
  female membership, 26*t*, 26-27
  mandatory membership, 23-24

Y

Young, B., 8-9

Z

Zimmer, M., 29-30